j812.041 The Big book of
BIG   large-cast plays.

$18.95

DATE			

JUL -- 1995

The Big Book

of

Large-Cast Plays

Other titles in the "Big Book" series

THE BIG BOOK OF DRAMATIZED CLASSICS
THE BIG BOOK OF FOLKTALE PLAYS
THE BIG BOOK OF HOLIDAY PLAYS
THE BIG BOOK OF COMEDIES
THE BIG BOOK OF CHRISTMAS PLAYS

Contents

Junior and Senior High

Middle and Lower Grades

Curtain Raisers

Special Christmas Program

The Big Book
of
Large-Cast Plays

Junior and Senior High

❧Spy for a Day

by Betty Tracy Huff

A spoof on foreign intrigue . . .

Characters

MR. PRENDERGAST, *tour guide*
PATTY GREEN ⎫
JIMMY STOCKS ⎪
MRS. TOWER ⎬ *tourists*
MISS LEON ⎭
BORIS ⎫
OMAR ⎬ *spies from OUCH*
MARIA ⎭
KONRAD ⎫ *spies from ICK*
VINCENT ⎭
MAX, *a waiter*
CARLA, *a souvenir peddler*
OTHER TOURISTS, *extras*

SETTING: *Sidewalk café in a foreign city. Sign at back reads:* CAFÉ INTERNATIONAL. ESPIONAGE CENTER OF THE WORLD. SPIES WELCOME.

AT RISE: BORIS, OMAR, *and* MARIA, *wearing trench coats with turned-up collars, hats with turned-down brims, and dark glasses, are seated at table down left, heads together.* VINCENT, *hidden behind newspaper, is seated at nearby table. From time to time, he peers over paper, trying to overhear* BORIS *and the others.* MR. PRENDERGAST, *followed by* MRS. TOWER, MISS LEON, *and* OTHER TOURISTS, *enters.* MR. PRENDERGAST *wears a huge badge reading:* OFFICIAL GUIDE, SUNSHINE TOUR COMPANY. *All tourists carry guide books, cameras, etc.*

MR. PRENDERGAST: Look to your left, folks, down the road. (*Tourists turn heads left in unison.*) The Art Museum, built in 1760.

MRS. TOWER (*Scoffing*): Huh! Out of date! Not nearly as nice as our new art museum back home in Soggy Falls, Oregon!

MISS LEON (*Timidly*): It's all very interesting, Mr. Prendergast. But where do you suppose those nice young people, Jimmy Stocks and Patty Green, have gone? They started out with us this morning.

MR. PRENDERGAST (*Reassuringly*): Don't worry, Miss Leon. They'll catch up with us soon, I'm sure. (CARLA *enters, carrying tray of souvenirs.*)

CARLA (*Chanting*): Chocolates, souvenirs, postcards.

MR. PRENDERGAST (*To* CARLA): Not now, thank you. (CARLA *wanders off among tables.*) Look to your right, folks. (*Tourists look right.*) There you see the famous fish market *al fresco.*

MRS. TOWER (*Sniffing*): We could have guessed that without the help of a tour guide!

MR. PRENDERGAST (*Firmly*): The fish market is going to be the highlight of our tour.

MISS LEON: But don't you think we ought to wait for Patty and Jimmy?

MR. PRENDERGAST (*Indignantly*): Not if we want to get to the market while it's still open.

MRS. TOWER (*Sniffing again*): Oh, it's open all right.

MR. PRENDERGAST: If you will kindly follow me, ladies and gentlemen . . . (MR. PRENDERGAST *and tourists exit.* MRS. TOWER *lags behind.*)

MRS. TOWER: Might as well see all there is to see, I suppose. (*Looks about café disdainfully*) Nothing exciting going on around *here,* that's for sure! (*Exits*)

CARLA (*Wandering over to* BORIS): Chocolates, souvenirs, state secrets? Safe-cracking tools, anyone?

BORIS (*Brusquely*): Not now, thank you, Carla. We're busy. (CARLA *wanders off.*)

MARIA: But, Boris, how will we recognize our man from OUCH?

OMAR (*Nervously*): If we give secret message revealing hiding place of plans for the new Wiener Schnitzel machine to the wrong person, it will cause great trouble!

BORIS: Is no trouble, Omar! Man from OUCH, the Organization of Universal Conspirators and Ham Radio Operators, will give password—*Ouch!*—and he will get a message from us.

MARIA (*Excitedly*): Good, Boris! And then?

BORIS: Then our agent gets plans from their hiding place and takes them to our headquarters. Success will be ours!

OMAR (*Clapping his hands; ecstatically*): Oh, yes, yes!

BORIS (*Putting hand warningly on* OMAR's *shoulder, looking around café*): Keep voice down, Omar! Spies from the rival organization, International Conspirators' Klub, known as ICK, may be all around. They would try anything to intercept the message to Agent Number Thirteen, and to find out where the plans for the Wiener Schnitzel machine are hidden! (BORIS, OMAR, *and* MARIA *put their heads together, and whisper.* PATTY GREEN *and* JIMMY STOCKS *enter, dressed as typical tourists and loaded down with cameras, guide books, etc.* JIMMY *carries sunglasses in his breast pocket.* PATTY *wears a pair of low-heeled pumps.*)

JIMMY (*Distastefully*): This café seems kind of odd, Patty. Don't you think we ought to walk on a bit farther and catch up with the rest of the tour group?

PATTY (*Flopping down in chair at table near* BORIS): Jimmy Stocks, did you say *walk?* You have to be kidding! Another step and I'll become one of the sights on the tour! (MAX *enters, wearing apron and carrying pad and pencil. He stands behind* PATTY.)

MAX (*In deep, sinister voice*): Something for you?

PATTY (*Startled*): What in the world! (*Turns to face* MAX, *who smiles grimly at her*) Er—I mean—there's nothing in the world I'd like more than a cup of coffee! Right, Jimmy?

JIMMY (*Shrugging*): Might as well, now that we're here.

MAX (*Clicking his heels and bowing*): Certainly! (*He exits.* JIMMY *puts camera down on table and sits.*)

PATTY (*Groaning*): This tour is exhausting. I used to think

college was hard work! I can hardly wait for next semester so
I can get a rest.

JIMMY (*Pointing to her shoes*): If you didn't insist on wearing
those new shoes . . .

PATTY (*Eagerly*): You mean you noticed?

JIMMY (*Dryly*): Not until you stepped on my foot this morning.

PATTY (*Aside*): It figures! It would take that for some people to
pay attention.

JIMMY: Did you say something?

PATTY (*Brightly*): I said I'd be happy if I never had to pay
attention to another tourist attraction.

JIMMY (*Looking over at MARIA*): Oh, I don't know. Some foreign sights aren't bad. (*Admiringly*) Not bad at all!

PATTY (*Wistfully; looking at MARIA*): And she didn't even have
to step on him. (*She reaches into JIMMY's breast pocket for
his sunglasses, and puts them on him.*) There, that'll cut the
dazzle!

JIMMY (*Turning back to PATTY; innocently*): I thought it was
kind of overcast, myself. Here, let me help you untangle some
of those camera straps. (*Starts to straighten straps when her
purse falls on his foot.*) Ouch! (*Hops around in pain*) Ouch!

MARIA (*Grabbing OMAR's shoulder*): Omar, Boris, did you
hear?

OMAR (*Excitedly*): The password! He said "Ouch!"

BORIS: He must be Agent Number Thirteen from our organization!

MARIA: Are you sure, Boris?

BORIS: Yes, Maria. He is wearing sunglasses when there is no
sun, just like the rest of us secret agents.

OMAR: He's a spy, all right!

BORIS (*Severely*): Is *secret agent,* Omar! Remember, *they* are
spies! *We* are secret agents!

OMAR (*Contritely*): Yes, Boris. (*Excitedly*) Where's the message,
Boris? Write the message for the man from OUCH.

BORIS (*Hurrying off*): Max! Max! Bring me paper, pen, and code
book! (*He exits as MARIA and OMAR watch JIMMY closely.*)

PATTY: Jimmy, are you sure you're all right now?

JIMMY (*With icy politeness*): Luckily it wasn't the same foot you stepped on this morning. (*Dramatically*) With care, time, and a small miracle, I may walk again one day. What do you carry in your purse, anyway? A spare anchor for the cruise ship?

PATTY (*Lightly*): Silly! All I have in here are one or two light-weight souvenirs. (*She opens her purse and takes out a horse-shoe.*) See? For good luck!

JIMMY (*Taking horseshoe from her, then nearly dropping it, as though it were too heavy*): It was good luck for the horse, all right—when he lost this thing.

PATTY (*Quickly grabbing horseshoe from him and slipping it into her purse*): Oh, Jimmy! It's not a *real* horseshoe! (CARLA *wanders over to them.*)

CARLA: Chocolates, souvenirs, postcards?

JIMMY (*Dryly*): Not now, thank you. We have all the souvenirs we can carry. (CARLA *wanders off among tables.* JIMMY *and* PATTY *mime conversation.* BORIS *reenters with paper and pen.*)

BORIS (*Sitting down at his table*): I write message for man from OUCH now. (*Reading aloud as he writes*) Dear Agent Number Thirteen: The plans for the new Wiener Schnitzel machine are hidden in . . . (*He lowers voice to a murmur, putting his arm over the writing to hide it from* OMAR *and* MARIA.) No fair peeking! (BORIS *hunches over his paper, continues to write, then claps his hand down on it.* MAX *reenters with tray of coffee and four dishes of ice cream.*)

MAX: The ice cream you ordered. (*He serves* BORIS *and* MARIA *ice cream and spoons.*)

BORIS (*Sarcastically*): We ordered it so long ago we'd forgotten about it!

OMAR (*Eagerly*): Did you remember the extra serving for me, Max?

MAX: I remember. (*He sets down dish.*) Strawberry. (*Setting down another dish*) Pistachio. Now your spoon. (*Fumbling in apron pocket for spoon*)

BORIS: Max!

MAX (*Clicking his heels and bowing*): Sir?

BORIS (*Folding up message*): Please take this to the man from the Organization of Universal Conspirators and Ham Radio Operators, over there. (*He indicates* JIMMY.)

MAX (*Looking at* JIMMY): *That* is man from OUCH? Looks more like common tourist to me.

BORIS: Such is the brilliance of our chief in sending this agent. If this tourist, college-type boy were not wearing dark glasses and giving countersign, I would not have dreamed he is Agent Number Thirteen.

MARIA: Be extra careful how you pass on the message, Max. Remember that our enemies from the rival organization known as ICK may be observing every move we make. (*At this*, VINCENT *peers over his newspaper, then quickly hides behind it again.*)

BORIS: ICK must not read the message, *and* they must not find out the true identity of Agent Number Thirteen, or all is lost!

MAX: Trust in me! ICK shall never know the message has been given! (*He picks up* OMAR's *two dishes of ice cream, and puts message into dish of pistachio.*)

OMAR (*Shocked*): He . . . he took my ice cream!

BORIS: Quiet! Everyone has to make sacrifices for the good of our organization! (*He begins to eat his own ice cream.* MAX *goes over to* JIMMY.)

MAX (*Clicking heels and bowing*): Coffee and ice cream, sir.

JIMMY: But we only ordered coffee.

MAX: Ice cream with compliments of the house, sir. (*He serves coffee.*)

OMAR (*Indignantly*): What does this mean, "compliments of the house"? Out of my pocket is the money coming! OUCH does not allow expense accounts!

BORIS: Are you implying OUCH is cheap-skate organization, Omar?

OMAR (*Spiritedly*): Implying nothing! I am stating fact!

MAX (*To* PATTY): Strawberry, miss. (*He serves her.*) Try the pistachio, sir. (*Puts dish in front of* JIMMY)

JIMMY: Thanks just the same, but I don't really care for pistachio.

MAX (*Emphatically*): You do now, sir! (*Pleadingly*) Please, please, try the pistachio!

JIMMY: All right, if it means that much to you! (*He picks up spoon.*)

MAX (*Suddenly grabbing* JIMMY's *spoon*): Wait! Wait, I forgot to take the usual precautions!

JIMMY: Huh?

MAX: Oh, sir, you never know what they'll do next! (*He picks up spoons, examines them intently, then peers into the sugar bowl.*) They are all around us!

JIMMY: They . . . they are?

MAX (*Motioning for* PATTY *and* JIMMY *to stand*): Electronic devices, sir! What else?

JIMMY (*Stepping away from table*): Yeah, what else? (*Laughs uncertainly*)

PATTY (*Aside*): It's probably some sort of local custom, Jimmy. (MAX *is now down on his hands and knees, feeling around the edge of the table.*)

MAX (*Triumphantly*): Ah-ha! (*He draws out suction cup, with a microphone and long cord attached to it, from underside of table.* MAX *begins winding up cord into a neat ball, pushing* MARIA, OMAR, *and* BORIS *out of way as he follows cord. When* MAX *reaches an empty table, he lifts up tablecloth to reveal* KONRAD *sitting cross-legged on floor fiddling with a large tape recorder.* KONRAD *does not notice* MAX, *who taps him on the shoulder.*) Heard any good secrets lately, Konrad?

KONRAD: Sh-h! Can't you see I'm busy eavesdropping? (*He taps his earphones.*) These things seem to have gone dead.

MAX (*Suavely*): Maybe it would help if you replaced the microphone under the table. (*He twirls microphone on end of cord.*)

KONRAD (*Absently taking microphone*): Thanks, Max. (*He suddenly realizes he has been spotted and crawls out from under table.*) It isn't fair, Max. I spend hours bugging this joint for ICK, and you come along and unbug it every time! It's frustrating! It's giving me a complex! (PATTY *and* JIMMY *watch bewildered as* KONRAD *gathers up his equipment and storms off, shaking his head.* MAX *follows him off.* JIMMY *and* PATTY *mime conversation, moving away from their table to look after* KONRAD.)

BORIS (*Profoundly shocked*): Oh, the wicked machinations of the International Conspirators Klub! Bugging the place! How underhanded can you get? How can they stoop so low? And why didn't we think of doing it first?

MARIA: Boris, does this mean Konrad from ICK has heard that handsome college type is really our man from OUCH?

BORIS (*Grimly*): Yes, Maria. I fear ICK knows all.

MARIA: Then handsome tourist-type espionage agent is now in deadly danger!

OMAR: And ICK knows the message is concealed in the pistachio ice cream!

VINCENT (*Looking over top of his newspaper; aside*): So that's where it is!

BORIS: If ICK gets hold of that message, they will discover the secret hiding place of the plans of the new Wiener Schnitzel machine! But ICK shall never know! (BORIS, MARIA, *and* OMAR *mime whispered conversation.* VINCENT *puts down his newspaper, picks up plate of spaghetti from his own table, and, peering furtively all around and whistling nonchalantly, switches the spaghetti for* JIMMY's *ice cream. He pulls a "cord" of spaghetti from the plate, pulling until it is long enough to reach his own table. He sits, holding one end of the cord to his ear, and listens intently.* PATTY *and* JIMMY *return to their table and sit.*)

JIMMY: I don't care what you say! There's something odd going on here.

PATTY: Don't be so provincial! It's just that the local customs are different. As Mrs. Tower says, this isn't Soggy Falls, Oregon.

JIMMY: You can say that again! (*Takes a bite of spaghetti*) Ugh! I knew I didn't like pistachio!

PATTY (*Tasting her ice cream*): My ice cream tastes fine.

JIMMY: Well *mine* tastes like spaghetti! (*Peering closely at his dish*) It looks like spaghetti, too.

PATTY: Of course, with those dark glasses on, you can't tell what anything really looks like.

JIMMY: You were the one who made me wear them. (*He takes off sunglasses, looks again at his dish.*) Yikes! It *is* spaghetti! Waiter, waiter! (MAX *enters.*)

MAX (*Clicking heels and bowing*): Sir? (JIMMY *points to spaghetti.*) Oh, sir, they *will* do it! (*He fishes microphone out of the middle of* JIMMY's *food, then whistles shrilly into microphone.* VINCENT *shrieks, pulls end of cord from ear, and puts his hand over his ear.*)

VINCENT: No fair, Max!

MAX: That will teach you to bug the noodles, Vincent!

VINCENT (*Miffed*): You needn't think I heard anything! All that spaghetti sauce in the microphone! "Squish, squish, squish" was all I heard.

OMAR (*Jumping up excitedly, pointing to ice cream at* VINCENT's *table*): Somebody grab the pistachio, quick! (VINCENT *grabs ice cream dish and runs off.*) Not you, Vincent! Wait, wait! (OMAR *dashes off after* VINCENT.)

JIMMY (*Stunned*): You'd better believe it's different from Soggy Falls!

PATTY (*Struggling to stay calm*): The mark of a sophisticated world traveler is to show no surprise at anything. Other lands, other customs!

JIMMY (*Excitedly*): I just want to know what's going on!

PATTY (*Disdainfully*): Don't be uncouth. Drink your coffee, and pretend you're used to world travel!

JIMMY (*Grumbling*): That's going to take some doing. (*Drinks his coffee*)

MARIA: Boris, handsome college-type is in deadly danger. He must be warned!

BORIS: *He* is in danger? What about us? If OUCH finds out ICK has stolen message we will be in plenty trouble.

MARIA: Maria thinks only of how to save handsome college-type agent. ICK will never let him get away alive.

BORIS (*Slyly*): Unless his exit is covered with our special smokescreen!

MARIA (*Expectantly*): You mean . . . ?

BORIS (*Nodding vigorously*): Yes, yes, pencil-type container of harmless smoke must be placed at disposal of Agent Number Thirteen. Under cover of the smoke he can make his getaway.

MARIA: Yes, yes! (*Rummaging in her handbag*) Aha! Here it is—pencil number 1212. (*Holding up pencil*)

BORIS (*Aghast*): Not that one! Number 1212 is harmless sleep
  gas! (JIMMY *turns to watch them with interest.*)

MARIA (*Bringing out more pencils*): How about 1314?

BORIS (*Shaking his head*): Truth serum!

MARIA (*Bringing out pencil after pencil*): 736? 5861? (BORIS
  shakes head.) What with codes, and ciphers, and disguises,
  and care and feeding of homing pigeons, electronics and oper-
  ating ham radio, is not easy being career-girl type spy! (*She
  holds up another pencil.*)

BORIS: That is pencil for writing! (*Takes another pencil from
  her handbag*) Here is right one. Now, get it to Agent Number thirteen.

PATTY (*Admonishingly*): All right, Jimmy Stocks, you put
  those dark glasses back on!

JIMMY (*Dreamily*): Huh?

PATTY: You're looking at that girl again!

JIMMY (*Turning*): You mean that pencil saleslady who's showing her samples?

PATTY: Oh, never mind. (*Jumping up suddenly, pointing off*)
  Look, Jimmy! Here comes Mr. Prendergast and Mrs. Tower,
  and the others! I knew they'd be looking for us sooner or later.
  I'll go ask them to join us. (*Calls and waves off*) Hello, Mr.
  Prendergast! Hello! (*She runs off. MARIA slinks over to
  JIMMY's table.*)

MARIA: Speak cautiously and in an undertone! If we are ob-
  served, it is, how you say, curtains.

JIMMY: Oh, I don't think Patty's *that* jealous. Miss . . . er . . .
  Miss . . . ?

MARIA: Call me Maria. I have something for you. (*She hands
  him a pencil.*)

JIMMY (*Dumbfounded*): A pencil, for me? Thanks. (CARLA
  hurries over.)

CARLA: Allow me to gift wrap that!

MARIA (*Grabbing pencil*): No, thanks, Carla. (CARLA *shrugs,
  then starts toward exit as* PATTY, MR. PRENDERGAST,
  MRS. TOWER, MISS LEON, *and* OTHER TOURISTS *enter.
  MARIA stuffs pencil into JIMMY's pocket.*) There! You know
  what it's for, don't you?

JIMMY: Sure, we use them all the time where I come from.

MARIA: Remember, do not use it until the last minute! Also, order the meatballs! They are transistorized.

JIMMY: Huh? (MARIA *puts her finger to her lips, and returns to her table. She and* BORIS *watch* JIMMY *closely.*)

MR. PRENDERGAST (*Sitting down at* JIMMY'*s table with* MRS. TOWER, MISS LEON, *and* PATTY): Keep together, I told you! But, no, you had to wander off and get lost.

PATTY: We're sorry, Mr. Prendergast!

MR. PRENDERGAST: Ah, well, I suppose you have been punished enough, Miss Green, missing the fish market!

PATTY (*To* MRS. TOWER): Did you enjoy the tour, Mrs. Tower?

MRS. TOWER (*Dryly*): What can I say? Except to tell you that the flounders are ripe and the kippered herrings are in bloom again!

MISS LEON (*Sighing*): It's nice to sit down for a bit. (MAX *enters to take their order.*) Do let's order some of the divine native dishes!

JIMMY: They're strong on meatballs here, so I was told.

MRS. TOWER: Anything, as long as it isn't fish! (MAX *takes their orders quietly as dialogue continues.*)

MISS LEON (*Brightly*): Such a splendid chance to write some postcards home! (CARLA *wanders over.*)

CARLA: Postcards, pens, stamps . . .

MISS LEON (*Appreciatively*): Such a splendid girl. Always here when you need her! (*They all purchase postcards from* CARLA.)

PATTY (*Holding out hand*): Could I borrow a pencil, Jimmy? (JIMMY *hands her pencil from his pocket.*)

MARIA (*Gasping*): Boris! The . . . the smokescreen pencil!

BORIS: Wait, Maria! (CARLA *grabs pencil.*)

CARLA: Do let me gift wrap this!

PATTY (*Grabbing pencil back*): No, thank you. It's fine just the way it is. (CARLA *shrugs and exits as* OMAR *enters, breathing hard.*)

BORIS: Omar, did you rescue pistachio?

OMAR (*Shaking head sorrowfully*): Alas, Vincent, the spy from ICK escaped into the fish market!

MARIA (*Mournfully*): All is lost, then!

BORIS (*Kindly*): Do not worry, Maria. Boris has plan for us all to escape the clutches of ICK. Our man from OUCH now has the smokescreen-type pencil, yes?

MARIA: His girlfriend is writing postcards with it!

BORIS: Now, here's the plan. (*Tracing diagram on the tablecloth with his finger*) Here at Point A, man from OUCH has smoke-screen. Now, in exactly twenty-five minutes, we will meet at point B, the western entrance to fish market. We will then send a message to headquarters at point C. Then at point D, man from OUCH throws up smokescreen, which hides get-away point E. We will meet at point F, or, better still, at point G, where we will make our escape by live bait barge to point H. (*He sits back, beaming with satisfaction.*) All clear? Any questions?

OMAR: Yes. (*Pause*) What comes after Point A?

BORIS (*Groaning*): Omar, sometimes I am thinking you are not quite cut out for cloak-and-dagger-type stuff. (*They discuss plans aside, as* MAX *enters carrying tray of water glasses and plates of meatballs. He serves some to* MARIA, BORIS, *and* OMAR, *then to* PATTY, JIMMY, *and others.* BORIS *holds up meatball on a toothpick and speaks into it.*) Calling OUCH! Calling Agent Number Thirteen. Come in! Come in! Over! (*He puts meatball to his ear and listens attentively.*)

MARIA (*Anxiously*): Any reply?

BORIS: Not yet. I cannot understand it. Maria, are you sure you told our man the meatballs are really two-way transis-tor radios?

MARIA: I tell handsome college-type all!

BORIS: I shall try again. (*To meatball*) Calling man from OUCH! Now is the time to use the smokescreen, and make your getaway! Come in, Agent Number Thirteen!

MRS. TOWER (*Staring at* JIMMY's *plate*): Did ... did you hear anything?

JIMMY: Hear what, Mrs. Tower?

MRS. TOWER: A sound like snap, crackle, and pop ... coming from your plate.

JIMMY: You're thinking of breakfast cereal, Mrs. Tower.

MRS. TOWER (*Insistently*): No—it's the meatballs. (*Cups her hands to her ear*) Listen! (*Pause*) It . . . it must be a touch of the sun, that's what it is. (*She rises, smiling dazedly.*) Steady now, Mabel, old girl. Get a grip on yourself! (*Hysterically*) People might not understand if you tell them you heard the meatballs talking. (*She laughs wildly and pours a glass of water over JIMMY's plate.*) There! That'll keep you quiet.

MISS LEON (*Leading her aside*): There, there, dear. We'll sit here where it's nice and shady. (*They turn chairs away from group and sit.*)

BORIS (*Putting down meatball microphone*): Blast! Another transistor drowned by unsuspecting tourist lady!

OMAR (*Suspiciously*): I wonder, what if tourist lady who foiled our plan to warn man from OUCH is really a spy from ICK?

BORIS (*Solemnly, clapping OMAR on shoulder*): Omar, you redeem self by brainwave! Now, here is plan for moving in. (*They all bend over table again, as BORIS sketches plan on tablecloth with his finger.*)

MRS. TOWER (*Fanning herself with postcard*): I think I'll write a postcard to the old folks at home in Soggy Falls, just to settle my nerves! Could I borrow that pencil, Patty? (PATTY *starts to hand her pencil.*)

OMAR (*Leaping to his feet*): No! No! Is not giving smokescreen-type pencil to spy lady from ICK! (MR. PRENDERGAST *grabs pencil.*)

MR. PRENDERGAST: Aha! I have it! ICK has succeeded! The plans of the Wiener Schnitzel machine will be ours.

MISS LEON: Mr. Prendergast, what is all this?

OMAR: We have made big mistake! Mrs. Tower really is nice tourist lady! Mr. Prendergast is spy from dastardly rival organization, ICK!

MR. PRENDERGAST (*Going to BORIS*): And now, Boris, the plans for the machine, please. Then I shall use this pencil smokescreen to cover my exit and be on my way!

MARIA (*Running over to JIMMY*): Agent Thirteen, do something! Don't let ICK get away with the plans! (JIMMY *looks around, bewildered.*)

PATTY (*To MARIA*): He isn't Agent Thirteen! I am! (*To*

JIMMY) I'm sorry I got you mixed up in this, Jimmy, but I had to use you as my cover so I wouldn't be recognized. You see, I'm working my way through college as a spy for OUCH. Our government is interested in the Wiener Schnitzel machine, and OUCH agreed to get the plans for us.

JIMMY (*Overwhelmed*): In that case, I quite understand, of course. But how are we going to stop Prendergast from getting away?

PATTY (*Taking horseshoe from her purse*): I shall call reinforcements on my cellular horseshoe phone!

MR. PRENDERGAST (*Fingering badge on his lapel*): And I shall call up reinforcements on my cellular badge! So there! Anything OUCH can do, ICK can do better! Now, Boris, the plans. Where are they?

BORIS (*Sighing*): Is no good holding out. Plans are on the bottom of Carla's tray. (CARLA *turns up tray to show plans taped to it.*)

CARLA: I'm from OUCH myself, also working my way through college.

MR. PRENDERGAST: The plans, please! (CARLA *peels off plans and rolls them up.* PRENDERGAST *takes them from her.*) Aha! At last!

JIMMY: I can't let you get away with those plans, Mr. Prendergast! (*He tackles* PRENDERGAST, *and takes plans from him.*)

PATTY *and* MARIA (*Together*): My hero! (PATTY *scowls at* MARIA, *who shrugs.*)

MR. PRENDERGAST: You have the plans, but I will use the pencil container of smoke to cover my exit! (*He presses pencil's eraser, and then starts to yawn.*) What, no smoke? Oooh, am I tired. (*He slumps into chair, closes his eyes, and starts to snore.*)

BORIS: Maria!

MARIA (*Delighted*): I gave wrong pencil! Is not smoke-type; is sleep-type! All those numbers to remember! It's difficult to remember own telephone number these days.

BORIS: Never mind, Maria! Is good thing you did mix up pencils! Now we have captured spy from ICK!

MRS. TOWER: But we have lost our guide!

OMAR: Never mind that, nice tourist lady. Omar will show you around city.

BORIS: Max, coffee for everyone! We must make new plans. (MAX *serves coffee, fishing microphones out of sugar bowl, cream jug, etc., as he does so.*)

MAX (*Shaking his head*): Always, they try it! (KONRAD *and* VINCENT *enter with their equipment and big coils of wire. Unnoticed by anyone, they crawl in and out from under tables, stringing wire and tangling themselves up in it.* MRS. TOWER *and* OMAR *talk aside.* BORIS *and* MARIA *draw plans on tablecloth.* CARLA *wanders around with her tray.*)

PATTY: You know, Jimmy, I think you'd make a great espionage agent. Just think of all the places we could travel. We could sit in cafés like this all around the world!

JIMMY: No thanks, Patty. I couldn't take another meal like this as long as I live! (*Reaching across table for her hand*) But I could sure go for a burger at the Soggy Falls Diner—that is, if you'd care to join me.

PATTY (*Delighted*): Really? Oh, Jimmy! (*Fumbling in her bag and pulling out horseshoe*) I'll call the diner right now and make us a reservation! (*She drops horseshoe on* JIMMY's *foot.*)

JIMMY (*Yelling*): *Ouch!* (BORIS, OMAR, *and* MARIA *rush forward.*)

MARIA: He said *ouch!* Is giving password again! (*She and BORIS and* OMAR *look at one other in astonishment, shrugging.* JIMMY *jumps up and down, holding foot, while* PATTY *fusses over him. Curtain*)

THE END

Production Notes

SPY FOR A DAY

Characters: 7 male; 5 female; as many extras as desired for Other Tourists.

Playing Time: 30 minutes.

Costumes: Modern, everyday dress. Spies wear trench coats, hats with floppy brims, and dark glasses. Maria has a handbag containing pencils. Mr. Prendergast wears a badge reading: OFFICIAL GUIDE, SUNSHINE TOUR COMPANY. Tourists carry cameras, guide books, etc. Patty wears new-looking low-heeled pumps. Jimmy has dark glasses in his jacket pocket. Max wears waiter's uniform with apron.

Properties: Souvenir tray with "plans" taped to bottom; tray is filled with postcards, chocolates, trinkets, etc. Serving tray with dishes of ice cream, spoons, coffee cups, sugar bowl and creamer filled with coiled wire, glasses, meatballs, plate of "spaghetti" with long string and microphone hidden in it; microphone on suction cup attached by long cord to tape recorder; newspaper; coils of wire; paper and pen; pencils.

Setting: A sidewalk café in a foreign city. At back is a sign: CAFÉ INTERNATIONAL. ESPIONAGE CENTER OF THE WORLD. SPIES WELCOME. Chairs and tables with tablecloths that reach the ground are placed about café. Exits are at right and left. Konrad and his tape recorder are hidden under one of the tables, and a microphone with cord is hidden under Jimmy's table.

Lighting and Sound: No special effects.

❧Belinda and the Beast

by Claire Boiko

A wild and woolly version of a favorite folktale . . .

Characters

JIMMY TONSILS
HU HEE
RUNNING WATER
CAPTAIN ABLE McREADY
TROOPER HENRY HOOPER
ABIGAIL HUCKLEBERRY
PEPITO
SASSAFRAS
B. J. BEAST
VARMINT } *Beast's henchmen*
VIPER }
BUCK BUCKTHORNE
BELINDA BUCKTHORNE
MRS. POMPOSIA SMYTHE-SMITHERS
FASTIDIA } *her daughters*
GAUDIA }
PARSON WORTHY
BEAST'S BAD MEN, *extras*

SCENE 1

TIME: *When the West was young.*
SETTING: *No-Man's Land, in the Old West.*
BEFORE RISE: *At center is pole with sign reading,* NO-MAN'S
 LAND. NO WOMAN'S NEITHER. BEWARE OF BEAST. *There is large
 rock at right. At left is water tower.* HU HEE *stands on steps of*

19

water tower, holding small gong and striker. He looks offstage, shading eyes with hand. JIMMY TONSILS, *holding guitar, enters.*

JIMMY (*To audience*): Howdy. They call me Jimmy Tonsils, the wanderin' song and dance man. (*Singing to tune of "Down in the Valley"*)

Oh, I'm a lone cowboy,

A-travelin' far,

Up highways and byways,

With my trusty guitar.

(*Points to sign; speaking*) See that sign? That's new in this territory. Used to be nice and peaceful hereabouts. Then the Beast came. (*Sings again*)

The Beast came from nowhere

Gobblin' towns one by one,

With hordes of bad hombres,

Like Attila the Hun.

(*Speaking*) They say that when that outlaw comes near, strong men quiver, women quail, and even fearless Injuns faint dead away.

HU HEE (*Pointing; excitedly*): Jimmy, look! In far distance, cloud of suspicious dust. (*Beats gong*) Beast alert! Beast alert! First-stage beast alert!

JIMMY (*Alarmed*): Yikes! Thanks for the warning, Hu Hee. I'm going to make myself scarce. (*He exits, as* RUNNING WATER *enters through center curtain on hands and knees. He stands, wets finger and holds it up to wind, then hoots three times.* CAPTAIN McREADY, TROOPER HOOPER, *and* ABIGAIL HUCKLEBERRY *enter.*)

McREADY: Not much time for a marriage proposal. (*To* HOOPER) Hurry, Trooper Hooper.

HOOPER: Yes, sir. That blasted Beast has interrupted us every time I've tried to pop the question to Miss Abigail. (HOOPER *offers flowers to* ABIGAIL. *She accepts them shyly.* McREADY, RUNNING WATER, *and* HU HEE *watch with interest.*) Ahem, ahem.

McREADY: Go on!

HU HEE: Time running out. Beast come soon.

HOOPER: I didn't expect an audience. (*Sound of hoof beats is heard offstage.*)

ABIGAIL: Was that an earthquake or a *beastquake?*

McREADY: Hurry, Henry. Propose! Before it's too late! (*Sound of hoof beats gets louder.*)

HU HEE (*Hitting gong*): Second stage! Head for the hills! The Beast! The Beast! (HOOPER *begins to usher* ABIGAIL *off.*)

HOOPER: I'm sorry, Miss Abigail. No proposal today.

ABIGAIL (*Wailing*): Oh, Henry. Shall we ever wed? (HOOPER *and* ABIGAIL *rush off right.* HU HEE *climbs down ladder, beating gong rapidly.*)

HU HEE: Run! Run for your lives! (*He exits.*)

McREADY (*Nervously*): Did you hear that, Running Water? The Beast is coming! (RUNNING WATER *faints.* McREADY *catches him.*) Sound the retreat! March to the rear! (*He backs off right, dragging* RUNNING WATER, *as sound of hoof beats grows louder.* BELINDA BUCKTHORNE *runs on left, followed by* PEPITO *and* SASSAFRAS, *howling in fear.* BELINDA *clutches a book.*)

BELINDA: Hurry, children. The Beast's henchmen are right behind us!

SASSAFRAS: Miss Belinda, they snatched the picnic basket right out of my hands. (*She bawls.*)

PEPITO: Señorita Belinda, I am so afraid. I have heard that the Beast is twelve feet tall and covered with green hair like Spanish moss!

BELINDA: There, there, children. Don't worry. I will protect you. (VIPER *and* VARMINT *run in, left.* VARMINT *carries flag with skull and crossbones.* VIPER *holds picnic basket and gun, which he shoots into air.* PEPITO *and* SASSAFRAS *scream and cower behind* BELINDA, *who faces outlaws bravely.*)

VARMINT (*Uprooting sign and planting flag in its place*): I claim this land for King Beast.

VIPER (*Advancing on* BELINDA): And I claim this gal for King Beast. Come along nice and quiet, little lady. (*He advances menacingly toward* BELINDA, *who holds up book like a talisman.*)

BELINDA (*Boldly*): Stop! (*Outlaws stop, bewildered.*) Stop in the name of Homer, Plato, and Aristotle!

VIPER (*Baffled*): *Who?*

VARMINT: Must be three dudes she's got hidden to ambush us.

BELINDA (*Advancing to* VIPER *and yanking picnic basket from his arm*): I will take back our picnic basket in the name of Ovid, Seneca, and Julius Caesar!

VARMINT (*Nervously*): Let's get out of here, Viper. Make tracks! (*They run off left.* BELINDA *laughs.*)

PEPITO: You were so brave, Miss Belinda!

SASSAFRAS (*Awed*): Bravest thing I ever saw. Weren't you scared?

BELINDA: Librarians are never scared, Sassafras. (*She laughs.*) Perhaps I should have let them have the picnic basket. What do you think is in it?

PEPITO: Delicious chickens?

BELINDA: No, delicious *Dickens.* (*Taking books from basket, showing them to children*) See? The only food a librarian ever has on a picnic—food for thought. Books! (*All laugh.*) Now, it's time to go home. Back to the Bar-B-Q Ranch. Father will be arriving home from St. Louis today. Come along. (*They exit right. "She'll Be Comin' Round the Mountain" is played fast tempo as curtains open.*)

* * * * *

TIME: *A few minutes later.*

SETTING: *Rustic parlor of the Bar-B-Q Ranch. Door up right leads outside. Up left and right of center are windows draped in chintz. Center is fireplace, with portrait of Texas Longhorn on wall above it, and bust of Homer and two hurricane lamps on mantelpiece. Down left are desk, chair, and bookcase crammed with books. Down right and left are exits to other rooms.*

AT RISE: BELINDA *stands down center, telegram in hand.* ABIGAIL *and* SASSAFRAS, *wearing aprons, stand as if in tableau:* ABIGAIL *holds broom;* SASSAFRAS *kneels with dustpan;* PEPITO *holds wicker trash basket;* HU HEE, *feather duster upraised, stands left.*

BELINDA: Why, this telegram is from Father. Listen. (*Reads*) "Big news, honey. Stop. You're going to have a stepmother and stepsisters. Stop. Father and fiancée arriving on four o'clock stage. Stop." (*Looks up*) Dear Father! I'm so happy for him. (*Silence*) Aren't you all happy, too?

HU HEE (*Shaking head*): Remains to be seen, Miss Belinda. Must first see wife-to-be.

BELINDA: Why, Hu Hee, don't you trust Father's judgment? Anyone he'd choose to be Mrs. Buckthorne is certain to be perfectly lovely. Just think, new sisters, too! (*She and others sing following lines slowly to tune of "She'll Be Comin' Round the Mountain."*)
A sublimely happy family, we will be.

OTHERS (*Doubtfully*):
We will see.

BELINDA :
With a mother to confide in, just for me.

OTHERS:
We will see.

BELINDA :
With two sisters for a bonus—
What a miracle's been shown us!
We will live together, oh, so lovingly.

OTHERS:
We will *see*.

BELINDA (*Speaking*): Do cheer up, all of you. This is good news.
(*Music to same song begins to play in background.*)

SASSAFRAS: We sure could use some good news around here.
(*Does some jig steps and sings as music tempo increases*)
Good news makes me feel like dancin'—

OTHERS (*Jigging in place*):
So do we! So do we!

SASSAFRAS (*Grabbing* PEPITO *to dance, center*):
Strut your stuff with fancy prancin',
One-two-three—

OTHERS:
One-two-three.

SASSAFRAS (*Singing*):

With the happiness we're feelin'
We'll go rockin' and a-reelin'
Lift the top right off the ceilin'—
Glo-ry be!

OTHERS (*Singing*):

Glo-ry be!

(*All form line, dance jig steps center. At conclusion of dance,* HU HEE *steps forward, speaking reflectively.*)

HU HEE: New lady-wife and daughters come from faraway St. Louis. Maybe they are like frightened little flowers. Perhaps pine for home. We make them welcome here. We help new lady-wife. (HU HEE *and others sing following lines.*)
We must aid her and abet her—

OTHERS:

Yes, siree!

SASSAFRAS:

There is nothin' I won't get her—

OTHERS: Yes, siree.

BELINDA :

We'll be happy that we met her,

OTHERS:

Mark this day with a big red letter,

PEPITO:

And *mañana* will be better,

OTHERS:

We'll soon see. Yes, siree.

(*Music continues, dance tempo, as all swing into a reel,* BELINDA *do-si-do-ing down the line. Loud knocking, then door bursts open.* MRS. POMPOSIA SMYTHE-SMITHERS *sweeps in haughtily, followed by* FASTIDIA *and* GAUDIA. *Music stops mid-beat. Others gasp.*)

POMPOSIA: Pray tell us, where is the Buckthorne mansion? I am Pomposia Smythe-Smithers the Third, and these are my daughters, Fastidia and Gaudia.

BELINDA: Why, this *is* the Buckthorne ranch.

FASTIDIA: This hovel?

GAUDIA: What a dump!

POMPOSIA: Is *this* Mr. Buckthorne's domicile? (*Snootily*)

How—quaint. (*She and daughters simultaneously hold up lorgnettes, staring at* BELINDA.) You must be Belinda Buckthorne.

BELINDA (*Cordially*): And you must be my stepmother-to-be. (*Crosses to embrace* POMPOSIA, *who draws away with distaste, and extends a limp hand. As if on signal, daughters extend their hands.*) We certainly do welcome you with open arms. (*To others*) Don't we?

ALL (*Looking at each other with foreboding*): We certainly do.

BELINDA (*Eagerly*): Is Father with you?

POMPOSIA (*Vaguely*): No. Your papa took a short cut across a stretch of desert called No-Man's Land.

ALL (*Together*): No-Man's Land!

PEPITO: The Beast just claimed that land!

FASTIDIA (*Alarmed*): Beast?

GAUDIA: What Beast?

POMPOSIA: Mr. Buckthorne never mentioned any Beast.

BELINDA (*Hastily*): It's nothing to worry about, truly, Stepmother.

POMPOSIA (*Haughtily*): Call me *Mrs. Smythe-Smithers*, Belinda dear. (*Indicating* SASSAFRAS, PEPITO, *and* HU HEE) Are these your hired help? Have them bring in our luggage immediately.

SASSAFRAS (*Arms on hips; saucily*): Miss Belinda, I don't tote luggage.

HU HEE *and* PEPITO (*Ad lib*): I won't carry their luggage. No, sir! (*Etc.*)

BELINDA: Please. Do it for me. (SASSAFRAS, HU HEE, *and* PEPITO *exit, grumbling, down right.* POMPOSIA *moves about room imperiously, looking at furnishings through lorgnette.* FASTIDIA *and* GAUDIA *follow her around, doing same.* BELINDA *stands apart, down left, arms folded.* "Tavern in the Town" *plays through action and under narration.*)

POMPOSIA: We have our work cut out for us, girls. We must turn this hovel into an abode fit for women of our station in life.

BELINDA: A hovel? Why, I decorated this house myself!

FASTIDIA: With your eyes shut, no doubt.

POMPOSIA: Take out your notebooks, girls. Make lists. (FAS-
TIDIA *and* GAUDIA *take notebooks and small pencils from
purses, following* POMPOSIA *as she whips out tape measure
from purse and measures curtains, benches, door, and floor.*
BELINDA *stands upstage, watching unhappily.* POMPOSIA
and others sing following lines to tune of "Tavern in the Town."
Those dreadful drapes, they must come down,
DAUGHTERS:
Must come down.
POMPOSIA:
We'll have portieres sent in from town.
DAUGHTERS:
In from town.
POMPOSIA:
And a suite complete with Duncan Phyfe—
BELINDA (*Stamping foot*):
You won't. You won't. Not on your life!
POMPOSIA (*Gazing upward*):
I'll want a crystal chandelier—
BELINDA:
Not in here!
POMPOSIA (*Crossing to sideboard*):
Some silver made by Paul Revere—
BELINDA:
Much too dear!
POMPOSIA:
And some servants from the British Isles,
All curtsies, bows, and cheerful smiles.
(*She crosses to bookshelf, running finger over books, looking
distastefully at fingertip.*)
This shabby bookshelf cannot stay.
BELINDA (*Running to bookshelf, arms outstretched protec-
tively*):
Yes, I say!
POMPOSIA:
Put in a charming window bay—
DAUGHTERS:
Window bay—
POMPOSIA (*Strolling downstage*):

There'll be Persian rugs upon the floors,
And carved pearl handles on the doors!

BELINDA (*Crossing center; speaking*): I don't believe this is happening. It's a nightmare. Oh, Father, Father. What have you done to us? (*Sound of hoof beats, shots, and whoops is heard offstage. Door bursts open, and* BUCK BUCKTHORNE *runs in with* VARMINT, *who is holding pistol to his head.* VIPER *follows with rifle. He forces women down left.*) Father!

POMPOSIA: Why, Mr. Buckthorne! What happened?

BUCK: The Beast's men caught me at the pass. (*To* VARMINT) Go on, shoot me. I'd rather be dead than tell these women what the Beast suggested.

VARMINT: I'd just as soon shoot you, Buckthorne, but King Beast wants his proposition delivered to these women.

POMPOSIA: What proposition? We'll do anything if you'll spare dear Mr. Buckthorne.

FASTIDIA *and* GAUDIA: *Anything.*

VIPER: King Beast wants one of you women to marry up with him. He wants a Queen Beast.

POMPOSIA, FASTIDIA, *and* GAUDIA (*Gasping; ad lib*): Anything but that! How dreadful! (*Etc.*)

BELINDA (*Stepping forward*): Stop—wait. *I* will go with you.

BUCK: No. I won't let you do it.

POMPOSIA: Yes, yes, Belinda. How *sweet.* How *commendable.* Go to save your father.

BELINDA (*To* VARMINT *and* VIPER): Take me to your Beast! (*She marches offstage.*)

VARMINT (*To* BUCK): Don't try to follow us, if you know what's good for you. (*Exits with* VIPER)

BUCK (*Running to door*): I'll get you back, Belinda!

POMPOSIA (*Aside to* FASTIDIA *and* GAUDIA; *smirking*): With Belinda out of the way, Mr. Buckthorne is all *mine.*

FASTIDIA: All *ours,* Mama.

GAUDIA: All *ours.* (*Curtain*)

* * * * *

SCENE 2

TIME: *Later that day.*
SETTING: *Beast's cave. Black backdrop is painted with stalac-*

tites and stalagmites. At center is rock throne, with crown,
bearskin robe, and club on it. Right and left of throne are
trunks and boxes of loot. Down right is campfire.

AT RISE: *Some of* BEAST'S BADMEN *are seated at fire, toast-*
ing chunks of meat on long sticks. Others are at table, playing
cards. Sound of roar is heard offstage. BADMEN *spring to at-*
tention.

1ST BADMAN: Attention. King Beast is comin'!

BADMEN (*Together*): Make way for King Beast. (*Another roar*
is heard offstage. B. J. BEAST *enters down left, swaggers to*
throne. He is ill-kempt and crude, but appealing.)

BEAST: Hail me.

BADMEN (*Together*): Hail, King Beast.

BEAST: Crown me.

1ST BADMAN (*Putting crown on* BEAST's *head*): Yes, sir,
King Beast.

BEAST: Robe me. (2ND BADMAN *puts robe around* BEAST's
shoulders.)

2ND BADMAN: Yes, sir, King Beast.

BEAST: Gimme my club.

3RD BADMAN: Right away, King Beast. (*Hands club to*
BEAST)

BEAST: Now sing me the Beastly Anthem.

BADMEN (*Singing to tune of "Tramp! Tramp! Tramp!"*):
Tramp! Tramp! Tramp! King Beast is coming.
Don't make trouble or he'll shoot!
Just bow low and call him "King,"
(*All bow.*)

BEAST:
All I want is *everything*—

BADMEN:
So give up, give in, and give him all your loot!
(BADMEN *begin marching in place, while singing.*)
Tramp! Tramp! Tramp! King Beast is coming.
Give up, there's no use to fight.
All your worldly goods forsake,

BEAST:
What I want is what I take,

BADMEN:
For the motto of King beast is:
Might makes right!

BEAST (*Speaking*): Right! (VARMINT *enters, followed reluctantly by* BELINDA, *with* VIPER *prodding her with rifle.*)

VARMINT *and* VIPER (*Together*): Hail, King Beast.

BEAST: Did you bring me some loot?

VARMINT: Better'n that, King Beast. I brought you a *bride.* (BADMEN *whoop and whistle.*)

BEAST (*Roaring*): Quiet! Don't you know how to behave in front of a lady? Vamoose, the lot of you. We're going to have a private parley. (BADMEN *exit down left.* VARMINT *and* VIPER *remain.* VIPER *nudges* BELINDA *up center with rifle.* BELINDA *folds arms defiantly.*)

VIPER: This is Buckthorne's daughter, Belinda.

VARMINT: She'll make a good queen for you.

BEAST (*Circling* BELINDA; *ogling her, then whistling approvingly*): Well, hello, Belinda. How'd you like to be Queen of the West, gal? (BELINDA *is silent; to* VARMINT) Can't she talk?

VARMINT: She can talk, all right. She could put a parrot out of business.

BEAST: Good. Then let's get the marryin' over with. Where's the parson? (VARMINT *and* VIPER *look at each other nervously.*)

VARMINT: Viper, you were supposed to hog-tie a parson and bring him here.

VIPER: Oh, no. *You* were supposed to get the parson.

BEAST: Get me a parson. *Now!*

VIPER *and* VARMINT (*Together*): Yessir, King Beast. (*Run off right*)

BEAST (*To* BELINDA; *indicating throne*): Sit down. Make yourself to home.

BELINDA: No, thank you. I have a home. This is not it.

BEAST (*Taken aback*): Huh! Feisty little gal, aren't you, Belinda?

BELINDA (*Frostily*): You may call me *Miss* Buckthorne.

BEAST: *Miss* Buckthorne, eh? Well, you can call me—King.

BELINDA: Never.

BEAST (*Angrily*): What makes you so contrary? Here I am being nicer to you than I am to anybody except my ma, and
you're as cold as ice. Now, why won't you call me King? I can
make you call me King. (*He thumps chest and yells like Tarzan.* BELINDA *yawns.*) How come you didn't faint? Women
always faint when I roar.

BELINDA (*Matter-of-factly*): I am a librarian. Librarians do
not faint.

BEAST (*Fetching necklace from jewel box and dangling it in
front of her; craftily*): Come on, gal. I'll give you this if you'll
call me King.

BELINDA: No.

BEAST (*Crossing to trunk, holding up gown; wheedling*): How
'bout this pretty purple dress? I stole it myself.

BELINDA: No.

BEAST (*Exasperated*): Then what'll it take to make you call me
King? (BELINDA *and* BEAST *sing following lines to tune of
"The Flowers that Bloom in the Spring."*)

BELINDA:
For you to be monarch of all, O Beast,
A remedial program you need.
With a knowledge of right and of wrong, at least,
An awareness of matters of state, increased,
And these words for your wisdom please heed:
You must certainly learn to *read.*

BEAST (*Turning away, disgruntled*):
Well, I ain't gonna listen,
By Ginger! By Sam!
'Cause I like the kind of a King
That I am.

BELINDA (*Stamping foot*):
I find you appalling!
Your manners are galling!
You're beastly and vulgar and sly.

BEAST (*Facing her; hotly*):
Well, don't rearrange me,
You never will change me,
I'll always be me. Don't try!

BELINDA (*Wagging finger at him*):
  For you to be head of society,
  Your manners must be more refined.
  You *must* change your shirts and bathe frequently,
  You must use fine china when you're at tea,
  And a napkin whenever you dine,
  And be reverent, courageous, and kind.
BEAST (*Fingers in ears*):
  Well, I ain't gonna listen,
  By Ginger! By Sam!
  'Cause I like the kind of a King
  That I am.
BELINDA (*Stamping foot again*):
  I find you appalling!
  I'll never stop calling—
  You Beast, 'til the day that I die—
BEAST:
  Well, don't rearrange me,
  You never will change me.
  I'll always be me. So don't try!
BELINDA (*Speaking*): You are impossible!
BEAST: You aren't any too *possible* yourself!
BELINDA: There are certain things I will require if you are going to keep me prisoner here.
BEAST: For instance?
BELINDA: Books. I must occupy my mind, and I intend to start a library right here.
BEAST: A library? Listen, gal. I got along my whole life without readin', and I'm not startin' now.
BELINDA (*With determination*): That remains to be seen. (*Curtain. Reprise of "The Flowers That Bloom in the Spring" and western songs may be played while scenery is changed.*)

* * * * *

SCENE 3

TIME: *Some months later.*
SETTING: *Same as Scene 2, but cave has been spruced up. Loot*

is stacked neatly at right. Campfire is gone. Bookshelf, table, and chair are down left.

AT RISE: BADMEN, *in clean, plaid shirts, hair combed, books open in their hands, sit on cushions across stage.* BELINDA *sits at table.*

BELINDA: You gentlemen have made phenomenal progress these past months.

BADMEN (*Together*): Thank you, Miss Buckthorne.

BELINDA: Now, let us all read from the Declaration of Independence. (*Roar is heard offstage.* BADMEN *pay no attention.*)

BADMEN (*Together*): "We hold these truths to be self-evident: that all men are created equal . . ." (BEAST *enters grandly, still unkempt, thumping chest, giving Tarzan yell.*)

BEAST: Hail me!

BADMEN (*Continuing to read*): "That they are endowed by their creator with certain unalienable rights . . ."

BEAST (*Louder*): Crown me! Robe me! Give me my club!

BADMEN (*Still reading*): "That among these are life, liberty, and the pursuit of happiness."

BEAST (*Roaring*): Quiet! This is *King Beast* talkin'!

1ST BADMAN (*To* BEAST): Simmer down, B.J. Accordin' to this book we are not your subjects anymore.

2ND BADMAN: We're your equals. See? (*Points to book*) Right here on page twenty-five.

BEAST (*Sarcastically*): Equals? I'm more equal than any six of you! Now, go out and grab me some land.

2ND BADMAN: We don't *grab* land anymore.

3RD BADMAN: We buy it and pay for it, fair and square.

BEAST: That's against all my principles! (*To* BADMEN) You smell like soap and shavin' lotion. Get out!

4TH BADMAN (*To* BELINDA): May we be excused, Miss Buckthorne?

BELINDA: You may. (BADMEN *put books in neat pile on table.*)

BADMEN (*Together*): Afternoon, Miss Buckthorne. So long, B.J. (*All except* 1ST BADMAN *bow to* BELINDA *and exit down right.*)

1ST BADMAN (*To* BEAST): We're going to pursue us some happiness.

BEAST (*Furious*): Get out and stay out! (1ST BADMAN *rushes out*. BEAST *throws book after him, crosses down left, stands with arms folded*. BELINDA *crosses down right*. BEAST *speaks aside*.) She's *ruinin'* me. And what's worse—she's gettin' to me. Yesterday I almost opened a book. Tomorrow I might take a bath.

BELINDA (*Aside*): Though I have won over his men, he remains aloof and apart. A beast to the end. How can I win him over?

BEAST (*Aside*): I could shut her in a dark room. But then she'd hate me. She's none too fond of me now, but I couldn't live if she hated me.

BELINDA (*Aside*): He has such potential. What a king he'd be! I could grow almost—fond—of him. (*Final measures of "The Flowers That Bloom in the Spring" are heard*. BELINDA *starts to sing*.)
If I could but reach him—
The things I could teach him!
How proud and how princely he'd be.

BEAST (*Singing*):
I'd talk to her often,
If only she'd soften—
I might even drink her *tea*!
(BEAST *crosses slowly to* BELINDA, *who turns to meet him. He addresses her shyly*.) Belinda—I mean, Miss Buckthorne.

BELINDA: Why, that's the first time you have addressed me as "Miss Buckthorne," Beast—that is—B.J.

BEAST: I won't beat around any bushes. I want to know straight out. Can you love a beast? Because that's what I am and that's what I'll always be.

BELINDA (*Hesitating, then sadly*): No, B.J., I cannot love you as a beast. (BEAST *turns away, crushed. Sounds of whoops are heard*.)

BEAST (*Starting off left*): That's Varmint and Viper. Something's up. (*He pauses, turns, bows awkwardly to* BELINDA.) Excuse me, Miss Buckthorne?

BELINDA (*Touched*): Of course, B.J. (BEAST *exits right*. RUNNING WATER *crawls in cautiously, down left, looks around, sniffs air, wets finger, holds it up, then hoots softly three times*.)

Running Water! (*He motions her to silence. SASSAFRAS enters, finger to lips.*) Sassafras! (BELINDA *motions them down right.*) I can't tell you how glad I am to see you! (BEAST, VARMINT, *and* VIPER *enter, unseen by others.*) How is Father?

SASSAFRAS: He's got trouble, Miss Belinda.

RUNNING WATER: That widder woman, Pomposia Smythe-Smithers, is a *crook!*

BEAST (*Aside*): Pomposia Smythe-Smithers! Aha!

BELINDA: What do you mean?

SASSAFRAS: She and her daughters travel around the country marryin' up with fellers. Then when she's got their money, she runs off, changes her name, and leaves 'em with empty pockets and empty hearts.

BELINDA: She mustn't marry my father!

RUNNING WATER: Too late! Wedding tonight!

BELINDA: What? Running Water, lead me out of this cave. Hurry! *I must stop that wedding!* (RUNNING WATER *runs off right, followed by* BELINDA *and* SASSAFRAS. VARMINT *and* VIPER *run center.* BEAST *follows them slowly, rubbing chin.*)

VARMINT (*Pointing off*): She's running out on you, boss!

VIPER: Want us to stop her? (BEAST *is silent.*)

BEAST (*To himself*): So, Pomposia Smythe-Smithers, our paths cross again. The only thing you understand is force, and you'll get it. (*To* VARMINT *and* VIPER) Fetch me my gun belt and my silver-studded six-guns.

VARMINT (*Eagerly*): Are you ridin' with us, boss? (BEAST *nods.*)

VIPER: Hot diggity dog! We're going to go grabbin' and robbin' again!

BEAST (*Aside*): Belinda will hate me for what I'm going to do. Still, I have to be a beast, so I can rescue her pa. (*Takes small book from table and slips it inside vest, above heart*) I'll take one of her books for luck. (*Thumping chest and roaring*) King Beast rides again! (VARMINT *and* VIPER *shout approval, shooting pistols into air. Quick curtain*)

* * * * *

SCENE 4

TIME: *That night.*

SETTING: *Same as Scene 1, but parlor is redecorated, with drapes at windows, and candelabra and bouquets on mantel. Ornate picture of a castle hangs over fireplace. Paper fan is in fireplace. On sideboard are punch bowl and cups. Folding chairs are set up, facing fireplace.*

AT RISE: BELINDA *tiptoes in, surveys decor.*

BELINDA: What deplorable taste! Why, these new furnishings must have cost Father a fortune!

POMPOSIA (*Offstage*): Come along, girls. We must see if Parson Worthy has arrived. (BELINDA *runs upstage and hides behind drapes, left, as* POMPOSIA, FASTIDIA, *and* GAUDIA, *wearing long gowns, enter, carrying long scarves.* POMPOSIA *carries bank book and bouquet with toy revolver hidden in it.*) The parson's not here yet. Just as well. Let's just run through our plans. (*Nods significantly at* GAUDIA *and* FASTIDIA)

GAUDIA: Are we doing the bank caper this time? Clean him out after the ceremony?

POMPOSIA: Exactly. (*Waves bank book*) As soon as the parson pronounces us man and wife, Buckthorne's entire fortune will be mine.

FASTIDIA: *Ours,* Mama. . . . We have the horses waiting out back.

POMPOSIA: Good. After the wedding, we'll meet in the kitchen—

FASTIDIA: Slip out the back door—

GAUDIA: Ride like sixty to the bank, and clean out the Buckthorne account.

POMPOSIA: And then—we'll go to California, to find a rich miner with a lonesome look.

ALL (*Together*): California, here we come! (*As they laugh,* BELINDA *marches out from behind curtain.*)

BELINDA: On the contrary! You are going nowhere—except to *jail.*

FASTIDIA *and* GAUDIA (*Ad lib*): Belinda! What are you doing here? (*Etc.* POMPOSIA *crosses upstage.*)

POMPOSIA (*Purring*): There, there, Belinda! We were only joking. Weren't we, girls? (*Aside, to* FASTIDIA *and* GAUDIA) Quick! The old scarf trick! And hurry! I hear someone coming. (FASTIDIA *and* GAUDIA *catch* BELINDA *by surprise.* FASTIDIA *gags her,* GAUDIA *binds her hands,* POMPOSIA *ties her feet. They push her behind drapes, left, as* BUCK *enters with* PARSON WORTHY, *who carries small black book.*)

BUCK: Pomposia, darlin', looky here, Parson Worthy's come, so the weddin' can commence to begin.

POMPOSIA: How wonderful! (PARSON *stands up center.* POMPOSIA *and daughters stand left,* BUCK, *right.* ABIGAIL, SASSAFRAS, PEPITO, HU HEE, RUNNING WATER, TROOPER HOOPER, *and* CAPTAIN McREADY *enter left and right and sit on folding chairs.* JIMMY TONSILS *enters and stands right, strumming "Wedding March" on guitar.*)

BUCK: If only Belinda were here!

FASTIDIA: She would have been—

GAUDIA: But she's all tied up.

SASSAFRAS: She's here somewhere (POMPOSIA *looks at her sharply.*) in spirit.

PARSON: Dearly beloved, we are gathered here to join these folks in holy wedlock. Afore I begin, is there anyone here who knows any reason why these two lovebirds may not be joined in marriage? (BELINDA *moans, struggles; drapes move.*)

PEPITO (*Pointing to drapes*): A ghost!

POMPOSIA (*As* FASTIDIA *and* GAUDIA *nudge drapes into place.*) Continue, parson.

FASTIDIA: It's only the wind. (*Sound of hoof beats is heard.* POMPOSIA *nudges* PARSON.)

POMPOSIA: Hurry up.

PARSON: Do you, Pomposia Smythe-Smithers the Third . . .

POMPOSIA (*Interrupting*): I do. So does he. Quickly, pronounce us wed.

PARSON: Hold your horses. Let me find the place. (*Examines book*) Here it is. I now pronounce you—(*Shots and whoops are heard.* BEAST *bursts on up right, shooting into air, followed by* VARMINT *and* VIPER.)

BEAST: Stop the weddin'!

POMPOSIA: Bartholomew! Bartholomew Jasper Beast!

BEAST: Pomposia Smythe-Smithers the Third, alias Gilda the Gold Digger. You had me under your spell once. You made me the Beast I am today. Well, the weddin' is off. You've bilked your last bozo, Gilda. (*Others gasp.*)

BUCK: What's going on here, Pomposia? (POMPOSIA *pulls revolver from bouquet as she moves toward drapes, where BE-LINDA is hidden.*)

POMPOSIA: Don't move, or I'll shoot. Yes, I am Gilda the Gold Digger. As long as there's a sucker in this world, I intend to go on diggin' gold. (*To* FASTIDIA *and* GAUDIA) Get Belinda and bring her with us.

BUCK (*As* FASTIDIA *and* GAUDIA *pull* BELINDA *from drapes*): Belinda! My little Belinda, tied up like a steer going to market. Somebody—save her!

BEAST (*Running upstage*): I'll save her, Buckthorne. (*Places himself between* BELINDA *and* POMPOSIA) Get away from my gal! (POMPOSIA *shoots* BEAST *and he crumples to floor.* BELINDA *moans through her gag.* HOOPER *drags* BEAST *down center, as* RUNNING WATER *and* McREADY *grab* POMPOSIA, FASTIDIA, *and* GAUDIA. BUCK *unties* BE-LINDA.)

McREADY (*To* POMPOSIA): Gilda the Gold Digger, you and your lowdown accomplices are under arrest. (*Hands gun to* RUNNING WATER) March 'em over to the jail, Running Water. (RUNNING WATER *marches* POMPOSIA, FASTIDIA, *and* GAUDIA *off left.* BELINDA *rushes to* BEAST, *kneels and puts his head on her lap.* VARMINT *and* VIPER *kneel beside her.* McREADY *takes* BEAST's *pulse as* HOOPER *fans him with hat.* BELINDA *sobs,* McREADY *consoles her.*) There, there, little lady, his pulse is still goin' strong. He's not dead yet. (*Music to "The Flowers That Bloom in the Spring" plays softly.*)

BELINDA: Courage, dear Beast. Courage!

VARMINT: Aw, shucks, Boss. Don't go and die on us.

VIPER: We need you, Boss. Who's gonna snatch ranches and grab land when you're gone?

BEAST (*Raising on elbow*): No more snatching and grabbing.

Promise me you'll give back every inch of land I've taken, and all that loot.

VARMINT: But, Boss—

BEAST: Promise!

VARMINT *and* VIPER (*Together*): We promise.

BEAST (*To* BELINDA): Can you forgive me, Belinda? I didn't want to be a beast anymore, but I had to be, just one more time, to save you and your pa from a fate worse than death: bankruptcy. (*Falls back*)

BELINDA: My poor, dear Beast! There is nothing to forgive. Why, you have proved yourself noble and generous and brave. In fact, with a clear conscience, I can now call you—King!

BEAST (*Grinning, raising head*): Did you hear that, folks? At last—she called me King. I can die happy! (*He goes limp. All gasp and press closer around* BEAST.)

HOOPER: Has he breathed his last, Captain?

McREADY: I don't know. He was shot in the chest, but there's not a drop of blood; something stopped that bullet cold. (*Pulling book with hole in it from* BEAST's *vest*) It's a book! Why, this is a miracle. (*All applaud and cheer, as* BEAST *staggers to his feet, assisted by* BELINDA, *who holds book for all to see.*)

BELINDA: A miracle indeed. It's Shakespeare's play—"All's Well That Ends Well"! (*All cheer.*)

PARSON (*Starting off right*): If you've no further need of a parson, I'll be going.

HU HEE: Please wait, Parson. (*Crosses down center, joins hands of* ABIGAIL *and* HOOPER, BELINDA *and* BEAST) Ancient sage say: "Never put off marrying until tomorrow when you can marry today."

ABIGAIL: Truer words were never spoken. (*To* HOOPER) Henry, pop the question.

HOOPER (*On one knee*): Miss Abigail, will you—

ABIGAIL (*Interrupting*): You know I will, Henry.

BEAST (*Hand on heart*): Miss Buckthorne, will you do me the honor of marryin' up with me?

BELINDA: B.J., will you learn to read?

BEAST: I'll swallow an entire encyclopedia and a dictionary if it'll please you.

BELINDA (*Joyfully*): Then I will consent to be your true and faithful partner with the greatest pleasure.

BEAST: Was that a "yes"?

BUCK: Take it or leave it, son. That's the closest to a yes you'll get from Belinda Buckthorne.

BEAST: I'll take it! (*All cheer.* PARSON *and two couples cross up center, forming tableau, with* McREADY *standing next to* ABIGAIL *and* HOOPER, BUCK *next to* BELINDA *and* BEAST. *Others turn to audience, and sing to tune of "She'll Be Comin' Round the Mountain.")*

Everything is fine and dandy,
Got no doubt.
Spread the word there's smiles
And sunshine, hereabout.
Every wrong has been all-righted,
And our lovers are united,
Naturally we're plumb dee-lighted,
Shout it out! Shout it out!

JIMMY TONSILS (*Singing*):

Swing your partner,
Promenade her when I call—
Do si do, away you go,
Around the hall,
Raise the roof and raise the rafter,
Raise some cane with joy and
    laughter,
We'll live happy—ever after,
After all!

(*Music continues, faster, as all dance. Curtain*)

·THE END

Production Notes

BELINDA AND THE BEAST

Characters: 12 male; 5 female; male extras for Beast's Bad Men.

Playing Time: 35 minutes.

Costumes: Jimmy Tonsils, cowboy outfit and guitar; Hu Hee, coolie costume; Running Water, Indian costume; Captain McReady and Trooper Hooper, Cavalry uniforms; Abigail, simple print dress, flowers in hair; Belinda, plain dress, hair in bun; Pepito and Sassafras, tattered clothes, may be barefoot; B.J. Beast, Varmint, Viper, and Badmen, scraggly hair, beards, and a generally crude appearance. In Scene 3, Badmen change to clean plaid shirts and jeans, and hair is combed. Pomposia, Fastidia, and Gaudia, ostentatious dresses, lorgnettes; they carry purses containing small notebooks and pencils. They change to wedding finery, carry long scarves, in Scene 4. Buck is well-dressed, with string tie and gold belt buckle; Parson Worthy, black suit, white collar.

Properties: Gong and striker; books; flag with skull and crossbones; prop rifle; picnic basket containing books; telegram; dustpan; broom; wicker trash basket; feather duster; tape measure; long sticks holding chunks of meat; playing cards; necklace; dress; bouquet with toy revolver hidden in it; bank book; Bible.

Setting: Scene 1, Before Rise: Pole at center has sign reading, NO MAN'S LAND. NO WOMAN'S NEITHER. BEWARE OF BEAST. Large rock is right, water tower left. At Rise: Parlor of the Bar-B-Q Ranch. Door outside is up right; exits to other rooms, down right and left. Up left and right, windows draped in chintz. Fireplace is center, with portrait of Texas Longhorn on wall above it. Mantel holds bust of Homer and two hurricane lamps. Desk and chair, and bookcase crammed with books, are down left. Scene 2: Beast's cave. Black backdrop has stalactites and stalagmites painted on it. Rock throne is center, with crown, bearskin robe, and club on it. Trunks and boxes of loot are right and left of throne. Campfire is down right. Scene 3: Same as Scene 2, but loot is stacked neatly at right, campfire is gone, and bookshelf, table and chair are down left. Scene 4: Same as Scene 1, but parlor is redecorated, with new drapes at windows, and candelabra and bouquets on mantel. Pretentious picture of castle hangs over fireplace. On sideboard are punch bowl and cups. Folding chairs are set up, facing fireplace, with aisle center and red runner.

Lighting: No special effects.

Sound: Hoof beats, gunshots, etc.

∾An American Story

by Arlene J. Morris

A pageant of great moments in America's history . . .

Characters

UNCLE SAM
CHORUS
TOWN CRIER
FOUR COLONISTS
THOMAS JEFFERSON
BEN FRANKLIN
JOHN ADAMS
GEORGE WASHINGTON
REPORTER
TWENTY NARRATORS
DANCERS
WILLIAM LLOYD GARRISON
FREDERICK DOUGLASS
SLAVE
ABRAHAM LINCOLN
STROLLING COUPLE
BARBERSHOP QUARTET
ELIZABETH CADY STANTON
APPLE SELLER
TWO MEN
STUDENTS
MARTIN LUTHER KING

BEFORE RISE: UNCLE SAM *enters in front of curtain.*
UNCLE SAM (*To audience*): Well, well, well, so I'm over two
    hundred years old! It seems like only yesterday that I was

41

born. (*Points to child in audience*) You're whispering, young man. (*Pauses as if listening*) Oh, I see. You think I'm an old man. Why, son, I've only just begun to live. My future is crammed full of promises. And why not? Think of all those noble pledges I've made and kept these past two hundred years! Once a mere child of mother country England, I grew so that now I am a power in my own right. I am . . . perhaps not all that I wish to be yet; mighty powerful today, ah, but tomorrow, the perfect union for all the people of this great land. (*Points to another child in audience*) What's that? What have I done to deserve the right to exist this long? Oh, the tales I could tell you if I had the time! This United States, its heroes and heroines, its glorious deeds, its fearless pioneers . . . Oh, yes, I remember it all so well. (UNCLE SAM *exits. Curtain opens.*)

* * * * *

SETTING: *At four angles of stage stand four flats, each depicting two figures in costumes representative of successive American fashions from 1775 to present. Backdrop is projection screen for slides (optional).*

AT RISE: CHORUS *may be seated on stage.* TOWN CRIER *enters, carrying placard reading,* 1775. *He moves across stage, ringing bell as he walks. As* CRIER *exits,* FOUR COLONISTS *enter, crossing to center. They gesture angrily.*

1ST COLONIST: The English have no right to tax us!

2ND COLONIST: England is our mother country. The King knows what's best for us.

3RD COLONIST: No man, not even the great King George, has the right to tax without representation.

4TH COLONIST: I say that we should oppose his decree. The tea shall be sipped only by the fish in the sea. (COLONISTS *exit, still gesturing angrily.* TOWN CRIER *reenters carrying placard reading,* 1776. *He rings bell as he crosses stage. As* CRIER *exits,* THOMAS JEFFERSON, BENJAMIN FRANKLIN, *and* JOHN ADAMS *enter.* JEFFERSON *holds unrolled parchment. Other men read over his shoulder.*)

FRANKLIN: Mr. Jefferson, are you prepared to read us your statement, this declaration we are going to send to King George?

JEFFERSON: I most certainly am.

ADAMS: Mr. Franklin, what shall we call this document Mr. Jefferson has composed?

FRANKLIN: There is no better name, Mr. Adams, than the one which best states our purpose. We shall call this noble scroll the Declaration of Independence.

ALL (*Ad lib*): Excellent. Fine. Yes, that's perfect. (*Etc.* JEFFERSON *exits, holding paper before him, as if reading, and others follow him off.*)

VOICE (*Offstage*): "We hold these truths to be self-evident, that all men are created equal, that they are endowed by their Creator with certain unalienable Rights, that among these are Life, Liberty and the pursuit of Happiness." (TOWN CRIER *enters, ringing bell, carrying placard reading,* VALLEY FORGE. *As* TOWN CRIER *exits,* GEORGE WASHINGTON *enters, holding and reading from large roll of parchment. He appears worried, and paces.* REPORTER *enters, carrying quill pen and piece of parchment.*)

REPORTER: General Washington, sir, about this war. Do you think we can defeat the British?

WASHINGTON: Sir, we have no choice. Lest there be those who do not feel the desire to govern themselves; lest there be those who wish to remain fledglings till eternity, then we must do battle. Freedom, sir, is our right. We will be free men in a free land or we will die.

REPORTER: Good luck, sir. (*He shakes hands with* WASHINGTON *and exits.* WASHINGTON *resumes his pacing. Curtain closes. If* CHORUS *is not seated onstage, they enter at this point and exit after song. They enter and exit in similar fashion for remainder of play.*)

CHORUS (*Singing "Johnny Has Gone for a Soldier"*):
Here I sit on Buttermilk Hill,
Who could blame me, cry my fill?
And every tear would turn a mill,
Johnny has gone for a soldier.

(When song is completed, 1ST NARRATOR *enters before curtain.)*

1ST NARRATOR:

The war was fought.

The American Revolution.

A sad and grueling war.

A dream, a victory, freedom.

The chains of a colonial past were broken.

We were a nation on our own.

The Constitution was born.

Strength, goals, ideals,

They abounded in this new land.

America had grown

From a helpless infant to an adult.

(1ST NARRATOR *exits. Curtain opens. If desired,* DANCERS *may enter and perform minuet to appropriate music of Revolutionary period. At conclusion of dance,* DANCERS *exit.* 2ND NARRATOR *enters.)*

2ND NARRATOR: It was 1812. The United States was reaching out to define itself as a nation. It was the time of the Industrial Revolution, bringing many new inventions. Robert Fulton had built his steamboat. Eli Whitney's cotton gin was being used with increasing popularity. We were planning how to use our natural resources. The Erie Canal opened. Cargo shipping would be easier and faster now. The United States was becoming recognized as an independent country. It was time to explore our frontier lands. Pioneers were moving into the Northwest Territory. They were settling the land. Brave people, Lewis and Clark, Daniel Boone, and Sacajawea, the Indian woman, dared to search for trails that few had traveled. *(Stage lights go out.* 2ND NARRATOR *exits. Slides of steamboat, Robert Fulton, Daniel Boone, and/or Lewis and Clark, are flashed on backdrop. Stage lights come on. Curtain closes.)*

CHORUS (*Singing "Erie Canal"*):

I've got a mule, her name is Sal,

Fifteen years on the Erie Canal. . . .

(At conclusion of song, 3RD NARRATOR *enters in front of curtain.)*

3RD NARRATOR:
Our country was growing
In knowledge and size.
But a burning question
Pierced the heart
Of this country.
Slavery . . .
Passions, fears, hatred, distrust . . .
It was the issue
That almost destroyed
The nation founded on
Equality for all.
(*Curtain opens, revealing* WILLIAM LLOYD GARRISON, FREDERICK DOUGLASS, *and* SLAVE, *with backs to audience.*)

GARRISON (*Turning toward audience, holding out placard reading,* ABOLISH SLAVERY): I am William Lloyd Garrison. I am an abolitionist.

DOUGLASS (*Turning to audience; holding placard reading,* DOWN WITH SLAVERY): I am Frederick Douglass, a former slave who escaped from a plantation to Massachusetts. I work as an abolitionist because I believe slavery is inhuman. (SLAVE, *with head bent, plods across stage, while* 3RD NARRATOR *recites following dialogue.*)

3RD NARRATOR:
My pen cannot remain idle, nor my voice be suppressed,
My heart cannot cease to bleed
While two million of my fellow beings
Wear the chains of slavery.
(3RD NARRATOR *exits. Stage lights go out.* 4TH NARRATOR *enters and speaks as slides of gold miners and pioneers in wagons are flashed on backdrop.*)

4TH NARRATOR:
The United States expanded.
Our territories were stretching from coast to coast.
"Remember the Alamo," they cried in Texas.
"We must be free of Mexico."
"Gold," they cried in California.

The Oregon Trail, the Santa Fe Trail, "Pike's Peak or Bust."
This was our Manifest Destiny,
To control from Atlantic to Pacific.
(4TH NARRATOR *exits*. 5TH NARRATOR *enters*.)
5TH NARRATOR:
But still the bitterness hung over.
We were a nation united,
But divided.
The North proposed freedom
For all men.
The South cried,
"We will keep our slaves."
Could this country survive?
A divided nation
Was like a man
Without a soul.
(5TH NARRATOR *exits. Stage lights come up.* DANCERS *enter and perform dance to "My Old Kentucky Home" or other music. At conclusion,* DANCERS *exit.* 6TH NARRATOR *enters*.)
6TH NARRATOR:
But the Court ruled a slave
Was a slave. He was at his master's mercy.
The abolitionists denounced that claim,
But only a few listened.
Then the South took its stand.
There would be no more union.
Abe Lincoln, the President then,
Refused to accept that decision.
A war was fought—
The Civil War.
Brother against brother,
A life for a life.
It was a shameful blot
On a past filled with so much glory.
(ABRAHAM LINCOLN *enters*.)
LINCOLN: "Fourscore and seven years ago our fathers brought
forth on this continent a new nation, conceived in Liberty, and

dedicated to the proposition that all men are created equal."
(LINCOLN *freezes in position. Curtain closes.* 6TH NARRA-
TOR *exits.*)
CHORUS (*Singing "Battle Hymn of the Republic"*):
"Mine eyes have seen the glory of the coming of the Lord. . . . "
(7TH NARRATOR *enters.*)
7TH NARRATOR:
By 1865 the Civil War was over.
The South remained a part of the Union.
The slaves were now free.
And . . . Abraham Lincoln was dead,
Killed by an assassin's bullet.
(*Curtain opens. Stage lights go off. Slide of Abraham Lincoln
flashes on screen for several moments, then is removed.* 7TH
NARRATOR *exits. "Home on the Range" is heard off.* 8TH
NARRATOR *enters. Stage lights go up.*)
8TH NARRATOR:
It was 1865. The United States was growing up.
It was a time for movement.
But sometimes dreams are
Not for everyone.
The Indian people
Bore the pain
Of America's westward calling.
They were moved to reservation towns.
Cowboys, miners, farmers
Yearned for the open spaces
And the gold.
But how,
How could the United States
Connect its eastern settlers
With its western pioneers?
The Union Pacific, the railroads
Solved this country's problems.
And so the West was settled.
CHORUS (*Singing "I've Been Working on the Railroad"*):
"I've been working on the railroad
All the live-long day. . . ."

(*Stage lights go off at conclusion of song, and* 8TH NARRA-
TOR *exits.* 9TH NARRATOR *enters in spotlight downstage.*)
9TH NARRATOR:
What is America? Literature, art, music?
Mark Twain, Stephen Foster?
A pioneer spirit, a determination, an inventive mind?
Thomas Edison, Alexander Graham Bell,
The Wright Brothers, Henry Ford.
These were just a few. It was a new type of living in America.
It was industry's turn now.
(*Slides of Model T and first airplane flash on screen.* 9TH
NARRATOR *exits. Stage lights come up.* 10TH NARRATOR
enters.)
10TH NARRATOR:
America was over a hundred years old.
She was no longer an agricultural land.
Factories were booming.
Big money names screamed through the land.
Pittsburgh's Andrew Carnegie and his steel mills;
Henry Clay Frick and his coke ovens;
John D. Rockefeller, the oil tycoon.
Ida M. Tarbell, the journalist, writing, trying to keep a big
　　business honest—
This was America at the turn of the century.
Oh, yes, those were the times.
Factories meant pollution, strikes, slums, child labor.
But they meant jobs and money for all,
Especially those people coming to America from Europe,
The immigrants.
(10TH NARRATOR *exits.* DANCERS *enter and perform ap-
propriate folk dance, then exit.* 11TH NARRATOR *enters.*)
11TH NARRATOR:
It was an exciting time for America.
The immigrants came to their new home,
Tired and poor.
But they believed in a dream, freedom from
Terror and want.
An American ethnic parade, the old and the new.

A melting pot, they called it.
There were hard times, and sad times, and moments of regret.
But they tried to succeed; they wouldn't give up.
Life here was busy.
There were moments of fun,
Strolls through the park.
Ice cream parlor dates.
And the singing songs of those barbershop quartets.
(STROLLING COUPLE *enters, arm in arm, and crosses to side of stage, where they freeze in position.* BARBERSHOP QUARTET *enters, stands center. They sing "Down By the Old Mill Stream," or other typical selection. At end of song, curtain closes.* 11TH NARRATOR *exits.* 12TH NARRATOR *enters.*)

12TH NARRATOR:

It was 1917 . . .
Europe was fighting a war, to save democracy.
We in the United States wouldn't sit back
And watch our friends die.
"Never," said Woodrow Wilson.
And so it was.
Our boys went over.
Their strength and spirit helped win World War I.
But our nation had learned a lesson.
Let us make a commitment
For World Peace.
And the League of Nations was begun
To prevent any more bloodshed.
(12TH NARRATOR *exits.* CHORUS *sings "Over There."* 13TH NARRATOR *enters.*)

13TH NARRATOR:

Americans were becoming world famous.
Lindbergh made air history
In a flight across the Atlantic.
There were fights for women's rights.
Elizabeth Cady Stanton, Susan B. Anthony
Led those daring women,
The Suffragettes.

(*Curtain opens.* ELIZABETH CADY STANTON *stands on box.*)

STANTON (*Gesturing*): It is time we women take a stand. We must no longer be denied the right to vote. We will battle until victory is achieved. (*Freezes in position*)

13TH NARRATOR: And it was. In 1920 the nineteenth amendment was passed. Women were a part of the democratic process. (*Curtain closes.* 13TH NARRATOR *exits.* 14TH NARRATOR *enters.*)

14TH NARRATOR:

But for most,
It was a time
To pursue fun.
Movies with sound,
"Talkies" became the rage.
Dancing The Charleston
Was the nation's pastime.
Flappers and curls . . .
Oldsmobile rides . . .
"The Roaring Twenties."

(14TH NARRATOR *exits.* DANCERS *enter and perform the Charleston to appropriate music.* DANCERS *exit.* 15TH NARRATOR *enters.*)

15TH NARRATOR:

The twenties ended.
A decade of peace had passed.
Depression set in. Americans faced a test.
There were no jobs, no money.
Men selling apples on street corners
Were the common sight now.

(APPLE SELLER *enters slowly, carrying bushel basket. From the other side of stage* TWO MEN *enter, heads down, moving slowly. The three figures meet, center.* APPLE SELLER *pantomimes peddling apples.* 1ST MAN *refuses;* 2ND MAN *pantomimes buying apple.* APPLE SELLER *exits, and* TWO MEN *resume walking. During this scene,* CHORUS *sings "Brother, Can You Spare A Dime?"*)

It took a great leader to calm the nation's fears.

Don't worry, folks. Franklin Delano Roosevelt is here.
(*Curtain opens. Lights go out. Slide of Roosevelt flashes on. "Happy Days Are Here Again" is heard. Music plays during following dialogue.*)
Franklin Delano Roosevelt, a man who was strong,
Helped guide this unhappy nation.
Work programs, jobs, a sense of pride—
FDR worked to solve our nation's woes.
Slowly, with work, we recovered,
And FDR became the people's hero.
(*Music stops.* 15TH NARRATOR *exits.* 16TH NARRATOR *enters.*)

16TH NARRATOR: But another crisis was at hand. In Europe, another war, another threat to democracy. We sat back for a while, sadly watching Europe crumble, until—(*Sound of three loud tom-tom beats is heard.*) December 7, 1941. Pearl Harbor, a U.S. naval base in the Hawaiian Islands, was attacked by Japan. It was war. FDR wouldn't allow anyone to destroy this nation's honor. We entered a war with Japan and joined Europe's battle. Finally, it was 1945. The war was over in Europe. Our boys were coming home. A few months later it would be over in the Pacific, but not before America had uncovered a terrifying new weapon, the atomic bomb. (DANCERS *enter and perform the Lindy. They exit.* 16TH NARRATOR *exits. Curtain closes.* 17TH NARRATOR *enters before curtain.*)

17TH NARRATOR: Post World War II. . . . It was our job now to maintain peace. The United Nations was formed to help the world keep a permanent peace. And we began a new type of expansion. We began to explore space. This would be our new frontier. Explorer I soared through space, searching. . . .
(17TH NARRATOR *exits.* 18TH NARRATOR *enters.*)

18TH NARRATOR:
The fifties . . .
It was a new way of life.
TV was tops.
"It's Howdy Doody time."
"M-I-C-K-E-Y—M-O-U-S-E."

But there were other noises:
"Hey, man, like, cool, Daddy."
Skirts and sweaters, slicked-back duck-tail hair. . . .
"You Ain't Nothin' But a Hound Dog."
The teenager became an American symbol.
It was 1956.
Elvis Presley introduced the world to rock and roll.
(*Curtain opens. A slide of Elvis Presley flashes on screen. Lights come up. Music to "Jailhouse Rock" is heard.* DANCERS *enter, perform jitterbug, then exit.* 18TH NARRATOR *exits.* 19TH NARRATOR *enters.* CHORUS *sings a few bars of "Camelot.")*
19TH NARRATOR:
1960 . . .
John F. Kennedy, President.
Camelot is a beautiful place where nothing is ever wrong.
Ah, yes, the sixties began as Camelot,
And ended . . . with the nation torn apart.
John F. Kennedy was assassinated.
Then Martin Luther King.
Unrest in the United States had begun.
"All men are created equal. . . . "
This slogan stood for Civil Rights.
"We are a part of America too"—
This was the sound of women's lib.
Yes, those were the events. . . .
So were rioting in the ghettos,
Bloodshed on the campuses.
"Peace," cried the young.
It became an obsession.
And yet, perhaps it was time to settle the score.
Black men and women led on by King
Dared to dream dreams they had never dreamed.
(STUDENTS *enter, carrying signs reading,* PEACE, WOMEN'S LIB, GET OUT OF VIETNAM, BLACK RIGHTS. MARTIN LUTHER KING, JR. *enters opposite side.)*
KING: I have a dream. I have a dream that all God's children. . . . (KING *and* STUDENTS *meet center. In pantomime*

KING *addresses* STUDENTS *while they motion angrily. Then in background* CHORUS *sings, "We Shall Overcome." All freeze until song finishes. Curtain slowly closes.* 19TH NARRATOR *exits.* 20TH NARRATOR *enters.*)

20TH NARRATOR:

But, we had made great strides.
Apollo II landed on the moon.
It was one small step for man,
One giant leap for mankind.
And we were cleaning our own house.
We were working together toward
Making all men and women equal.
We were a vibrant nation once again.
The years passed.
It was the seventies.
The American nation revisited its past. . . .
The Bicentennial year 1976.
The heroes of old came to life.
America looked back and smiled.
For with every minute of pain
There was an hour of glory.
America . . . born from a seed,
Grown to a giant oak.

(20TH NARRATOR *exits.* CHORUS *sings, "This Land Is Your Land."* UNCLE SAM *enters through curtain, center.*)

UNCLE SAM (*To audience*): Over two hundred years old, am I? Why, I still feel young. I couldn't think of retirement. There's too much left to be done. Disease to conquer, poverty to eliminate, health care for all. Those are my challenges. And there's more. How can we conserve our natural resources? How can our mighty nation help the world realize all people must be treated with dignity? We will find those answers as the century closes, just the way we solved other problems. (*Points to child in audience*) What did you say? No, I can't do it myself. Who's left? Who's able enough? Who can make America the more perfect Union? Why, the solution is simple. Uncle Sam needs you! (*Points into audience, then crosses to side of stage. Lights go off. Curtain opens. "America the Beautiful" is heard.*

Six slides representing moments in American history flash on screen, then go off. Entire cast marches on and sings "America the Beautiful." Curtain)

THE END

Production Notes

AN AMERICAN STORY

Characters: 12 male; 2 female; 34 or more male or female for Narrators, Town
Crier, Colonists, Reporter, Slave, Barbershop Quartet, Apple Seller, Students, Chorus, and Dancers.

Playing Time: 35 minutes.

Costumes: Narrators wear modern dress. Uncle Sam, red, white, and blue
suit, and traditional top hat. Town Crier, Colonists, Franklin, Jefferson,
Adams, Washington, and Reporter wear stockings, knickers, white shirts,
and tri-cornered hats. Abolitionists wear Victorian period costumes. Slave
wears torn, cut-off pants, torn shirt, and kerchief. Abraham Lincoln wears
top hat and black suit. Barbershop Quartet wears striped jackets and straw
hats. Strolling Couple: male is in suit, female in long dress and gloves.
Elizabeth Cady Stanton wears long skirt and blouse. Apple Seller and Depression Era Men wear old sports jackets and worn pants and shirts. Martin
Luther King, suit and tie. Students, street clothes.

Properties: Bell; parchment; quill pen; box; bushel basket; placards reading,
1775, 1776, VALLEY FORGE, ABOLISH SLAVERY, DOWN WITH SLAVERY, PEACE,
WOMEN'S LIB, GET OUT OF VIETNAM, and BLACK RIGHTS.

Setting: Placed on four angles of stage are four flats—wooden frames covered
with muslin, each depicting two figures in costumes representing different
successive eras in American fashion, e.g., Colonial, Civil War, Victorian,
etc. There is a backdrop which is the projection screen for slides (optional).

Lighting: Lights on and off; optional slides.

Sound: Various musical selections representative of American song and dance
through various periods. Recorded music may be substituted for Chorus.

∾ Titanic: Destination Disaster

by John L. Lipp

A dramatic account of a tragic day at sea . . .

Characters

FIRST OFFICER MURDOCK
QUARTERMASTER HITCHENS
FLEET, *the lookout*
LAWRENCE BEESLEY
CAPTAIN SMITH
THREE PASSENGERS
THOMAS ANDREWS
OFFICER WILDE
OFFICER BOXHALL
MARY SLOAN
EDITH RUSSELL
JOHN JACOB ASTOR
MRS. JOHN JACOB ASTOR
ISADOR STRAUS
MRS. ISADOR STRAUS
BENJAMIN GUGGENHEIM
FIRST OFFICER LIGHTOLLER
ETCHES, *the steward*

TIME: *Sunday, April 14 and Monday, April 15, 1912.*
SETTING: *Split stage: at left, the engine room, and at right, boat deck of the* Titanic. *Chair left represents lookout's tower at front of ship.*
AT RISE: *Stage is dimly lit. Spotlight comes up left. FLEET, the*

lookout, is staring intently off left. FIRST OFFICER MUR-
DOCK *and* QUARTERMASTER HITCHENS *stand behind
him, in engine room.*

FLEET (*Yelling*): Iceberg, dead ahead!

MURDOCK (*Urgently*): Turn the wheel starboard, Hitchens.
(HITCHENS *motions, as if turning wheel.*)

HITCHENS: Aye, aye, sir.

MURDOCK: Now, full speed ahead. (HITCHENS *motions, as if
pulling throttle.*)

HITCHENS: Aye, sir. . . . What next?

MURDOCK: We've done all that is humanly possible, Hitchens.
All we can do now is wait. (MURDOCK *and* HITCHENS *continue to look off left.* BEESLEY *enters, crosses center, and addresses audience.*)

BEESLEY: And thirty-seven seconds later, we hit. (BEESLEY,
FLEET, HITCHENS, *and* MURDOCK *jolt slightly to left, as
if feeling the impact.* CAPTAIN SMITH *rushes in and
crosses left.*)

CAPTAIN SMITH (*Tensely*): Mr. Murdock, what happened?

MURDOCK (*Pointing, panicky*): An iceberg, sir. We did all we
could, but she was too close.

SMITH: Close the emergency doors!

MURDOCK: Done, sir.

BEESLEY: But by then it was already too late. (*Spotlight goes
out left, comes up on* TWO PASSENGERS, *who enter right.*)

1ST PASSENGER (*Panicky*): What was that?

2ND PASSENGER: I think we hit something.

1ST PASSENGER (*Puzzled*): But what? It was only a slight jolt.

2ND PASSENGER: Perhaps some debris from another ship?

1ST PASSENGER: Well, whatever it was, it can't be anything
too serious.

2ND PASSENGER: I'm sure it's nothing to worry about. After
all, this is the world's most luxurious ocean liner! (*They ad
lib quietly, as* BEESLEY *speaks.*)

BEESLEY: Welcome to the *Titanic*. She is not only the world's
most luxurious ocean liner, but at ninety-two feet wide, 882
feet long, and eleven stories high, she is the world's largest.

(PASSENGERS, MURDOCK, HITCHENS, SMITH, *and* FLEET *turn to audience.*)

ALL: Unsinkable!

BEESLEY (*Sighing deeply*): Or so we thought. (FLEET, HITCH-ENS, MURDOCK, *and* SMITH *exit.*) But on the *Titanic's* maiden voyage of April 14, 1912, she hit an iceberg and sank two and a half miles to the bottom of the Atlantic Ocean, taking with her 1,522 men, women, and children.

1ST PASSENGER: Including me. (*Exits*)

2ND PASSENGER: And me. (*Exits*)

BEESLEY: I was one of the lucky ones. One of only 700 people who survived that night. Why me? I've often wondered that. Perhaps it's just that I was in the right place at the right time—and the *Titanic* was in the wrong place. (*Pause*) My name is Lawrence Beesley, and I am a schoolteacher making my first trip to America, a second-class passenger. (*Pause*) I'll never forget that night on the *Titanic*. The sea was dead calm, barely a ripple. And the air was ice-cold. Without a moon to shed light, the ship was surrounded by darkness. But the sky was so incredibly clear. Each star that night was exceptionally bright. It was almost as if they were alive, talking to each other, and all the while watching helplessly the catastrophe that was unfolding on the earth below. (BEESLEY *moves upstage, passing* THOMAS ANDREWS *as he enters.* ANDREWS *and* SMITH *move center.* BEESLEY *turns his head to audience.*) That's Mr. Thomas Andrews (ANDREWS *nods.*), the managing director of White Star Lines, the company that designed and built the *Titanic*. It was said that Mr. Andrews knew every rivet, every nail, every piece of steel, and every piece of fabric that went into the creation of the *Titanic*. He is talking with Edward J. Smith, the Captain of the *Titanic*, who had planned to retire after taking the *Titanic* on her maiden voyage. Of all the people who died that night, I don't think any two were quite as tragic as Mr. Andrews and Captain Smith. It is now 12:00 a.m., twenty minutes after the *Titanic* hit the iceberg. (BEESLEY *exits.*)

SMITH: Mr. Andrews, what is your assessment of the damage, sir?

ANDREWS: Captain Smith, after inspecting the damage, I'd say we have maybe one, one and a half hours left. When we hit the iceberg on the right-hand side, it created an opening that has filled the first four watertight compartments with water. The water has slowly overflowed from one compartment to the next. As each compartment fills, the ship is slowly tipping forward, allowing the weight of the water to bring her down. Within an hour, I estimate her entire bow will be under water.

SMITH (*Gravely*): If only I had heeded the ice warnings that came in earlier. Perhaps . . .

ANDREWS: Captain Smith, we've no time to think about what should have been done or might have happened. As each moment passes, the speed at which she's sinking will increase until . . . (ANDREWS *stops, shakes head.*)

SMITH (*Yelling urgently*): Officer Wilde! Officer Boxhall! (OFFICERS WILDE *and* BOXHALL *rush on, cross to* CAPTAIN.)

WILDE: Yes, sir.

SMITH: Officer Wilde, uncover the lifeboats. We will begin evacuating the *Titanic* in an orderly and controlled fashion. There are to be no rumors, no panic. Is that understood?

WILDE: Yes, sir. (WILDE *exits.*)

SMITH: Officer Boxhall, wake up Second Officer Lightoller, Third Officer Pitman, and Fifth Officer Lowe. I will need each of you to assist with the orderly evacuation of the passengers.

BOXHALL: Sir?

SMITH: Yes, Officer Boxhall?

BOXHALL: We have only enough lifeboats to accommodate 1,178 of the passengers, sir.

SMITH: Yes, Officer Boxhall?

BOXHALL: And we have over 2,200 passengers on board, sir!

SMITH (*Grimly*): Women and children first, Mr. Boxhall. Women and children first.

BOXHALL: Yes, sir. (BOXHALL *exits.*)

ANDREWS: Incredible, isn't it, Captain Smith. There are enough lifeboats to accommodate only half our passengers, yet that's more than the British Board of Trade ever required.

SMITH: Perhaps future generations will learn from our errors,

Mr. Andrews. . . . If you'll excuse me, I need to have the wireless room send out distress calls. Our only hope now is for another ship in the vicinity to rescue the remaining passengers, before the ship disappears forever. (SMITH *exits*.)

ANDREWS: Disappears . . . forever. (ANDREWS *exits, passing* BEESLEY, *who enters, stands upstage*.)

BEESLEY: It was at that moment that Mr. Andrews realized the *Titanic*, his monument to the twentieth century and the power of technology, was as fragile as the men who had built her, as fragile as the people who would disappear with her . . . forever. (MARY SLOAN *enters with* 3RD PASSENGER. *They cross center*.)

SLOAN: Now, don't worry, it couldn't be that bad. (SLOAN *and* 3RD PASSENGER *ad lib quietly as* BEESLEY *speaks*.)

BEESLEY: That is Mary Sloan, a stewardess on the *Titanic*, and one of its many heroes that night.

3RD PASSENGER (*Nervously*): But Miss Sloan, why have we stopped?

SLOAN: Well, whatever hit us probably did some minor damage to the ship. And knowing how thorough the captain is, he probably doesn't want to continue on until he's sure that she is in tip-top shape.

3RD PASSENGER: But what if there's leakage?

SLOAN (*Reassuringly*): The pumps will handle it. Now, don't worry. (3RD PASSENGER *exits, passing* ANDREWS, *who enters*.) Mr. Andrews?

ANDREWS: Yes, Miss Sloan?

SLOAN: Is everything all right, sir?

ANDREWS: I'm afraid not, Miss Sloan. I think it would be wise to have everyone put their life jackets on over warm clothing and have them assemble on the boat deck. But, please, I don't want panic. It's imperative that we handle this with complete dignity. After all, we are British.

SLOAN: Yes, sir. (*She starts toward exit*.)

ANDREWS (*Calling after her*): Oh, and Miss Sloan? When I say everyone must put on life jackets, I mean you as well. (SLOAN *looks at him, nods, then exits. After a moment, ANDREWS follows her out*.)

BEESLEY (*Crossing center*): Mary Sloan would stay on the ship until 1:45 in the morning, helping passengers onto the lifeboats. If Mr. Andrews had not seen her, she would have stayed and gone down with the ship. He ordered her onto the last lifeboat to leave the *Titanic*, number four. All that remained were collapsible boats, actually large rafts. Not nearly enough for the fifteen hundred people who remained. Ironically, when lifeboat number four was lowered, twenty places in the boat were left empty. Why? (EDITH RUSSELL *enters, crosses to stand next to* BEESLEY.)

RUSSELL: I don't think we'll ever know why. But it wasn't just lifeboat four. Lifeboat number seven, the first lifeboat to be lowered into the cold Atlantic approximately one hour after the *Titanic* first hit the iceberg, had only twenty-eight people aboard.

BEESLEY: It was made to carry sixty-five.

RUSSELL: And it happened again and again on that terrible night.

BEESLEY: This is Miss Edith Russell, a fashion correspondent for *Women's Wear* magazine.

RUSSELL: The *Titanic* was the most fantastic ocean liner I had ever seen. Yet, from the minute I stepped aboard, I felt it was almost too fantastic. It seemed as if man had perhaps gone too far this time. As beautiful as the *Titanic* was, I couldn't help but feel that something terrible was going to happen. How I wish I had been wrong! (*As* RUSSELL *exits, she passes* MR. *and* MRS. JOHN JACOB ASTOR, MR. *and* MRS. ISADOR STRAUS, *and* BENJAMIN GUGGENHEIM.)

BEESLEY: Among those who were aboard the *Titanic* that night were some of the wealthiest people in the world. One in particular could have bought the *Titanic* several times over. His name was John Jacob Astor. (JOHN JACOB ASTOR *and* MRS. ASTOR *move center.*)

MRS. ASTOR: They say we should put these life jackets on. I don't understand, darling. How could such a simple device keep one afloat in the ocean?

ASTOR: No need to worry. Why, you'll be quite dry and very much afloat in a lifeboat, my dear.

MRS. ASTOR: You'll come with me, won't you?

ASTOR: I'm afraid not. The officers have informed me that women and children must board the lifeboats first. I'm sure it's just a precaution, but after all, I wouldn't be much of a gentleman if I refused their orders, would I?

BEESLEY: And so Mrs. Astor entered lifeboat number four without her husband.

ASTOR (*As* MRS. ASTOR *exits*): Don't worry, my dear. I'll get another boat and follow just behind you. I promise.

BEESLEY: But by then it was too late. Of the men who were allowed on a lifeboat, most were crew members who were placed on the boats as oarsmen. John Jacob Astor would never see his wife again. (ASTOR *exits.* MR. *and* MRS. ISADOR STRAUS *move center as* FIRST OFFICER LIGHTOLLER *enters.*)

LIGHTOLLER: Mrs. Straus, please, you must come with me.

MRS. STRAUS: And leave my husband? Never!

BEESLEY (*Motioning toward* MR. *and* MRS. STRAUS): Mr. and Mrs. Isador Straus, the owners of Macy's department stores. They had been married for over forty years.

STRAUS: Please, my dear. You must take your place in one of the lifeboats. It's your only chance.

MRS. STRAUS: I have spent my life with you, Isador. Where you go, I go. (LIGHTOLLER, *upset, exits.* MR. *and* MRS. STRAUS, *arm in arm, immediately follow him out.*)

BEESLEY: The last anyone ever saw of Mr. and Mrs. Straus, they were on the promenade deck, sitting side by side in deck chairs, peacefully waiting for the end. (BENJAMIN GUGGENHEIM *moves center.*)

GUGGENHEIM: Steward Etches? (STEWARD ETCHES *enters.*)

ETCHES: Yes, Mr. Guggenheim?

BEESLEY: Mr. Benjamin Guggenheim, an industrial giant who was traveling without his wife on this journey. Like all first-class passengers, he was rarely without a private steward at his side.

GUGGENHEIM: I shall require your assistance changing into my evening clothes.

ETCHES (*Surprised*): Sir?

GUGGENHEIM: Etches, you've taken good care of me on this journey. I have only one more request for you.

ETCHES: Anything, sir.

GUGGENHEIM: If you should survive, please locate my wife and tell her that I have done my duty and have gone down like a gentleman. (GUGGENHEIM *and* ETCHES *exit*.)

BEESLEY: Etches did indeed survive, and relayed to Mr. Guggenheim's family just how distinguished he looked in his full dress evening clothes. (EDITH RUSSELL *enters*.)

RUSSELL: It was now 2:17 a.m., and those of us who had found a place in a lifeboat watched with horror as the *Titanic*'s brief but magnificent life came to an end.

BEESLEY: First, Captain Smith released from duty the remaining brave crew members. (SMITH *enters*.)

SMITH: Gentlemen, you have done all that is humanly possible. You are hereby released from duty. It is now every man for himself. (SMITH *exits*.)

RUSSELL: And then he was gone. As sea captains had done for generations before him, Captain Smith prepared to go down with his ship.

BEESLEY: At 2:18 a.m. the ship's bow was completely underwater, the stern tilted up in the air. There was a tremendous crash as everything that wasn't bolted down careened forward. And then the ship broke in half, the bow crashing 12,460 feet to the bottom of the sea.

RUSSELL: The stern then slowly righted itself, almost as if it were going to resist the forces of nature and float forever. But soon it, too, filled with water and began to tilt forward.

BEESLEY: And at 2:20 a.m., it disappeared completely. The *Titanic* was gone, and for a brief moment there was only silence.

RUSSELL: The water was now filled with hundreds of people, clinging to whatever piece of wreckage they could find. One clung to a boat chair, another to a piece of wood.

BEESLEY: But the water was freezing cold that night, and most people lasted for only a short time before the cold and shock overtook them. One by one they became victims of the frigid north Atlantic.

RUSSELL: The lifeboats floated in the water for nearly two hours before another ship, *The Carpathia*, came to our rescue. One by one the lifeboats were unloaded until finally the Captain of the *Carpathia* was convinced that all the survivors were on board.

BEESLEY: At 8:50 the following morning, the *Carpathia* headed to New York, carrying 705 survivors from the great unsinkable ship, the *Titanic*.

RUSSELL: One thousand, five hundred and twenty-two people died that night. Men, women, and children.

BEESLEY: The majority of those who died were third-class passengers. Many were not allowed onto the upper decks until it was too late. By the time they did manage to reach the deck, all the lifeboats were gone.

RUSSELL: Most were immigrants who were coming to America in search of a better life.

BEESLEY: It was a dream that never came true.

RUSSELL: They say that some good comes from all tragedies, and the *Titanic* was no exception.

BEESLEY: An International Conference for the Safety of Life at Sea was held in London in 1913. At that conference, several regulations were passed—regulations meant to prevent future tragedies like the *Titanic*. (FLEET, FIRST OFFICER MURDOCK, QUARTERMASTER HITCHENS, THREE PASSENGERS, THOMAS ANDREWS, CAPTAIN SMITH, OFFICER WILDE, OFFICER BOXHALL, MARY SLOAN, MR. *and* MRS. ASTOR, MR. *and* MRS. STRAUS, FIRST OFFICER LIGHTOLLER, BENJAMIN GUGGENHEIM, *and* STEWARD ETCHES *reenter*.)

1ST PASSENGER: From then on, all ocean-going ships were required to have enough lifeboats to accommodate all passengers and crew.

2ND PASSENGER: All ships were to be outfitted with wireless sets.

FLEET: The firing of rockets or distress calls was to be done only for actual emergencies.

SMITH: Captains would never again ignore ice warnings. They would slow down and, if necessary, change the ship's course.

WILDE: An International Ice Patrol was created.

BOXHALL: Eventually this international patrol became part of the United States Coast Guard.

ANDREWS: In memory of the *Titanic* and those who were lost at sea, every year the Coast Guard drops a wreath on the site where the *Titanic* was last seen before going down.

SLOAN: But what happened to the *Titanic* after she disappeared below the ocean's surface on that cold night?

3RD PASSENGER: We knew approximately where she was, 350 miles southeast of Newfoundland.

ASTOR: More than two miles below the surface.

MRS. ASTOR: But nobody knew the exact spot of her grave.

STRAUS: For years people talked of finding the *Titanic* and of the great treasures that went down with her.

MRS. STRAUS: But it wasn't until 1985 that a combination of technology and determination made such a dream a reality.

LIGHTOLLER: On September 1, 1985, Dr. Robert Ballad and his team of scientists found the wreck of the *Titanic*.

GUGGENHEIM: Using a submarine and a small robot with an attached camera, they went two and a half miles to the bottom of the ocean and once again human eyes were able to see the *Titanic*.

ETCHES: Only this time it was a much different ship.

MURDOCK: Lying in two sections, her hull was in remarkably good shape.

HITCHENS: The carved wood that once graced her interior had long since rotted away, yet her huge metal frame was still very much intact.

BEESLEY: But her stern was now nothing more than a twisted piece of wreckage.

RUSSELL: In between the two sections was a debris field of artifacts from the *Titanic*. Not just pieces from the ship, but mementos of the passengers. Each item was a memory of a human being.

SLOAN: A tea cup.

MRS. ASTOR: Silver serving dishes.

MRS. STRAUS: Wine bottles still corked.

ANDREWS: Bathtubs.

3RD PASSENGER: Deck chairs.

1ST PASSENGER: Hair brushes.

SMITH: And saddest of all, lying next to each other, were three pairs of shoes.

BEESLEY: Sometimes, as the years march on, I think back to that voyage and to the wonderful times we had before that awful moment when the *Titanic* hit the iceberg. I can still see people laughing, dancing, and celebrating the maiden voyage of the grandest ocean liner the world had ever known—the *Titanic!*

ALL (*Raising hands in tribute*): Unsinkable! (*All freeze as* SMITH *walks forward, looking at each actor. One by one, they exit, obviously sad, heads down. When* SMITH *is alone, he speaks his last line.*)

SMITH: Or so we thought. (*He exits as curtain falls.*)

THE END

AUTHOR'S NOTE

When the *Titanic* first set sail, it was considered the most luxurious, fastest, and, at 46,000 tons, the largest ship afloat. Among its many features were a Turkish bath, swimming pool, squash court, and a grand stairway that stood over six stories high from its base to the top of the domed glass skylight that covered it. Its hull was divided into sixteen watertight compartments designed to stay afloat even if any two of those compartments were flooded. Because of this special design, the *Titanic* was thought to be unsinkable.

Production Notes

TITANIC: DESTINATION DISASTER

Characters: 13 male; 4 female; 3 male or female.

Playing Time: 25 minutes.

Costumes: Traditional turn-of-the-century costumes. Appropriate uniforms for ship personnel.

Properties: None.

Setting: A bare stage to represent engine room and boat deck of the *Titanic*. Chair left represents lookout's station.

Lighting and Sound: No special effects.

∾Langston Hughes: Poet of the People

by Mary Satchell

Young writer defies his father to follow his dreams . . . .

Characters

LANGSTON HUGHES, *black American writer*
MR. JAMES HUGHES, *his father*
SEÑORA GARCIA, *housekeeper*
THAD, *medical student*
WAITER
LONGSHOREMAN
YOUNG COUPLE
FOUR MEN
YOUNG WOMAN
PASSERSBY
MRS. JONES
JOHNNY JONES
MRS. MARY MCLEOD BETHUNE, *Bethune-Cookman College founder*
HELEN, *her secretary*
ALICE JACKSON ⎫
JEAN BAXTER ⎬ *college students*
KEVIN DANIELS ⎭

SCENE 1

TIME: *Summer, 1920.*
SETTING: *Study in James Hughes's home near Mexico City. A desk, chair, and wastebasket are center. Accountant's ledger*

lies closed on edge of desk. Floor vase with tall pampas grass stands nearby.

AT RISE: LANGSTON HUGHES *sits writing at desk.* SEÑORA GARCIA *enters, holding feather duster.*

SEÑORA GARCIA: Señor Langston, how can you sit in one place for hours just writing?

LANGSTON (*Leaning back*): Señora Garcia, if I could spend my whole life writing, I'd be happy.

SEÑORA GARCIA (*Dusting vase*): You are a true artist, Señor Langston. (*Turns; sighs*) It is too bad that your father does not understand. You two belong to different worlds. You are a dreamer, and he is such a practical man.

LANGSTON (*Thoughtfully*): Father and I still don't know each other very well. (*Rises*) Since I arrived, he's been trying to make me into what *he* thinks I should be.

SEÑORA GARCIA (*Putting hands on hips*): I have been your father's housekeeper for a long time. I know Señor Hughes is a very stubborn man. But I'm sure he wants the best for you because you are *hijo querido*—his only son. (*Door slams off.*)

LANGSTON (*Tensely*): That must be Father, and I haven't finished those accounting problems he left for me.

SEÑORA GARCIA (*Giving ledger to* LANGSTON): Quickly, Señor Langston! Take this ledger and give me those papers you've been writing on before your father sees them. He will be angry to find you have been writing poems. (*She sweeps papers into desk drawer, but one falls unnoticed to the floor.*)

LANGSTON (*Earnestly*): But, Señora Garcia, I can't be a make-believe son for my father any longer.

SEÑORA GARCIA (*Pushing* LANGSTON *into chair*): Señor Langston, if you don't do as I say, you had better brace yourself for a thunderstorm. (MR. HUGHES *enters, frowning.* SEÑORA GARCIA *turns with big smile.*) *Buenas dias,* Señor Hughes. We were not expecting you back from Toluca so soon.

MR. HUGHES: Hello, Señora Garcia. (*As he removes his poncho*) Langston?

LANGSTON (*Rising; uncomfortably*): Hello, Father. (MR. HUGHES *gives poncho to* SEÑORA GARCIA, *who exits with it.*)

MR. HUGHES: Well, Langston, let me see what progress you've made with the accounting problems.

LANGSTON (*Hesitantly*): Father, I need to talk to you.

MR. HUGHES (*Pointing to ledger*): We should go over the accounting problems first, and after dinner, we'll work on your Spanish lessons.

LANGSTON (*Pleading*): Father, please listen to me . . .

MR. HUGHES: We can talk later, son. Let me see your bookkeeping. If you're going to run this ranch someday, you'll have to learn how to keep accounts. (*Sits at desk*)

LANGSTON (*Giving ledger to* MR. HUGHES): I'm afraid I didn't get much done.

MR. HUGHES (*Slowly turning pages; irritated*): Langston, you've hardly done any work on these at all.

LANGSTON (*Pleading*): I tried—I really did. (*Sighs*) Accounting just isn't for me. I'm more interested in other things (*Paces*)—like writing.

MR. HUGHES (*Slamming ledger shut*): So—just as I thought. I suppose you've been sitting around here since I left—daydreaming?

LANGSTON: Actually, I've been very busy.

MR. HUGHES (*Angrily*): I didn't bring you to Mexico just to waste your life, Langston.

LANGSTON: I appreciate what you're doing for me, but—

MR. HUGHES (*Banging desk*): *No excuses!* You can be as successful as I am. (*Rises*) I left the States and moved here to Mexico because here a black man can live like any other man. That's why I insisted you move here from Cleveland . . . so you can have more opportunities! Here if a man works hard, he can be a success at whatever he wants.

LANGSTON (*Confidently*): I plan to be a successful writer.

MR. HUGHES: Nonsense! You'll attend a good school and earn a degree in engineering.

LANGSTON (*Surprised*): Engineering?

MR. HUGHES: Of course. (*Proudly*) I can afford to send you to the finest schools in the world. (*Thoughtfully*) I hear there are excellent schools in Switzerland.

LANGSTON (*Stunned*): Switzerland! (*Agitated*) I don't want to go to school halfway around the world.

MR. HUGHES: All right, if you feel that strongly about it. Let's see. (*Thinks*) What are some schools with good engineering departments?

LANGSTON (*Eagerly*): What about Columbia?

MR. HUGHES: Columbia University in New York City?

LANGSTON: Yes. My grades were good in high school. I think Columbia would accept me.

MR. HUGHES (*Pleased*): That's more like it. Now, forget that silly writing business, and we'll see about getting you an application for Columbia. (SEÑORA GARCIA *enters.*)

SEÑORA GARCIA: Excuse me. Dinner is ready, Señor.

MR. HUGHES: We'll be right there. (*He turns, sees paper on floor.*) What's this?

LANGSTON (*Hurriedly*): It's nothing. I'll get it. (MR. HUGHES *picks up paper, glances at it, and frowns.*)

MR. HUGHES: Is this one of your poems?

LANGSTON (*Sheepishly*): Yes. (*Reaches for paper, but* MR. HUGHES *crumples it.*)

MR. HUGHES (*Sternly*): You won't have any more time for poetry. (*Drops paper into wastebasket and puts arm around* LANGSTON's *shoulders*) We'll talk later about what courses you'll take at Columbia University next year. You'll have to study a lot of science and math. (*They exit.* SEÑORA GARCIA *takes crumpled paper from wastebasket, smooths it out.*)

SEÑORA GARCIA (*Sadly*): Poor Señor Langston. Why can't his father just accept him the way he is? (*Puts paper in desk drawer and exits. Curtain*)

* * * * *

SCENE 2

TIME: *The next year.*

SETTING: *Langston's dormitory room at Columbia University. Bunk or twin beds and small bureau are upstage. Desk with papers, pencils, and books; two chairs; lamp, clock, and waste-*

basket are downstage. Closet door is in wall right. Exit is left. Large posters of Harlem street and café scenes are on wall upstage.

AT RISE: THAD *sits at desk, reading.* LANGSTON *enters.*

LANGSTON: Hi, Thad. I don't suppose my father has shown up yet.

THAD: No, he hasn't, Lang, but if I were you, I'd get out of town before he arrives.

LANGSTON (*With a forced laugh*): You talk as if you've already met him. (*Sighs*) He's probably very angry with me now.

THAD: Can't say I blame him. (*Closes book*) Lang, what gives with you? All you've been doing lately is skipping classes and spending all your time uptown in Harlem. You haven't touched a book in weeks.

LANGSTON (*Placing jacket on chair*): I've tried to stick to my studies, Thad, but—(*Sighs*) my heart's just not in engineering.

THAD (*Rising*): Do you think I enjoy studying all the time? Sometimes I'd like to forget this (*Points to book*) and go uptown with you. (*Pauses; glances at posters*) It sure would be great to hear some jazz and just unwind for a while. (*He moves back to desk.*) But I want to earn a decent living someday. A medical degree is my ticket to a good life.

LANGSTON: I always thought you really wanted to be a doctor.

THAD: I *do* want to be a doctor.

LANGSTON: But you just said that a medical degree is a *ticket* to somewhere.

THAD (*Defensively*): It's a ticket to a comfortable home, a fine car, and all the other things I want in life.

LANGSTON (*Disappointed*): I thought a man decided to become a doctor in order to help people.

THAD (*Shrugging*): You're too idealistic, Lang.

LANGSTON (*Thoughtfully*): Maybe a better word would be *honest*. And speaking of honesty, I've decided it's time to tell my father the truth.

THAD: What are you going to tell him?

LANGSTON (*Earnestly*): That I just don't want to be an engineer. I came here to be near the Harlem scene, but I'm study-ing engineering only to please him.

THAD (*Putting hand on* LANGSTON's *shoulder*): You've got to be practical, Lang. An engineering career makes sense.

LANGSTON: For me, everything has to come from the heart, or it's nothing. I want to write poems, stories, and plays about black Americans. Harlem's where I belong.

THAD (*Incredulously*): You'd give up a stable future to spend your time in Harlem?

LANGSTON: Yes.

THAD (*Concerned*): But if you make a foolish decision now . . .

LANGSTON (*Passionately*): At least I'll know I've been true to myself.

THAD (*Embarrassed; looking at clock*): I have a biology class soon. Your father will be here any minute.

LANGSTON (*Glumly; sitting*): I guess I'd better brace myself for a storm. (THAD *gets jacket from closet and picks up book.*)

THAD (*Trying to be cheerful*): Don't look so down, Lang. Once you're into your engineering courses, we'll both laugh about the way you feel now.

LANGSTON: I don't think so. (THAD *exits.* LANGSTON *picks up pencil and writes. Knocking is heard offstage.* LANGSTON, *preoccupied, does not answer. After a moment,* MR. HUGHES *enters.*)

MR. HUGHES (*Frowning*): Langston. (LANGSTON *looks up.*) I hope you were too deep in your studies to hear my knocking.

LANGSTON (*Rising*): Hello, Father. (*Uncomfortably*) I know you're here because of my grades.

MR. HUGHES: I don't have to tell you how disappointed I am. (*Sits*)

LANGSTON (*Sighing*): It's time for me to be honest with you. When I came to Columbia, I tried to convince myself that it was to earn a degree, but I really wanted to get to Harlem.

MR. HUGHES (*Bewildered*): What's Harlem got to do with this?

LANGSTON: Everything. Thousands of black Americans live in Harlem, and I want to live with them. I have a burning desire to write about black people—our joys, sorrows . . . everything.

MR. HUGHES (*Irritably; rising*): Langston, are you telling me you want to drop out of Columbia?

LANGSTON (*Calmly*): Yes. Writing is the only future for me.

MR. HUGHES (*Angrily*): If you quit school, you won't get another cent from me.

LANGSTON: It's not your money I need now, Father.

MR. HUGHES (*Softening*): Langston, I know I could never make up for all those years when you and your mother lived without me. But I tried to give you this opportunity—a ticket to success. (LANGSTON *shakes his head sadly.*)

LANGSTON: I have to strive for success in my own way.

MR. HUGHES: Is that your final decision?

LANGSTON (*Quietly*): Yes, it is.

MR. HUGHES: Then I won't argue with you anymore. (*Puts on hat*) I'm returning to Mexico City on the morning train. (*Turns to exit*)

LANGSTON: Is that all you're going to say?

MR. HUGHES (*Turning back; sadly*): I wish you well, Langston, but I feel you're making a foolish mistake. I honestly have my doubts that you'll ever become a successful writer. (*Exits. LANGSTON moves to closet, takes out suitcase, puts it on bed. He moves to bureau and starts packing. Lights slowly fade. Curtain*)

* * * * *

SCENE 3

TIME: *Years later.*

SETTING: *Harlem street scene. Backdrop has painted storefronts: drugstore window showing table, chairs, and jukebox; barbershop with pole; doorway with steps and bench nearby. At right is pier with boxes and crates. At center, street light and sign mark intersection of Lenox Avenue and 125th Street. Chair, small table with cup and saucer and man's hat on it, are downstage.*

AT RISE: *Tableau of Harlem residents:* MAN *sits on steps at doorway;* YOUNG COUPLE *holds hands in drugstore win-*

dow, sipping soda with two straws; THREE MEN *stand beneath street light;* LONGSHOREMAN *works on pier. Spotlight comes up on* LANGSTON, *who sits at table, writing in journal.* WAITER *enters, moves to table.*

WAITER: Can I bring you anything else, Mr. Hughes?

LANGSTON (*Glancing up*): No thanks, Frank. You make the best coffee in Harlem, but I've had enough for one day. (*Glances at wristwatch*) It's four o'clock already. I've been sitting here writing since noon. (*Rises*) I think I'll stretch my legs. (*Spotlight remains on* LANGSTON *during following monologue.*)

WAITER (*Smiling*): Suit yourself, Mr. Hughes. You're welcome at my place any time. (*Exits.* LANGSTON *places money on table, puts on hat, moves down center, carrying journal, then turns to audience.*)

LANGSTON: This is Harlem, my adopted home. (*Glances up, then turns back; with satisfaction*) It's a wonderful place. I've lived here for a long time, writing about the people. Young and old, they're my friends. Sometimes Harlem laughs, sings, and dances. (*Pensively*) Sometimes it's a struggle to survive. A lot of crying over broken dreams goes on in Harlem. (*Enthusiastically*) But whatever the situation, Harlem always teems with *life.* (*Gestures*) This is the Harlem of my poetry! (*Turns. Lights come up full. Other actors move naturally when* LANGSTON *walks upstage. He moves to* LONGSHOREMAN.)

LONGSHOREMAN: Hey there, Langston! Still writing your poems?

LANGSTON (*Nodding*): I can't seem to stop.

LONGSHOREMAN (*Glancing around; bewildered*): I don't see a thing here worth writing about. All I see are a polluted river and a lot of work for me to do.

LANGSTON (*Chuckling*): That's because you and I see things in different ways.

LONGSHOREMAN: You may be right, Langston. (*Sighs*) I'd better get back to work. (*Waves*) See you around. (*Stacks boxes; lights fade to show* LONGSHOREMAN *working in silhouette; sound of foghorn and clanging bell. Spotlight on* LANGSTON *as he moves down to audience, recites "The Ne-*

gro Speaks of Rivers."* At end of poem, LONGSHOREMAN *exits. Lights come up.* YOUNG COUPLE *moves center, hand in hand. Lively jazz tune is heard.* LANGSTON *watches as they dance briefly, then exit. Music stops.* LANGSTON *moves center to recite "Juke Box Love Song."* THREE MEN *under streetlight begin to argue loudly.*)

MEN (*Ad lib*): In this country, black people are treated like second-class citizens, as if we don't belong! Now, just one minute! There are a lot of good things I can say about our country. Oh, yeah? Yeah! (*Etc. They turn to* LANGSTON.)

1ST MAN (*Pointing*): There's Langston Hughes. Let's find out what he thinks about America.

2ND MAN (*Beckoning*): Langston!

LANGSTON (*Moving nearer*): What's going on?

3RD MAN: We're having a little debate, and we'd like to get your opinion.

1ST MAN: What do you think about America, Langston?

2ND MAN: We know you're a poet of the people, so we respect what you have to say.

LANGSTON: Quite frankly, I love America.

3RD MAN (*Dubious*): You can't mean that!

LANGSTON: Yes, I do. (*Earnestly*) I've traveled to many places—Latin America, Europe, Africa, Russia, the Far East—but I wouldn't want to call any of them home.

1ST MAN (*To others*): See? Langston agrees with me.

3RD MAN (*Grudgingly*): Well, if Langston Hughes can say good things about America, I'd better think about it some more. (*Beckoning*) Let's go. (MEN *exit;* LANGSTON *moves down center to recite "I, Too, Sing America."* YOUNG WOMAN *enters, wearing red dress and carrying umbrella. Sound of jazz notes from saxophone is heard off.* YOUNG WOMAN *moves past* LANGSTON, *who smiles at her.*)

YOUNG WOMAN (*Flirting*): Hello, Langston.

LANGSTON (*Smitten*): Hello, Sue. You sure look pretty in that red dress.

---

*This and other poems recited in this scene may be found in *Selected Poems of Langston Hughes* (Alfred A. Knopf, 1988).

YOUNG WOMAN (*Coyly*): Why, thank you. (*She walks away, glancing over her shoulder at* LANGSTON. *Jazz notes accompany* YOUNG WOMAN *off.* LANGSTON *recites "Harlem Night Song."* MAN *rises from steps and approaches* LANGSTON.)

MAN: I heard what you told those guys on the corner.

LANGSTON: You mean how I feel about America?

MAN: Yes.

LANGSTON: Do you agree with me?

MAN (*Shrugging*): Maybe I do. (*Pauses*) And maybe I don't. (*Knowingly*) I can dig all jive, but I mind my business to stay alive. (*Pulls hat over his eyes and slowly exits.* LANGSTON *comes down center and recites "Motto."* MRS. JONES *and* JOHNNY JONES, *carrying bag of groceries, enter.*)

MRS. JONES (*Cheerfully*): Good afternoon, Langston.

LANGSTON: Hello, Mrs. Jones. (*Puts hand on* JOHNNY's *shoulder*) How's everything going, Johnny?

JOHNNY (*Morosely*): O.K., I guess.

LANGSTON (*Teasing*): Aren't you sure?

JOHNNY (*Irritably*): Sure, I am. Why are you so interested in me, anyway?

MRS. JONES (*Scolding*): That's no way to talk, Johnny. Apologize to Mr. Hughes.

JOHNNY: I'm sorry.

MRS. JONES: I don't know what's gotten into this boy lately. He should be happy because he was just hired for a job today.

JOHNNY (*Angrily*): Mr. Frank hired me to wash dishes in his coffee shop. How can you call that a job?

MRS. JONES: It's honest work.

JOHNNY: I don't want to wash dishes all my life, Ma. I want to go to college.

MRS. JONES (*Sighing*): I don't see how, Johnny. We just don't have that kind of money. (*To* LANGSTON) Langston, will you have supper with us on Sunday?

LANGSTON: I wish I could, Mrs. Jones, but I'm leaving town tomorrow.

MRS. JONES: Where are you off to this time?

LANGSTON: Mrs. Mary McLeod Bethune has invited me to

visit her college in Florida. She wants me to read my poetry to her students.

JOHNNY (*Eagerly*): I wish I could go with you.

MRS. JONES: Maybe you'll go to college someday, Johnny. But for now, your dreams will have to wait. (*Takes groceries*) Have a good trip, Langston. (*Exits*)

JOHNNY (*Sitting dejectedly*): My dreams always have to wait.

LANGSTON: Johnny, did you know I worked as a dishwasher in a little café in Paris?

JOHNNY (*Surprised*): *You* were a dishwasher?

LANGSTON (*Nodding*): I've also worked as a kitchen helper and cabin boy on a ship, and a farmhand in California. And those jobs were better than many others I've had.

JOHNNY: You probably didn't make much money.

LANGSTON: I made *very* little money in those days. But I always knew those jobs were just stepping stones to get me where I wanted to go.

JOHNNY: Where were you going?

LANGSTON: Toward my dream. After years of working, I earned a college degree and became a writer.

JOHNNY (*Rising*): You never lost your dream. (*Confidently*) Mr. Hughes, if you could do it, *I* can, too!

LANGSTON (*Clapping* JOHNNY *on shoulder*): That's the spirit, Johnny!

JOHNNY: I have to go home and help Ma with dinner. Goodbye, Mr. Hughes. Say hello to Mrs. Bethune for me. (*Pauses*) And tell her that she just may be hearing from me one day. (*Exits.* LANGSTON *moves downstage to recite "Harlem." Lights begin to fade.* PASSERSBY *hurry past* LANGSTON *and call out greetings. He moves to table, sits down center.* WAITER *enters.*)

LANGSTON (*Taking off hat*): Could I have another pot of coffee, Frank?

WAITER: Sure thing, Mr. Hughes. What are you going to write about this time?

LANGSTON (*Gesturing*): Harlem, of course. What else?

WAITER (*Chuckling*): You could be our official poet, Mr. Hughes.

You're really the poet of the people. (*Exits.* LANGSTON *opens journal, writes. Curtain*)

* * * * *

SCENE 4

TIME: *Several days later.*

SETTING: *Bethune-Cookman College. Small bookcase, desk, and chair are left. Banner pinned to curtain reads,* BETHUNE-COOKMAN COLLEGE WELCOMES LANGSTON HUGHES.

BEFORE RISE: MRS. MARY MCLEOD BETHUNE *sits reading at desk.* HELEN *enters right.*

HELEN: Mrs. Bethune, Langston Hughes just arrived.

MRS. BETHUNE (*Rising; pleased*): Wonderful! Please bring him in, Helen. (HELEN *exits;* MRS. BETHUNE *takes book from bookcase, places it on desk. Anxiously, to herself*) I certainly hope Langston won't be angry when he discovers what I've done. (HELEN *reenters, followed by* LANGSTON. MRS. BETHUNE *greets* LANGSTON *heartily.*) Langston, I'm so happy to see you.

LANGSTON: It's a pleasure to visit your lovely campus again, Mrs. Bethune. (HELEN *exits.*)

MRS. BETHUNE: You're just the person we need now.

LANGSTON (*Puzzled*): Why do you say that?

MRS. BETHUNE: Our students need encouragement from someone who's become a success in spite of hard times.

LANGSTON: I haven't made a lot of money.

MRS. BETHUNE (*Waving hand*): Money's no true measure of success. Look at all the wonderful poems you've published. (*Pauses*) Sometimes, especially in moments of discouragement, I read your poems. They never fail to inspire me.

LANGSTON: I didn't think you ever felt discouraged.

MRS. BETHUNE (*Smiling*): Everyone needs a lift now and then.

LANGSTON: I wish I could reach more people with my poetry.

MRS. BETHUNE (*Suddenly*): Why, Langston, I should have thought of it before!

LANGSTON: Thought of what?

MRS. BETHUNE: I think you should travel around the country, reading your poetry. People need poetry, Langston; it would inspire them as it does me.

LANGSTON: If people are willing to listen, I'll be glad to read my poetry to them.

MRS. BETHUNE: Our students are certainly glad to have you here as their guest. (*Pauses, then mysteriously*) And speaking of guests, I've invited someone very special to enjoy your poetry.

LANGSTON (*Interested*): And who might that be?

MRS. BETHUNE: You'll find out soon enough. (*Picks up book*) Now, Langston. (*With a broad smile*) Would you please let me have your autograph?

LANGSTON: It's my pleasure. (*He signs book.*)

MRS. BETHUNE: I can't tell you what an important day this is for Bethune-Cookman College. The students are so looking forward to meeting you.

LANGSTON: And I'm looking forward to meeting them. (*They exit as curtain opens.*)

* * * * *

TIME: *A short time later.*

SETTING: *A high stool and lectern are at center.*

AT RISE: ALICE JACKSON, *carrying notebook,* JEAN BAX-TER, *and* KEVIN DANIELS *enter left.*

ALICE (*Excitedly*): Isn't it wonderful? We're going to meet Langston Hughes!

JEAN: I love his poem "The Negro Speaks of Rivers."

KEVIN: And what about "Harlem Night Song." I hope he recites that one today.

ALICE: I can't wait to talk to him about poetry.

KEVIN: Alice, what makes you think Mr. Hughes would talk to you about his poetry?

ALICE: I don't want to talk to him about *his* poetry, Kevin. (*Proudly*) I intend to talk about *my* poems.

KEVIN: Are you serious? Why would a writer like Langston Hughes read your poems?

ALICE (*Lifting chin*): Maybe he'll laugh at me, but I'm going to ask him anyway.

JEAN (*Grabbing* KEVIN's *hand*): Let's get out of here before Alice makes herself look ridiculous. (*They exit quickly.* ALICE *moves to lectern, opens notebook.* LANGSTON *appears, unnoticed, stands right.*)

ALICE (*Bowing*): Thank you, ladies and gentlemen, for coming to hear me read my original poems. (LANGSTON *coughs;* ALICE *turns quickly in embarrassment.*) Oh, Mr. Hughes! I didn't know you were here!

LANGSTON (*Moving nearer*): I didn't meant to interrupt you. (*Gestures and sits*) Please continue.

ALICE (*Stammering*): I—I couldn't recite my poems to you. (*Pauses, then breathlessly*) But I must admit that I came early to ask you to look at my work and tell me what you think of it.

LANGSTON (*Earnestly*): Why do you want to write poetry, Miss—

ALICE: Jackson. Alice Jackson. (*Shrugs*) I just can't think of doing anything else.

LANGSTON (*Nodding*): I understand. May I see your work? (*She gives him notebook; he reads silently, then glances up.*) These are much better than my first poems. (*Rises*) You and I have something in common.

ALICE (*Wide-eyed*): We do?

LANGSTON: We both write from our hearts, and we believe in what we're doing.

ALICE (*Fervently*): At last, someone who understands! My friends didn't think you'd take me seriously.

LANGSTON: Sometimes the people we love don't understand or have faith in us.

ALICE (*Curiously*): Did someone you love ever try to discourage you?

LANGSTON (*Sadly*): Yes, Alice—my father. (*Wistfully*) We haven't seen each other in many years.

ALICE: Well, I'm sure things would be different if he could see you now.

LANGSTON (*Uncomfortably; looking at watch*): The program will begin soon, but I still have time to look at a few more of your poems. (LANGSTON *moves upstage;* JEAN *and* KEVIN *enter.*)

JEAN: Alice, we came to apologize ... (*Sees* LANGSTON) It's Langston Hughes!

KEVIN: Did you show him your poetry, Alice?

ALICE (*Smiling*): That's what he's reading right now.

JEAN: Really? That's wonderful!

ALICE: You were all wrong about him. (*To* LANGSTON) Mr. Hughes, I'd like you to meet my best friends, Jean Baxter and Kevin Daniels.

JEAN *and* KEVIN (*Awestruck; ad lib*): Pleased to meet you, Mr. Hughes. This is a real honor. (*Etc.*)

JEAN: We owe you an apology, Mr. Hughes. We thought you might hurt Alice's feelings.

LANGSTON: I've been hurt many times by people who said I couldn't write. But their doubts just made me work harder. (MRS. BETHUNE *enters.*)

MRS. BETHUNE: The students are beginning to assemble in the auditorium, Langston. Are you ready?

LANGSTON: Quite ready, Mrs. Bethune. (*Gives journal to* ALICE) I've discovered a fellow poet here. She's very talented. (ALICE *beams.*)

MRS. BETHUNE (*Interested*): Is that so? (*To* ALICE) I'd like to hear more about your poetry. Why don't you and your friends join me and Langston for dinner after his program? (*Students ad lib thanks.*)

ALICE (*To* JEAN *and* KEVIN): Let's hurry so we can find seats down front. I don't want to miss a *word* of Mr. Hughes' poetry. (*Students exit.*)

MRS. BETHUNE: You've made this a very special day for that young lady.

LANGSTON: Today is special for me, too. I'm about to read my poetry in public for the first time. (HELEN *enters.*)

HELEN: Excuse me, Mrs. Bethune. Your other guest has just arrived. Should we come to the auditorium?

MRS. BETHUNE (*Quickly*): No, Helen. I'll go back to my office with you. (*To* LANGSTON) We'll start just as soon as I get back.

LANGSTON: All right, Mrs. Bethune. (MRS. BETHUNE *exits with* HELEN. LANGSTON *flips through pages.* MR. HUGHES *enters, carrying briefcase.*)

MR. HUGHES (*Hesitating*): Langston? (LANGSTON *turns, stunned.*)

LANGSTON: Father! (*Happily*) I can't believe it's really you! (*They move quickly to embrace.*)

MR. HUGHES (*Stepping back*): Let me look at you, Langston. (*Proudly*) Do you know, people I don't even know congratulate me and say what a lucky man I am when they find out that you're my son.

LANGSTON: How did you know I'd be here?

MR. HUGHES (*Chuckling*): Mrs. Bethune called me. (*Sincerely*) I've wanted to get in touch with you, but I was ashamed— after the way I left when you needed me most.

LANGSTON: That doesn't matter any more. I'm just glad you're here.

MR. HUGHES: Then, you forgive me?

LANGSTON: Of course. . . . I inherited your strong will. I guess that's why I could never let go of my dream.

MR. HUGHES: Your writing touches people's hearts, Langston. (*Opens briefcase, takes out several books*) I have all of your poetry books—and your plays, novels, essays . . . Would you autograph them for me?

LANGSTON (*Happily*): I'd be glad to.

MR. HUGHES: Wonderful! (MRS. BETHUNE *enters.*)

MRS. BETHUNE (*Relieved*): There you are! I didn't know what to think when I didn't find you in my office.

MR. HUGHES (*Apologetically*): Forgive me, Mrs. Bethune. I couldn't wait to see Langston, so I asked some students to show me how to get here.

LANGSTON (*To* MRS. BETHUNE; *knowingly*): So, my father is that very special guest.

MRS. BETHUNE: I've been planning this surprise for weeks, Langston.

LANGSTON: I can't thank you enough, Mrs. Bethune.

MRS. BETHUNE (*Beaming*): Well, shall we begin the program?

LANGSTON (*Eagerly*): Yes. You may open the curtains. (MRS.
BETHUNE *exits.*)

MR. HUGHES: I'd better hurry and get a front-row seat.

LANGSTON: Fine. See you after the program. (MR. HUGHES
exits; LANGSTON *turns.*) My dream of making my father
proud of me has finally come true. (*Thoughtfully*) Now I know
the real meaning of success. (*Enthusiastically*) I'm going to
take Mrs. Bethune's advice and travel all over this great country. (*Moves to lectern and faces audience*) I'll visit schools,
churches, and community groups, and share the message of
my poetry (*Gestures expansively*) with the people of America!
(*Opens journal as if to begin program. Curtain*)

THE END

Production Notes

LANGSTON HUGHES:
POET OF THE PEOPLE

Characters: 12 male; 8 female; at least 8 male and female for passersby.

Playing Time: 30 minutes.

Costumes: Scene 1, Mexican dress of the early 1920s: James Hughes wears poncho; Señora Garcia, long dress and apron. Scene 2, Langston wears jacket at opening of scene; Mr. Hughes, hat. Scenes 3 and 4, 1930s: Langston wears suit, wristwatch; Waiter, uniform; Longshoreman, work clothes; Young Woman, red dress. Others wear costumes appropriate for the period.

Properties: Feather duster; suitcase; soda glass with two straws; journal; paper money; umbrella; bag of groceries; notebook; briefcase holding books.

Setting: Scene 1: James Hughes's home near Mexico City. Desk, chair, wastebasket are center. Accountant's ledger lies closed on desk. Floor vase with tall pampas grass is nearby. Scene 2: Dormitory room, Columbia University. Bunk or twin beds and bureau are upstage. Downstage, desk with papers, pencils, books; two chairs; lamp, clock, wastebasket. Closet door in wall right. Exit left. Posters of Harlem street and café scenes on wall upstage. Scene 3: Harlem street scene. Backdrop has painted storefronts: drugstore window showing table, chairs, jukebox; barbershop with pole; doorway with steps and bench nearby. At right, pier with boxes and crates. Center, sign marks intersection of Lenox Avenue and 125th Street. Downstage, chair, small table with cup and saucer and man's hat on it. Scene 4: Bethune-Cookman College. Bookcase, desk, chair. At Rise, high stool and lectern.

Lighting: Lights fade at end of Scene 2; spotlight in Scene 3.

Sound: Door slamming; knock on door; foghorn; clanging bell; lively jazz.

❧ Campaign Fever

by *Frank Sandock*

The politics of popularity in a school election . . .

Characters

SUSAN BLAINE, *candidate for Senior Class President*
CATHY MORENO, *her campaign manager*
ANDY GILLIS, *another candidate*
EDDIE GRADY, *Andy's campaign manager*
KENNETH APPLEBAUM ⎫
MARY O'DEA ⎪
KIM INGALLS ⎬ *candidates*
TAMMY BARNETT ⎪
JASON WIDENER ⎭
MR. STEMPLE, *school principal*
VOTERS, *extras*

SCENE 1

SETTING: *Art room at Morgan High. Student art works and campaign posters adorn walls and tables. Chair and large desk with pad of paper and pen on it face audience, center.*
AT RISE: SUSAN BLAINE *is sitting at desk, a shoulderbag and books beside her. She picks up pen and paper, ponders, and writes a few words. Abruptly, she crumples paper and throws it into wastebasket. She repeats actions with another sheet of paper. Then she rises and paces. CATHY MORENO enters, carrying school books and large shoulderbag.*
CATHY (*Teasing*): Susan Blaine, can this be you? The next president of the senior class, frowning and pacing the floor?

86

SUSAN (*Annoyed*): Cathy, where have you been? You're half an hour late!

CATHY (*Sitting*): I'm sorry. I was talking to Larry Hart, and I lost track of time. Anyway, I'm here now. (*Brightly*) How are things going?

SUSAN (*In dismay*): My speech is going absolutely nowhere. I can't even write the first sentence.

CATHY: What's wrong?

SUSAN: Everything! I've tried, "Welcome, friends and associates," but that sounds terrible. "Good afternoon, fellow students" is stiff and stuffy. And "Hello, boys and girls" is just plain stupid. (*Frustrated*) I should give up. I'll never get it right.

CATHY: How about, "Greetings, fellow inmates"?

SUSAN: Very funny. Cathy, is it too much to ask you for some real help? After all, you are my campaign manager.

CATHY: Campaign manager, yes. But speech writer? That's not my thing. Besides, you're the best writer and speaker in class. You'll work it out.

SUSAN (*Sarcastically*): Sure, it'll be a snap. (*Annoyed*) Tell me—when are you going to get down to business?

CATHY: I know I haven't given you much help, but I've got problems. I don't even have a date for the prom.

SUSAN (*In disbelief*): The prom? That's six months away!

CATHY: I know, and it's getting closer every day. Sue, I know how much the campaign means to you, but I don't know why you're so worried. You're way ahead of the other candidates. (*Pulls sheet of paper out of her shoulderbag*)

SUSAN: You don't have to read that list again. I know it by heart.

CATHY: It's good for your morale. (CATHY *reads from list, looking up to make comments.*) Mary O'Dea: She hasn't come close in any election since she made freshman treasurer. Then there's Ken Applebaum, the class clown. Did you hear what he did today? He hung an enormous campaign sign out the window.

SUSAN: Typical. That must be why Mr. Stemple announced those limits on the size of signs and posters.

CATHY (*Shaking head*): Leave it to Applebaum. Then we have (*Reads from list*) Kim Ingalls, Tammy Barnett, and Jason Widener—average students, and not especially popular. And finally, you, Susan Blaine: Freshman and Sophomore Secretary. Student Council Chair, National Honor Society, countless clubs and volunteer groups. (*Earnestly*) Sue, nobody is more qualified than you are. Nobody cares more about Morgan High, and all the seniors know it.

SUSAN: We're certainly not going to win by sitting back and waiting for it to happen. I was up at 5:30 this morning making posters. I just wish you'd do your part.

CATHY: I think you're way ahead, but I suppose we shouldn't be too sure of ourselves. And just to put your mind at ease (*She stands and raises her right hand.*), I'll give you a solemn pledge: "I, Cathy Moreno, promise to work my fingers to the bone. I'll leave no stone unturned in my quest for votes. I hereby promise to treat this campaign as a matter of life and death." (CATHY *sits, stretches leisurely and puts her hands in back of her head.*) Then, on election day, you and I can enjoy the delicious and well-deserved fruits of our labor.

SUSAN (*Musing*): The fruits of our labor. (*She writes on pad.*) I like that. (KENNETH APPLEBAUM *enters, carrying bag of apples and holding one apple in right hand.*)

KENNETH: Apples, anyone? Applebaum apples! For seniors only!

CATHY: Kenneth Applebaum! What are you doing here?

KENNETH: Isn't it obvious? Delivering apples to seniors. You are seniors, aren't you?

CATHY: Crawl away, Crabapple. We have the art room until four-thirty.

KENNETH: Calm down, Cat Woman. Have an apple. (KENNETH *places apple in* CATHY's *hand and another before* SUSAN.) No obligation, of course. Just enjoy.

SUSAN: Ken, are you trading apples for votes?

KENNETH: No way, Blaine! That would be unethical.

CATHY: Your cause is always hopeless, Crabapple, but just for the record—how many seniors have these forbidden apples?

KENNETH: Every member of the senior class—well, almost

every member. A few wouldn't accept them. But the majority—get that, Sue?—the majority enjoyed them very much. They're good apples.

CATHY: Oh, by the way, Ken, tell us about the outrageous sign you brought to school today.

KENNETH (*Concerned*): Oh, the sign. A temporary setback. A strategic error. It blocked the view from Mr. Stemple's window. (SUSAN *and* CATHY *laugh.*) Go ahead, enjoy your mirth . . . but I have to see Mr. Stemple at four o'clock.

CATHY: Don't let us detain you. The truth is, we're working on a project of our own: the "Landslide for Susan" program.

KENNETH: Landslide, you say? Ah, such innocence. You haven't heard the latest, have you? A shame, really. Sue had a good chance. But I detest telling bad news, and it's time for me to go. Bye, losers. (KENNETH *starts for exit.*)

SUSAN: Wait, Ken! (*He stops and turns.*) You can't leave us like that.

KENNETH (*Uneasily*): Look, I really have to go.

SUSAN (*Warningly*): Tell us what you're talking about, or I'll take this apple to Mr. Stemple and complain like mad. I really will!

KENNETH (*Resigned*): You win. I'm in enough trouble already.

SUSAN: That's better. (KENNETH *walks back.*) Now, what were you saying?

KENNETH: Andy Gillis put his name in the running today.

SUSAN (*Surprised*): Andy Gillis?

KENNETH: The one and only. Handsome, bright, all-state basketball star—and the worst part, very popular. But you know all that.

CATHY (*Dreamily*): Do I! (*Seriously*) But he's never run for office before. Does he have a campaign manager?

KENNETH: Does he ever! None other than (*Wincing*) Grady.

SUSAN (*Shocked*): Not Slick Eddie Grady!

CATHY: Andy Gillis really hooked up with that creep?

KENNETH: The other way around. When Eddie heard that Andy was thinking about running, he couldn't wait to offer his services. He's sticking to Andy like glue.

CATHY (*In disgust*): The leech. He could never win anything for himself, so he latches onto Andy's coattails.

SUSAN: But Andy's never been interested in class affairs before. Why now?

KENNETH (*Shrugging*): He figures being class president will get him into a first-rate college. And all his friends are urging him on—especially Eddie.

SUSAN: So do you think he has a chance?

KENNETH (*Surprised*): The guy is golden! Haven't you noticed him smiling at all the girls and joking with the guys? He's a shoo-in. (*Looks at watch*) Five of four. I've got to dash. (*Moves toward exit*) By the way, bad luck to you both.

CATHY: Same to you, loser! (KENNETH *ignores this remark. As he reaches exit, he looks off and pauses.*)

KENNETH: Well, can you beat that! They're on their way down here.

SUSAN: You mean Andy and Eddie?

KENNETH: Who else? Remember, ladies—be kind to your enemies. (*Exits.* ANDY GILLIS *and* EDDIE GRADY, *each carrying posters, enter.*)

EDDIE: Well, well, well. Look who's here. The in-group.

ANDY: We're just dropping off these posters. You know, of course, that I'm running for president.

SUSAN: Yes, we heard.

ANDY: Do I detect a note of dismay? What's the matter—feel threatened?

CATHY (*Quickly*): Oh, no, not at all. (*Pauses*) We were surprised, that's all.

SUSAN: I didn't know you were interested in school affairs, Andy.

ANDY: I never was, till now. But sports aren't enough for me anymore. I need to broaden my horizons. Right, Eddie?

EDDIE: You tell 'em, A.G. (*To girls*) He'd be a fool not to take advantage of all the publicity and attention he gets from sports.

ANDY: And do you remember this from Latin I? "To the victor go the spoils." Yes, the spoils—getting out of class, more respect from the teachers. (*Preening*) I think I'll like that.

SUSAN: Tell me, Andy. Do you have a platform?

ANDY: A platform? All the world's my stage. I don't need a platform.

SUSAN: No, no! Let me translate that for you. A platform is a set of policies or positions—you know, ideas that will help Morgan High.

ANDY (*Uneasily*): What about it, Eddie? Do we have any of those?

EDDIE (*Confidently*): Sure, we have a platform—a platform for students, not for teachers and administrators.

CATHY (*Defensively*): What do you mean by that?

EDDIE: I mean that you and the rest of your know-it-all crowd have dominated this school long enough. Every time there's a new rule or restriction, the principal comes to people like you, and you buy it. And all our privileges disappear—like the after-school cafeteria for seniors, and an open campus.

SUSAN: You know perfectly well that those programs didn't work. Some students, including you, Eddie, abused the privileges. Maybe with a student court for violations, we can get those programs back.

EDDIE: You're right. We will get them back, but with Andy as president, and you as an onlooker. (*Puts his posters on work table*)

ANDY: Eddie gets excited sometimes, but he's right, you know. I don't dislike you, Sue, but we need a president who's on the side of the students—and someone who can get things done.

SUSAN: Meaning you, of course.

EDDIE: Face the facts, Sue. Andy's been captain of the football and basketball teams. He's used to being in charge. (ANDY *puts posters on worktable*.) Well, we're off to press some flesh. (*They exit.*)

CATHY: Have you ever heard anything so conceited? Too bad he's so good-looking. . . . Hey, that gives me an idea. I play up to Andy, go out with him. Then, I soften him up and get him to drop out of the race.

SUSAN (*Looking at* CATHY, *in disbelief*): Cathy, you're unreal!

CATHY: It was just a thought. (*Begins to leaf through posters*)

SUSAN (*Upset*): I was afraid something like this would happen!

Andy is bound to take a lot of our votes. What are we going to do?

CATHY (*Angrily*): I know what I'd *like* to do. Take a look at these posters: "Put the Blame on Blaine"; "Get Rid of Blaine—the Plain Jane."

SUSAN: Let me see those. (*Looks at posters*)

CATHY: Talk about negative campaigning!

SUSAN (*Holding up "Plain Jane" poster*): Smear tactics is more like it.

CATHY: Well, we can play that game, too. (*Starts to gather up posters*) We'll start with a bonfire, using these as fuel.

SUSAN: We can't beat them at their own game—and we won't stoop that low, either. Besides, Eddie is an expert. (*Sadly*) He knows what hurts, too. (*Pause*) This is just mean, calling me a Plain Jane!

CATHY: Yeah, as if that would make you a bad president.

SUSAN (*Angrily*): Cathy! What do you want me to do? Smear myself with makeup and act like those silly girls who strut around in front of the boys?

CATHY (*Gently*): Calm down, Sue. I didn't mean that I agreed with them.

SUSAN (*Agitated; picking up books*): This is all too much for one day! (*On the verge of tears*) I can't write a stupid speech; I'm insulted by Eddie Grady; Mr. All-State Popularity decides to run; and now my best friend informs me I'm a Plain Jane. I'm out of here. See you in a couple of years. (*She rushes out.* CATHY *watches her, then looks at posters, shaking her head. Curtain*)

* * * * *

SCENE 2

TIME: *One week later.*

SETTING: *The same, except that lectern is diagonally right, facing audience. Table back left has punch, cookies on it. There are several chairs center, facing lectern, but turned enough so audience can see actors sitting in them.*

AT RISE: *Candidates stand at table, talking quietly.* SUSAN *sits front center, alone.* CATHY *enters.*

CATHY: Hi, Sue.

SUSAN (*Nervously*): Cathy, what took you so long?

CATHY: On my way over I met Charlie Cutter, and we started talking. (*Frowning*) I hope you're not angry.

SUSAN (*Resigned*): No, I'm not angry.

CATHY: So this is the famous Morgan High tradition of waiting for election results.

SUSAN (*Glumly*): This is it. I'm glad you came. You can carry me home when I lose.

CATHY: Don't talk that way. You still have a good chance.

SUSAN: Take my advice, Cathy. Prepare for the worst. (CATHY *squeezes* SUSAN's *shoulder, then goes to get some punch.* ANDY *joins* SUSAN. *The others continue to converse, ad lib, in low tones.*)

ANDY: Well, Sue, how many votes are you counting on?

SUSAN (*Defiantly*): Just enough to win.

ANDY: You must hate me for deciding to run against you.

SUSAN: Don't be ridiculous, Andy. Of course I don't hate you.

ANDY: You act cool, Sue, but inside I'll bet you're a bundle of nerves.

SUSAN (*Grudgingly*): I'm a little on edge. Aren't you?

ANDY (*Also grudgingly*): A little. I have to confess, this waiting around does get to me. And there's something else—

SUSAN (*Quizzically*): You are acting sort of peculiar. Not like the confident Andy we all know. What's wrong?

ANDY: Well, it's the election. Of course, I'm sure I'm going to win, but I've been wondering lately about what I'll do when I take office.

SUSAN: So?

ANDY: Well, that's it. I don't really know what a president does. (*Hesitates*) Sue . . . could you be my advisor? You know your way around school matters. You've always been involved.

SUSAN (*Stunned*): You're asking *me* to be your advisor? That's crazy! All week long you've been attacking me and my ideas.

ANDY: That was just campaign talk. Eddie wrote most of my speeches, and I was dumb enough to say everything he told me. Actually, I like some of your ideas. The seniors want me, but you could make a real contribution as an assistant or an advisor. How about it?

SUSAN (*Angrily*): Look, Andy, I'm running for president, not assistant. I don't want to talk about it—or even think about it!

ANDY (*Holding up hand*): O.K., O.K., it was just an idea!

SUSAN (*Looking off; nervously*): Here comes Mr. Stemple. (MR. STEMPLE *enters, walks to lectern. Others go to chairs, sit.*)

MR. STEMPLE: Good morning, everyone. I know it's difficult to be patient at a time like this. Before I announce the results, I want to thank you all for your fine campaign efforts— marred only by a few incidents, such as a certain sign that eclipsed my view for several minutes. (*All look at* KENNETH, *who slumps in his chair.*) Well, I can tell you that as far as we can tell, we have a first in Morgan High history. The winners in the Senior Class President election are—Andy Gillis and Susan Blaine. It's a tie! (*All murmur excitedly.*)

CATHY: Terrific! There's still a chance!

SUSAN (*Relieved*): I can't believe it.

EDDIE: There'll have to be a runoff.

MR. STEMPLE: I must say that this development took me by surprise, too, but we've already devised a plan for breaking the tie. Those seniors who were absent during yesterday's election will vote in a special election this Friday. Susan and Andy, you will be the only candidates. Each of you will have a chance to address the voters just before the election. (*Shakes hands with* SUSAN *and* ANDY) Congratulations—and good luck—to both of you. (*Exits*)

CATHY (*To* SUSAN): We're back in business! Let's get right to work. I'll get a copy of yesterday's absentee list. (CATHY *exits.* ANDY, KENNETH, *and* EDDIE *walk to one side and chat.* MARY, KIM, TAMMY, *and* JASON *approach* SUSAN.)

MARY: Good luck, Sue. Of course, I'll have to wish Andy good luck, too. (*Looks at* ANDY) He's quite a guy.

KIM: Yeah—but he's putting on weight.

MARY (*Puzzled*): He is? I didn't notice.

KIM: Look at his head. It's getting big.

MARY: Well, he is confident—but that's important in a class president.

TAMMY: Best of luck, Sue.

SUSAN: Thanks, Tammy.

KIM (*To* SUSAN): I hope you win.

SUSAN: Thanks for your support, Kim.

JASON: Don't worry, Sue. Some of us are wise to that hypocrite Gillis. You just might make it. I hope you do.

SUSAN: Thanks, Jason. I'm going to give it my best shot. With such a small group of students voting in the runoff, at least we'll be able to sit down and talk with each one.

KIM, TAMMY, JASON (*Ad lib*): Bye. See you later. Good luck. (*Etc.*)

SUSAN: See you tomorrow. (KIM, TAMMY, JASON, MARY, KENNETH, *and* ANDY *exit.* CATHY *reenters, holding sheet of paper.*)

EDDIE (*Approaching* SUSAN; *in mocking tone*): Congratulations, Susan. Enjoy the taste of victory while you can. But it's only a taste. You'll never get this close again.

SUSAN: We'll see about that!

CATHY (*To* EDDIE): I'm surprised you have the time to bait Susan. Don't you and Andy have work to do?

EDDIE: Work? What work? There's nothing to do. You know, I've never had a feeling like this before. I mean being absolutely certain about something—completely convinced, no doubt in my mind. It's a nice feeling. See you later, Second-Raters.

CATHY (*As* EDDIE *exits*): So long, First Class Louse.

SUSAN: Did you hear that? They must be up to something big.

CATHY: Yes, and I think I know what it is. (*Holds up sheet*) Here's the attendance list. Listen to this: Absent or Dismissed: Bob Aiken, Don Allison, William Cato, Michael Holtzman—(*Breaking off; upset*) It's the basketball team! They were dismissed early yesterday for the game in Colebrook. Andy and his teammates missed the election. Out of 17 seniors who were out, 10 are on the team. I see only two we can count on.

SUSAN: Oh, no! Then Andy's definitely going to win.

CATHY: There's still hope. Maybe Andy's teammates are jealous of him.

SUSAN (*Gloomily*): Thanks for trying to cheer me up, Cathy, but Andy's buddies aren't going to vote for me.

CATHY: Don't give up, Sue. Please.

SUSAN: Look, Cathy, I may be Plain Jane, but I'm not stupid. I can read the handwriting on the wall, and so can you. (SUSAN *takes up her books.*) No sense hanging around here. Goodbye.

CATHY: Wait! I'll walk with you.

SUSAN: I'd rather be alone right now. (SUSAN *exits, head down, walking slowly. Curtain*)

* * * * *

SCENE 3

TIME: *Friday, three days later.*

SETTING: *Same as Scene 2. A chair is on each side of table front center, and another chair a few feet back. Worktable and two chairs stand left.*

AT RISE: CATHY *is writing at worktable.* SUSAN *enters, carrying folders.*

SUSAN: What are you doing here?

CATHY: I know I can't vote, but nobody said I couldn't watch.

SUSAN: I'm glad you're here. It'll be nice to have one fan in the crowd, at least.

CATHY: Listen, I tried to reach every voter today. Only Lori Cataldo and Bill Wiener said definitely they'd vote for you. The others wouldn't commit themselves, or else they're teammates or friends of Andy's.

SUSAN (*Patting CATHY's arm*): Thanks for trying, Cathy.

CATHY (*Indicating folder*): Is that your speech?

SUSAN: Yes. The tenth version. (*Laughs*) I change it every time I look at it.

CATHY: You seem so calm. I wish I could be, but every time I think about today's election I get so angry. It's just not fair.

Here you are, the perfect candidate, losing out to a pretender with a phony smile.

SUSAN: I guess underneath I'm as angry as you are. (*Pause*) You know, I have a perfect right to be angry. It *is* unfair. And I'm going to tell them so. (SUSAN *takes speech out of folder, starts ripping it up.*)

CATHY: Sue, what are you doing? Stop!

SUSAN: It's all right, Cathy. I don't need a script. I know just what to say.

CATHY: What's that?

SUSAN: I'm going to let them know how unfair this whole election has been. I'm the better candidate, and even if it means losing, I'm going to tell them why. (TWO VOTERS *enter, conversing ad lib.*)

CATHY: Here come the voters!

SUSAN: Good. This is one speech I'm ready for. (*More* VOTERS *enter, sit in chairs.* MR. STEMPLE *enters and stands by lectern.* ANDY *enters and sits to right of* MR. STEMPLE. SUSAN *walks to front and sits to left of* MR. STEMPLE.)

MR. STEMPLE: Good afternoon, seniors. I just want to remind you that you have a serious and important decision to make. Now, for the candidates. The first speaker is Susan Blaine. (*He sits.* SUSAN *approaches lectern. There is mild applause except for* CATHY, *who cheers loudly until others look back at her. She sinks into her seat.*)

SUSAN: Thank you, Mr. Stemple. (*Pause*) Fellow seniors, friends of Morgan High. Recently I met with each of you and told you what I would work for if elected president: a "Seniors Helping Freshmen" program, a hotline for troubled students, a program for volunteers at the city's homeless shelters, student representation on the school board, and other goals too numerous to mention here. It's an ambitious platform. I'm proud of it, and I stand behind it. (*Pause*) I ran a low-key campaign—maybe too low-key. I didn't want to appear conceited, and I may have given you a false impression. Today, I stand before you totally convinced that I should be your next president. I have knowledge and experience for the job. I love this school, and win or lose, I will try to serve it well. As you vote today, remember that you are not here to declare your friendship; you are here to do what's best for Morgan High. Thank you. (*Applause as* SUSAN *sits.* MR. STEMPLE *stands.*)

MR. STEMPLE: Thank you, Susan. Now, Andy Gillis. (*Generous applause and whistles.* ANDY *approaches lectern.*)

ANDY (*To* MR. STEMPLE): Thank you, Mr. Stemple. (*To audience*) Seniors and friends. A few weeks ago I had no interest in running for president, but my friends urged me to run. I was quite surprised at the amount of support I received. I know that much of it can be traced to my success in sports. Athletics teaches important lessons about competition, hard work, and determination. A good president needs these qualities, but he needs others as well. Morgan High deserves the best. We need someone with communication skills and administrative ability, someone with a record of school service and accomplishment. We need someone whose dedication to Morgan High is unquestioned. (*Pause*) We need Susan Blaine. (SUSAN *is startled. There is a buzz among* VOTERS. ANDY *waits for silence.*) Some of you came here today intending to vote for me. I appreciate that, but the truth is that I've been fooling myself. I'm not prepared to be president, and I know it. Susan has given years of unselfish service to Morgan High, and she deserves a victory. I want all of you to join me in a unanimous vote for Susan Blaine. Thank you.

SUSAN (*Rising; stunned*): I don't know what to say . . . except, thanks for supporting me, Andy.

ANDY: Come on, everyone. Stand up if you're for Susan Blaine. (*Several* VOTERS *stand. Others look around, uneasily.* ANDY *enthusiastically gestures his approval; he and* VOTERS *who are standing start to clap.* CATHY *stands, clapping wildly. Remaining* VOTERS *stand, until all are standing, clapping.*)

MR. STEMPLE (*Pleased*): Well, I guess it's unanimous. (*Applause stops.*) Morgan High's new Senior Class President is Susan Blaine.

SUSAN (*Crossing to* ANDY): Thanks, Andy. I think I've misjudged you. I can count on your help, I hope.

ANDY (*Shaking* SUSAN's *hand; smiling broadly*): You sure can, Susan.

CATHY *and* OTHERS (*Clapping and shouting ad lib as curtain closes*): All right! Congratulations, Susan! (*Etc. Curtain*)

THE END

Production Notes

CAMPAIGN FEVER

Characters: 5 female; 5 male; as many male or female extras as desired for
  Voters.
Playing Time: 35 minutes.
Costumes: Everyday dress. Mr. Stemple wears suit.
Properties: School books; papers and pen; shoulderbags; bag of apples; cam-
  paign posters, including one reading GET RID OF BLAINE—THE PLAIN JANE;
  folder with speech; attendance list; wastebasket.
Setting: Art room at Morgan High. Scene 1: Large desk and chair face audi-
  ence. Student art works, campaign posters adorn walls, tables. Scene 2:
  Table and lectern face audience. Several chairs face lectern. Scene 3: Chair
  is on each side of table and lectern, and another chair a few paces back. At
  front left are a worktable and two chairs.
Lighting and Sound: No special effects.

~Escape to the Blue Planet

by *Claire Boiko*

Earthlings must fight for their lives on a hostile planet . . . .

Characters

BEN HARPER
LORI LARSON, *his cousin*
MRS. JUNE HARPER, *Ben's mother*
LADY KALA, *The Shining One of Planet Paragon*
NIGHTSHADE, *The Deadly Tracker*
MAGNATE MALENIXUS, *The Ultimate Villain*
TECHNOS
SCAN
TWO GUARDS
FRITILLARIAN, *butterfly*
ROBOID, *robot*

SCENE 1

TIME: *The present. An autumn evening.*
SETTING: *A corner of the Harpers' backyard. Center stage, on a carton, is a "radio telescope" made of an upside-down opened umbrella covered in foil, its handle pointed skyward. A "radio receiver" made of a hair dryer, also covered in foil and with a metal rod set into its nozzle, is attached to umbrella by wires. Garbage can and patio table with can of insecticide on it are right.*
AT RISE: BEN HARPER, *wearing earphones, sits facing audience, intently listening to "receiver." Sound of static is heard.*

From time to time, he jots notes in notebook. Suddenly a short burst of whistling pulses is heard. BEN *jerks to attention, holding earphones closer.*

BEN (*Excitedly*): Hey! That's a signal! A definite signal from somewhere in space. (*Whistling fades, and static is heard again.* BEN *quickly makes notes in notebook.*) Lost it. But I know the source was: right ascension, 2220, declination, minus 0132. This radio telescope actually works! (*He does not notice* LORI LARSON, *who enters wearing sundress and crosses to stand in back of* BEN.) Let me see, there's a correction factor of minus two, and that changes the—

LORI (*Pulling earphones from* BEN's *ears*): Hello-o, Cousin Benny! It's Lori. I know you know I'm here.

BEN (*Outraged*): Lori Larson, get out of my hair! (*Grabs earphones from her*)

LORI (*Pointing to umbrella*): What's that thing?

BEN: It's not a thing. It's a radio telescope. (LORI *tries to squint through umbrella handle.*) No, Lori! (*Exasperated*) You can't *see* through it. It picks up radio waves. The aerial focuses the waves, and the radio receiver, here, turns them into sound waves. I can "hear" the stars. (LORI, *obviously bored, yawns.*)

LORI: Boring, boring, boring. You're supposed to be entertaining me, Ben. Your mother said so.

BEN: You're a big girl, Lori. Go entertain yourself.

LORI: You're so *mean*, Ben Harper. In California people are really kind and nice and mellow.

BEN (*Impatiently*): Well, this is a mean state, and I'm in a mean mood. So get lost!

LORI: I just *hate* you. You're a terrible cousin! I'm going to tell your mother. (*Marches down right, militantly*) I'll never invite you to my gorgeous beach house in Malibu. (*Calling off as she exits*) Aunt June!

BEN: Who cares? (*Whistling pulses resume, louder.* BEN *rises, grabs radar device.*) Please don't stop. Stick with me. I'll answer you. (*He replaces earphones, holds hair dryer at same angle as umbrella, turning left slowly so that his back is to* MRS. HARPER, *who enters right.*)

MRS. HARPER (*Sharply*): Benjamin! Are you hiding from Lori?

BEN (*Ignoring her*): Here goes. (*He turns on hair dryer. A high-pitched whine is heard in same rhythm as whistles.* MRS. HARPER *crosses quickly to* BEN, *grabs his shoulders and turns him around.*)

MRS. HARPER: Benjamin Harper, you answer me!

BEN (*Removing earphones, groaning*): Mom!

MRS. HARPER: What's going on? Lori is very upset and says you are ignoring her completely. What's the matter with you? (*Points to radio telescope*) And what is this mess?

BEN: It's my radio telescope. You're going to be proud of me when I win first prize in the science fair! See, the way it works is—

MRS. HARPER (*Interrupting*): That's my good umbrella! What have you done to it? (*Angrily*) And is that my hair dryer?

BEN (*Sheepishly*): I only borrowed them, Mom. I was going to put them back tomorrow.

MRS. HARPER: You're going to put them back now. I want that mess cleared away immediately. Then you're going to play Scrabble with Lori. (*Marches off right*)

BEN (*Disgruntled*): This is the absolute pits! I'll bet Einstein's mother would have lent him her hair dryer. (*Disconnects umbrella and hair dryer*) And I'll bet he didn't have a cousin from California interfering with his work. (*Mournfully*) Now I'll never find the source of those signals or win first prize at the science fair. (*Cups his hand to mouth and shouts skyward*) Hey, wherever you are, if there's a perfect planet out there I'm willing to join you. (*Lights flash, then a crescendo of whistling is heard.* BEN *cowers behind umbrella.*) Hey, wait. I was only kidding. (*Loud whistle is heard. Lights go out. When they come up again, large silver cone, with a sliding triangular door, stands down left.*) My gosh! An unidentified flying ice cream cone! (*Strange music is heard as door of cone slowly slides open.* LADY KALA, *wearing crown and diaphanous rainbow-colored robe, steps out, looks around curiously, and stretches.*)

LADY KALA: Safe, at last!

BEN (*In awe*): Wow! She must be the *real* Miss Universe.

LADY KALA (*Lifting her hand in greeting*): Cosmic greetings, Star Lord.

BEN (*Stammering*): C-c-cosmic greetings, whoever you are. (*Suddenly*) Hey, we're speaking English.

LADY KALA (*Laughing*): Hardly. We are communicating on the universal telepathic band. And thank you, Star Lord.

BEN: For what?

LADY KALA: For your signal. You guided me to this safe, blue planet. (*Points to herself*) I am Lady Kala, the Shining One, ruler of the planet Paragon. (BEN *bows awkwardly*.)

BEN: Welcome to Earth, Your Highness, ma'am.

LADY KALA: And who are you, Star Lord?

BEN (*Embarrassed*): Oh, I'm not a Star Lord. I'm just a kid. (*A soft, ominous hissing sound is heard off*.)

LADY KALA (*Frightened*): Hush! Did you hear that? (*Hissing grows louder*.)

BEN: That hissing sound? Sounds as if somebody's getting a flat tire.

LADY KALA (*More alarmed*): No, it's Nightshade, the deadly tracker. I am in dire peril. Will you help me?

BEN: Well, sure. But I thought you came to help *me*. Didn't you hear me calling for a perfect planet where there is no trouble?

LADY KALA: It is true, my planet is perfect. (*Sighs*) But there is trouble there. Terrible trouble for Paragon.

BEN: What kind of trouble?

LADY KALA: Let me ask you this. What happens on your planet when you possess a rare jewel?

BEN: Everybody tries to steal it.

LADY KALA: Precisely. My planet is a rare jewel. Magnate Malenixus of Stygios, the planet of shudders, has his wicked sights set on capturing my planet. But he cannot succeed unless he first makes me a prisoner. I have eluded him, so far. But Nightshade, his tracker, is near. (*Hissing grows louder*.) Oh . . . very near! Hide me!

BEN (*Indicating cone*): But won't he spot your ship?

LADY KALA: You're right. I must send it deep into space. (*Points to cone*) Go . . . go . . . hide in the dust of the remotest nebula. (*Lights flash on and off. Cone is removed.* LADY

KALA *speaks urgently*.) Now, Star Lord, you must hide me among your people.

BEN: But, Your Highness, you'll have to change into something less—er—conspicuous. (*Pause*) I know, I'll go borrow something from my cousin Lori. (*Hissing begins again very loudly*.)

LADY KALA: There is no time. I will imaginate the clothes.

BEN: "Imaginate"? What's that?

LADY KALA: Quickly. Look into my eyes. Imagine an Earth costume for me. Concentrate. (*She stares into* BEN's *eyes, making magical motions with her hands*.)

BEN (*Weaving back and forth, as if in a trance*): Sundress . . . sundress . . . sundress. (LADY KALA *removes her crown and drops her robe. Underneath she wears sundress exactly like* LORI's.) Great! You look just like Lori! (*He picks up her robe and crown and hides them in garbage can*.) Come on, Your Highness. We have to find a good hiding place for you.

LADY KALA: You must be careful. Do you have a weapon? Nightshade is dangerous. (BEN *looks around quickly, then runs right and picks up can of insecticide*.)

BEN (*Waving can around*): This bug spray will take care of him! See? (*He sprays quickly, then puts can in his pocket*.) Let's go! (*They exit right quickly. After a moment,* LORI *enters*.)

LORI (*Looking around*): Ben? Where are you? (*Crosses to garbage can*) I wouldn't put it past you to hide in the smelly old garbage can! (*Looks in can, gasps and pulls out robe and crown*) How gorgeous! (*As she dons robe and crown and preens,* NIGHTSHADE, *wearing black breeches, boots, tunic, and hood with white makeup and black-ringed eyes, sneaks onto stage and hides behind garbage can*.) Why, even the boutiques in Malibu don't have anything like this. (NIGHT-SHADE *stands, grabs* LORI's *wrist*.)

NIGHTSHADE (*Hissing*): S-s-so, Lady Kala. I have you in my power at las-s-st.

LORI (*Shrieking*): Oh! You scared me, Ben. What are you dressed up for, Halloween?

NIGHTSHADE (*Dragging her downstage*): Just come with me.

LORI (*Realizing*): Hey, wait! You're not Ben! (*Terrified; struggling*) Who are you? Where are you taking me?

NIGHTSHADE: Where do you s-s-suppose, my fine lady? To S-s-stygios, planet of shudders. (*Lights flash.*)

LORI: No! No! I want to go home—to California! (*Lights go out. Curtains close.*)

* * * * *

SCENE 2

TIME: *A short time later.*

SETTING: *Throne room of the Magnate Malenixus, on the planet Stygios. A giant silver web is painted on black backdrop. Bat-shaped throne stands center. Computer console and two chairs are left. There is a dark arch up right, with red, glowing interior. Sign above arch reads* EXTREME PERIL. ENTER AT YOUR OWN RISK. DUNGEON OF STYGIOS.

AT RISE: MAGNATE MALENIXUS, *clad in black tunic, breeches, boots, cape, and crown, is hunched down on throne. A silver ray gun is in his belt.* TECHNOS *and* SCAN, *who also wear black and close-fitting caps with antennae, are seated at computer console, busily working. View scope is on console in front of* SCAN. TWO GUARDS, *with ray guns in their belts, stand at attention, one at each side of arch.*

MALENIXUS (*Rising, pacing*): Where is he, Technos? Why is he taking so long? Where is my deadly tracker, Nightshade?

TECHNOS: I have picked up his signal on a remote, blue planet, Magnate Malenixus. He is returning now.

SCAN (*Looking into scope*): I've got visual contact, sir. You will be pleased to hear he has someone with him.

MALENIXUS (*Nodding*): Ah, the Lady Kala. (*Gloating*) For eons upon eons I have pursued the Lady Kala. Now she will be mine. I will force her to demonstrate her rare and special powers, and then—my ultimate triumph.

TECHNOS: What do you mean?

MALENIXUS: Marriage—to *me*. We will consolidate our two planets, and then (*Chuckles evilly*) the whole galaxy will be mine! (*Klaxon horn sounds offstage.*)

1ST GUARD (*Approaching* MALENIXUS, *putting finger to nose in salute*): The prisoners are ready for sentencing, mighty ruler.

MALENIXUS (*Returning "salute"*): Bring them here for my special justice. (2ND GUARD *exits.* MALENIXUS *sits on throne.*) Dispensing justice is my favorite part of the job. (2ND GUARD *reenters with* FRITILLARIAN, *a butterfly, and* ROBOID, *a robot.*)

2ND GUARD (*"Saluting"* MALENIXUS): Here are the worthless worms, O Magnate. (*Pushes* FRITILLARIAN *and* ROBOID *to their knees*)

MALENIXUS: Read the charges against them, Guard.

2ND GUARD (*Unrolling black scroll, reading loudly*): This Fritillarian was caught red-handed, making herself beautiful.

MALENIXUS (*In disgust*): Disgraceful! Fritillarian, do you not know it is against the law to beautify yourself?

FRITILLARIAN (*In quavering voice*): Mercy, O mighty Magnate. I cannot help being beautiful.

MALENIXUS: Mercy? Ha, ha, ha. (*With a sneer*) I will be merciful. I could have your wings pulled, but instead, you shall be zilphered.

FRITILLARIAN (*Distraught*): Oh, no, no! Not the zilpher! (1ST GUARD *pulls her to her feet and pushes her through the arch, then reenters.*)

2ND GUARD (*Pointing to* ROBOID): This Roboid is guilty of treason, mighty one. He disobeyed his master.

MALENIXUS: Well, well, this is a most serious crime. What have you to say for yourself, Roboid?

ROBOID (*Nervously*): It was self-defense, Magnate. My master was tormenting me. He threatened to short-circuit me.

MALENIXUS: No excuse! (*To* 2ND GUARD) Take him away. Scrap him.

ROBOID: Scrap me? Please, please don't scrap me! (2ND GUARD *pushes him to his feet and leads him off through arch, then reenters. Both* GUARDS *stand at attention. Klaxon sounds again.*)

TECHNOS (*Excitedly*): Nightshade the tracker has returned! (*Hissing sound is heard, as* NIGHTSHADE *enters, dragging* LORI *on.*)

LORI (*Protesting*): Let go of me, you snake!

NIGHTSHADE (*Proudly*): Behold—the Lady Kala!

OTHERS (*Ad lib*): The Lady Kala! How beautiful! (*Etc.* MA-
LENIXUS *rises, crosses to* LORI.)

MALENIXUS (*Grandly*): At last we meet, Lady Kala.

LORI: You'd better let me go. Just wait until the President hears
about this. You can't just kidnap people!

MALENIXUS: Come, Lady Kala. Show us your rare and special
powers, and you will have nothing to fear.

LORI (*Confused and upset*): What powers? I can't do anything.
Honest.

MALENIXUS: It is said you can teleport objects across the cosmos. It is said you can levitate. So—levitate a little.

OTHERS (*Chanting*): Lev–i–tate. Lev–i–tate.

LORI (*Incredulously*): Levitate? Me? I can't even jump very
high.

MALENIXUS (*Snarling*): Do something, before I hang your
head in my trophy room.

LORI (*Pleading*): Listen, I don't know who Lady Kala is, but
I'm telling you I can't do anything. I'm just your average kid.

MALENIXUS (*Raising his gun*): Perform!

LORI: O.K., O.K. (*Pauses, thinking*) I know. I'll spell. I'm a
good speller.

NIGHTSHADE (*Hissing*): A s-s-spell. Do you hear that, O powerful master. A s-s-spell.

MALENIXUS (*Eagerly*): Show me the spell.

OTHERS: The spell . . . the spell . . . the spell.

LORI (*Swallowing hard, nervously*): O.K. I'll do a hard one—
Mississippi. (*Spells*) M-i-s-s-i-s-s-i-p-p-i. (*Repeats word*) Mississippi. (*Looks around hopefully*)

OTHERS (*Ad lib*): That's all? What a disappointment! (*Etc.*)

MALENIXUS: Is that all? Is that your entire act?

LORI: I could spell "Honolulu" if you'd like.

MALENIXUS (*Grabbing* LORI's *arm and looking at her closely*):
The truth is—you have no powers.

LORI: Ouch! Let me go. That's what I've been trying to tell you.

MALENIXUS: The truth is (*Suddenly furious*)—*you are not
Lady Kala!*

OTHERS (*Ad lib; shocked*): Not Lady Kala! How can that be? Who is she? (*Etc.*)

LORI: That's the truth!

MALENIXUS (*Releasing* LORI, *advancing threateningly on* NIGHTSHADE): Nightshade, you bumbling fool. You have brought me a primitive from the blue planet. I will have you *rubbled!*

NIGHTSHADE (*Terrified*): Don't rubble me, sire. Anything, but don't rubble me. I will bring you Lady Kala shortly—

MALENIXUS (*Imperiously*): *Immediately,* do you hear?

NIGHTSHADE: Yes, of course, immediately. (MALENIXUS *sits on throne.* 1ST GUARD *pushes* LORI *off, through arch.* NIGHTSHADE *speaks haughtily to* TECHNOS *and* SCAN.) Scan, bring me my Tracker Scope. Technos, get me my Magnetic Attracto. (TECHNOS *and* SCAN *run off left.*)

MALENIXUS (*Threateningly*): Your Tracker Scope had better work, Nightshade—or else.

NIGHTSHADE: It has never failed me, mighty one. (TECHNOS *reenters, carrying giant horseshoe magnet with wires, coils, aerials attached to it.* SCAN *follows, carrying huge red goggles.*)

SCAN: Here is your Tracker Scope, deadly one.

TECHNOS: And your Magnetic Attracto. (NIGHTSHADE *takes items and crosses center. Lights dim; spotlight on* NIGHT-SHADE, *who puts on goggles and sweeps magnet around in semicircle.*)

NIGHTSHADE: S-s-seek. S-s-seek. (*Second spotlight comes up on apron down left revealing* BEN *and* LADY KALA.) Ah, I have found her. (*Points magnet at them*) Come to me. Come to me. Across the deep reaches of empty space. Come to me . . . (*Strobe light plays on* BEN *and* LADY KALA. *Ominous music is heard, as* GUARDS *rush to* BEN *and* LADY KALA *and pull them center roughly. Music stops and lights come up, full.* MALENIXUS *rushes to greet* LADY KALA.)

MALENIXUS (*Smoothly*): So, Lady Kala, we meet at last.

LADY KALA: So, Malenixus, we are face to face.

BEN (*Looking around; confused*): What's going on? Where are we? (*To* MALENIXUS) Who are you?

1ST GUARD (*Forcing* BEN *to his knees*): Bow when you greet the mighty Magnate Malenixus.

LADY KALA (*Protesting*): Leave the boy alone. He is only a harmless primitive.

MALENIXUS: As you say. (*To* BEN) You may rise. (BEN *rises*.) And now, Lady Kala, a special treat. You will entertain us with a demonstration of your special powers.

LADY KALA (*Vehemently*): Never!

MALENIXUS: Never is a long time, my lady. (*Rubs his chin, thinking*) I see you are fond of the little primitive. (*Indicates* BEN, *as he addresses* GUARDS, NIGHTSHADE, TECHNOS, *and* SCAN) Destroy the primitive. (*They surround* BEN.)

LADY KALA: Leave the primitive alone!

BEN: Hey, what is this? What did I ever do to you guys?

MALENIXUS: Zap him! (*All remove ray guns and point them at* BEN, *who suddenly flops on floor, and rolls over face up*.)

LADY KALA: Stop! Don't harm him. I will show you my powers.

1ST GUARD (*Poking* BEN *with his foot; puzzled*): We did not zap him, but he appears to be dead. (*As* GUARDS, TECHNOS, SCAN, *and* NIGHTSHADE *bend over* BEN *curiously, he gives a war whoop, jumps up, whips out spray can from pocket, and "sprays" them. They drop to floor, choking, then lie still.* MALENIXUS, *furious, raises his ray gun and descends on* BEN.)

MALENIXUS: Prepare to meet your doom! (BEN, *cornered, raises his arms.* MALENIXUS *laughs wickedly*.) I will annihilate you. (*Points ray gun at* BEN)

LADY KALA (*Standing on tip toe, calling out*): Malenixus— look. I am *levitating*. (MALENIXUS *turns to look at her.* BEN *quickly thrusts spray can under his nose and "sprays."* MALENIXUS *coughs, then writhes, and falls to floor with dramatic spasms, like an insect dying.* LADY KALA *claps her hands in delight*.) You did it! You conquered Malenixus!

BEN (*Waving can; exuberantly*): Wow! Now, that's what I call a powerful insecticide.

LADY KALA (*Putting her hand on his shoulder*): Insects. That is all they were. Just an ugly, wicked species of insect! (FRIT-

ILLARIAN *and* ROBOID *enter, followed by* LORI, *who runs to* BEN, *carrying robe and crown.*)

LORI: Ben! Oh, am I ever glad to see you. Take me home!

LADY KALA (*Loftily*): Give me my royal robe and crown, primitive.

LORI (*Awed*): Yes, ma'am. (*To* BEN) Who is *she*?

BEN: It's a long, long story, Lori. (FRITILLARIAN *and* RO-BOID *drop to their knees in front of* LADY KALA.)

FRITILLARIAN *and* ROBOID: Hail, Lady Kala, the Shining One. Stygios is yours forever.

LADY KALA (*Laughing; kindly*): Oh, no thank you. (*They rise.*) I have had quite enough of Stygios. Stygios is *yours* forever. I hereby appoint you regents of the planet. Go! Proclaim liberty to your inhabitants.

FRITILLARIAN *and* ROBOID (*Ad lib; gleefully*): Oh, thank you, Lady Kala! Free! Free at last! (*They run off happily.*)

LADY KALA (*Pointing to sky, calling*): Come, come to me, my starship. Out of the dust of the remotest nebula. (*Lights flash, as cone is placed onstage.* LADY KALA *crosses to cone.*)

BEN: Wait a minute, Lady Kala. What about Lori and me? We can't stay here.

LADY KALA: Of course not. You're coming with me—to Paragon. Let me show you what is in store for you. (*She crosses to them, looking into their eyes, waving her hands magically.*) Imaginate . . . Imaginate . . . (BEN *and* LORI *turn toward audience as if in a trance. Color wheel plays in the light on them, and exotic music is heard.*)

BEN: I see rainbows. Colors I've never seen before. It's beautiful.

LORI (*In wonder*): It's even more beautiful than California.

BEN (*Pointing*): Look at that. A crystal castle, floating on a cloud.

LADY KALA: That is your castle.

BEN (*Excitedly*): My own castle! (LORI *blinks, coming out of trance. She pulls* BEN *away from* LADY KALA.)

LORI: No, Ben. You can't go. You belong on Earth.

LADY KALA (*Pulling* BEN *toward cone*): You must come with

me. I owe you my very life. I will make you a Star Lord. You shall have a silver ship to sail the galaxy forever.

BEN (*Bemused*): A Star Lord! My own starship!

LORI (*Pulling him back*): What about your mother and father? What about your space project? What about me?

BEN (*Blinking, snapping out of trance*): You're right, Lori. I've got to go back home. (*To* LADY KALA, *who drops his hand, regretfully*) I'm sorry, Lady Kala. Maybe Earth is a primitive planet, but it's my planet.

LADY KALA (*Sighing*): So be it. I shall miss you. (*Wistfully*) You could have been a Star Lord. Ah, well. I shall transport you back to Earth. Close your eyes, clap your hands three times and say, "There's no place like Earth."

BEN *and* LORI (*Clapping hands, with eyes closed*): There's no place like Earth . . . There's no place like Earth . . . There's no place like Earth. (LADY KALA *moves upstage toward cone, as strobe light plays on stage. Curtain closes behind* BEN *and* LORI.)

BEN (*Opening eyes, looking around*): We're home, Lori! Home!

LORI (*Opening eyes; excitedly*): Oh, wonderful! (BEN *pulls* LORI *center.*) Where are we going?

BEN: To the backyard. Maybe we can see Lady Kala zooming across the sky in her starship. (*Curtains open on backyard scene. On the carton, center, is a small radio telescope.*)

LORI (*Pointing*): Ben—look!

BEN: A real radio telescope! But, who—? How—? (*Faint sound of music is heard.*) Lady Kala! It's a gift from Lady Kala.

LORI: She doesn't want you to forget her, Ben. (MRS. HARPER *enters, carrying tray with pitcher of milk, cups, and plate of cookies on it.*)

MRS. HARPER: Oh there you are. I've been looking all over for you two. (*Chuckling*) I knew you wouldn't go too far. (BEN *and* LORI *exchange knowing glances.*)

BEN (*Casually*): Oh, just to a nearby galaxy.

MRS. HARPER (*Playing along*): Oh, you've been traveling in space, have you? You must be starved after all that zooming about in the cosmos. Milk and cookies, anyone?

BEN *and* LORI (*Ad lib*): Thanks. Sounds great. (*Etc. They take cups and cookies.* MRS. HARPER *puts tray on table.*)

MRS. HARPER (*Examining telescope*): Isn't that clever! Ben, you simply amaze me. When I think of what you can do with a few coat hangers and some aluminum foil! (*Shakes her head*) I'll leave you two to your invention. (*Exits*)

LORI (*Crossing to telescope*): What were you telling me about radio waves, Ben? I think radio waves are fascinating.

BEN: Are you sure you want to hear about radio waves? (*Sarcastically*) Wouldn't you rather talk about California?

LORI: Oh, I only brag about California because it's the only interesting thing about my life. You're such a *genius,* and I'm just so—so *average.*

BEN (*Surprised*): You? Average? I wouldn't call a fellow space-voyager average. In fact, I think you're quite exceptional, Lori.

LORI (*Taken aback*): Exceptional. What a lovely word. (*Musing*) Exceptional. (*Pause*) Teach me about the radio telescope, Ben. I want to know all about it.

BEN (*Shaking his head*): That's what I call a small miracle. (*Looks skyward*) I'm going to set up a steady signal, Lady Kala. So, when you're ready to visit us, you can beam right in on Earth. We may be a primitive planet, but you've got to admit, we've got a lot of promise. (*Curtain*)

THE END

Production Notes

ESCAPE TO THE BLUE PLANET

Characters: 2 male; 3 female; 7 male or female for Nightshade, Technos, Scan, Guards, Fritillarian, and Roboid.

Playing Time: 35 minutes.

Costumes: Ben wears everyday clothes; Lori, a sundress; Lady Kala, rainbow-colored robe, with sundress exactly like Lori's underneath, and crown; Nightshade, Malenixus, Technos, Scan, and Guards, black breeches, tunics, boots. Malenixus also wears black cape and a crown. Nightshade wears white makeup with black-ringed eyes. Technos and Scan wear close-fitting caps with antennae. All carry ray guns in belts. Fritillarian wears butterfly wings. Roboid wears typical robot costume.

Properties: Earphones; notebook; pencil; large silver cone with sliding triangular door, large enough for Lady Kala to step through; black scroll; red goggles; large horseshoe magnet with wires, coils, aerials attached; tray with pitcher, cups and plate of cookies on it.

Setting: Scene 1: The Harpers' backyard. At center, on a large carton, is a "radio telescope" made of an upside-down umbrella covered with aluminum foil. Attached to this is a "radio receiver"—a hair dryer also covered in foil with a metal rod in its nozzle. Garbage can and patio table with can of insecticide on it are right. Scene 2: Throne room of the Magnate Malenixus, on the planet Stygios. Up center, on black backdrop, is a giant silver web. Center is bat-shaped throne. Computer console and two chairs are left. A "view scope," made of two paper towel tubes painted black and joined like binoculars, is on console. Up right is dark arch, with red glowing interior. Sign above arch reads, EXTREME PERIL. ENTER AT YOUR OWN RISK. DUNGEON OF STYGIOS. Later, scene switches to backyard again; realistic radio telescope is now on carton.

Lighting: Flashes, spotlight, strobe, and color wheel, as indicated in text.

Sound: Static; whistling; whining; exotic music; hissing; Klaxon horn; ominous music, as indicated in text.

ᵔThe Comeback Caper

by Anne Coulter Martens

A tense courtroom drama . . .

Characters

ALICE MARTIN, *mystery writer*
SUE KELSEY, *young actress*
PETE LANSING, *prop man*
MIKE BARSTOW, *TV "villain"*
DENNIS GRANT, *young actor*
BILL TAYLOR, *director*
VALERIE POWERS, *reporter*
GLORIA SHEPARD, *aging actress*
HOWARD WRIGHT, *prosecutor*
TOM ANDERSON, *police officer*
JANE GREENWAY, *defense attorney*
NANCY REDMOND, *her assistant*
OWEN FRASER, *judge*
MR. KELSEY ⎱ *Sue's parents*
MRS. KELSEY ⎰
COURT CLERK
STENOGRAPHER
TWO COURT OFFICERS

SCENE 1

TIME: *Early evening.*
SETTING: *TV studio. A few folding chairs are at one side. Rehearsal area, with floor lamp, easy chair, telephone, desk and chairs, is right. If desired, scene may be played in front of curtain.*
AT RISE: *ALICE MARTIN sits in folding chair left, script and*

115

pencil in her hand. SUE KELSEY *enters right with coffee mug.*

SUE KELSEY: Here's your coffee, Alice. (*Gives mug to* ALICE, *then paces nervously*)

ALICE: Thanks, Sue. (*Watching her*) You've been doing great in rehearsals. Not nervous all of a sudden, are you?

SUE (*Sharply*): Why do you ask that?

ALICE (*Shrugging*): Maybe because I'm a little out of sorts, myself. If the great Gloria Shepard demands one more change in this script, I think I'll scream. (PETE LANSING *enters right, carrying plant in ornamental pot. He puts it on desk, then moves lamp slightly.*)

SUE: Alice, I'm not just nervous, I'm panicked! Gloria wants to kick me off the show!

ALICE: Oh, no! Is that what she said?

SUE: Not in so many words, but she's been hinting at it all week. (PETE *adjusts position of plant, then exits.*)

ALICE: Well, don't worry. I won't let her do it. Why didn't you tell me about this earlier?

SUE: I've been trying to think of some way to stop her. (MIKE BARSTOW *enters right.*)

ALICE (*To* SUE): Have you told anyone else about Gloria?

MIKE (*Interrupting*): If you mean what Gloria's been up to, yes, Sue told me. And I'm furious!

SUE: Mike, please. You have your own job to think of. (*To* ALICE) Gloria says a man should play the part of her assistant in the series, not me.

ALICE (*Incensed*): She can't do that! I wrote the script, and it stays the way it is!

MIKE: Want to bet? Nothing can stop her from having her own sweet way.

ALICE: Any idea who she wants for the part? (DENNIS GRANT *enters right.*)

SUE (*Indicating* DENNIS; *softly*): Can't you guess?

DENNIS (*Coming forward*): Hi, gang. Rehearsal over yet?

ALICE: Hi, Dennis. Almost. We're taking a break. (BILL TAY-LOR *enters right.*)

BILL: Places, everyone! Let's do a smooth job this time. Tomorrow we tape. (*Looks around*) Where's Miss Shepard?

SUE: In her dressing room.

MIKE: I'm ready whenever you are.

BILL: Good. Now, Mike, when you make your entrance to attack Maude Fenwick and steal the ruby, fake your action. Miss Shepard doesn't want her hair mussed.

MIKE (*Shrugging*): O.K. (*Leans against desk.* SUE *joins him.*)

DENNIS (*To* BILL): Mind if I watch? I came to pick up Miss Shepard for our dinner date.

BILL: That's fine. Just keep out of my hair. (*Calls out*) Gloria! Let's go! (*He is about to exit right when* VALERIE POWERS *enters left.*)

VAL: Oh, Mr. Taylor? (BILL *stops, nods.*) I'm Valerie Powers of *The Daily Bulletin*. Would it be possible for me to get an interview with Gloria Shepard?

BILL: I don't know. You'll have to ask her after the rehearsal. (*Exits*)

VAL (*To* ALICE): It must be fascinating to work with an actress like Gloria Shepard.

ALICE (*Dryly*): Never a dull moment.

VAL: I've been a fan of hers from way back. I've seen every one of her movies. She was so beautiful!

DENNIS: Miss Shepard is more beautiful now than she ever was.

VAL: It's so exciting that she's making a comeback. What's the name of the new series?

ALICE: *Maude Fenwick, Private Eye*. It's based on my detective books.

VAL: Tell me, is she going to wear the fabulous Rajah Ruby pendant?

ALICE: Of course. She wears it in all her public appearances. It's her trademark, really.

VAL: I'd be afraid to have something so valuable around my neck. They say it's worth half a million dollars. Is that true?

ALICE: Yes. In fact, I've made that ruby the focal point of this first episode.

VAL (*Turning to* DENNIS): You're Dennis Grant, aren't you?

DENNIS: That's right.

VAL: Are you in the series?

DENNIS: No, I'm not.

VAL: Rumor has it that you and Gloria have a romance going.

DENNIS (*Smiling*): We're just good friends.

VAL (*To* MIKE): Are you in the series?

MIKE: I play the bad guy.

VAL (*Turning to* SUE): And you're Sue Kelsey. I understand you play the assistant to the private eye. (SUE *nods.*) Don't you just love working with Gloria Shepard?

SUE: I just love working! This part is my first big break.

VAL: That's great. Well, I'll just sit down and keep quiet until the rehearsal is over. (*Sits far left as others gather at set right.* GLORIA SHEPARD, *attractive older woman, enters right, followed by* BILL. *She wears large ruby pendant on chain around her neck.*)

GLORIA: Dennis, darling. How are you? (*Kisses him on cheek*)

DENNIS: Gloria, you look lovely.

GLORIA: Thank you, pet. (*Sighs*) It's so stuffy in my little trailer. When I made movies, I always had a dresser and a hair stylist.

BILL: This is TV, remember?

GLORIA: Darling, I'm not complaining. I'm crazy about my part. Imagine me playing a private eye! (*Laughs; turns to* DENNIS) Dennis, pet, could I borrow your handkerchief? (DENNIS *goes to her, takes out handkerchief.*) Just pat my forehead lightly, would you, dear? (*He does so.*) Thanks, sweet. (DENNIS *goes left.*) Shall we start?

BILL: Take it from where you're on the phone to the police lieutenant. (SUE *and* MIKE *exit right.* GLORIA *picks up phone and sits on front side of desk, legs crossed.*) No, no, sit behind the desk, not on it.

GLORIA: What's the matter? Don't you think I have nice enough legs?

BILL: Just do it my way, O.K.?

GLORIA (*Petulantly*): Oh, all right. (*Sits in desk chair, speaks on phone*) Let me speak to Lieutenant Snyder. This is Maude

Fenwick. (*Breaks off; to* BILL) Maude. Oh, I hate that name! Can't we change it to Gloria?

ALICE (*Firmly*): This character is Maude Fenwick in my books, and Maude Fenwick she stays.

BILL: I don't see any point in changing the name.

GLORIA: Oh, but there is. Next season, when this series is a big success, we can change the title to *The Gloria Shepard Show.*

ALICE (*Angrily*): Gloria, I've written six books about Maude Fenwick, and they were all best sellers. *My* Maude Fenwick was a retired schoolteacher. But I rewrote the part for you, making Maude (*Gives* GLORIA *an appraising look*) somewhat younger. I made your ruby an important part of the plot. But I will *not* change my character's name.

GLORIA (*Sarcastically*): We're a little testy today, aren't we? (*Annoyed*) All right. I'll agree to be Maude—for now. (*In her part, on phone*) Let me speak to Lieutenant Snyder. This is Maude Fenwick. . . . (*Excitedly*) Lieutenant, I know who the jewel thief is! (SUE *enters right.*) Yes, yes, I'm sure. Come to my office right away. And one more thing—(*Breaks off, then her voice rises*) Lieutenant! Can you hear me? (*Waits, then hangs up*) The line just went dead!

SUE (*In her part*): Maude, I'm worried. Suppose he finds out that you know?

GLORIA (*As herself, to* BILL): Bill, will I get a close-up here?

BILL: No, here the camera zooms in on Sue, looking worried.

GLORIA (*Annoyed*): You're giving her too many close-ups. (*Angrily*) I may as well tell you now, Bill, that Sue's just not right for the part. I think it's better to have a young man play my assistant. More contrast.

SUE (*Flaring*): Miss Shepard, I have a contract.

GLORIA (*Sweetly*): So do I, dear. No Gloria Shepard, no series.

SUE: You want me to back out? Well, I won't!

GLORIA (*In bored tone*): But, darling, you're so inexperienced! All you've ever done are TV commercials.

SUE: And some bit parts. If you're thinking about replacing me with Dennis Grant, that's all the experience he's had.

GLORIA: Did I say anything about Dennis?

DENNIS: Ladies, please leave me out of this.

SUE (*To* GLORIA): I know what you're up to! Don't try it.

ALICE (*Angrily; to* BILL): Bill, my script calls for a female assistant, and I won't have Gloria rewriting it to suit herself.

BILL (*Looking at watch*): Listen, it's getting late. Can we please go through the scene the way it is and talk about this later?

GLORIA (*Sweetly*): Of course, darling. You know I've always been easy to work with. But I *am* the star, right? (*To* SUE, *brusquely*) You missed your cue a minute ago.

SUE: I did not! I said my lines! (*In her part*) Maude, I'm worried. Suppose he finds out that you know? (*Behind them,* MIKE *enters right. He has dark hood over his head and wears gloves. He comes forward quietly, arms outstretched.*)

GLORIA (*In her part*): Nonsense! He couldn't possibly find out. (MIKE's *hands almost reach her neck when lamp goes out, and stage is in darkness.* SUE *and* GLORIA *gasp. Everyone starts to mill about, talking excitedly.*)

BILL: What happened to the light?

MIKE: Maybe the bulb burned out.

BILL (*Loudly*): Check the light, somebody!

PETE (*Entering*): I'm checking, I'm checking.

MIKE: Who bumped into me?

DENNIS: Hey, careful! (GLORIA *screams.*)

SUE: Gloria, what's wrong?

GLORIA: Oh, no! No, no, no! (*Lights come on.* SUE *is at far right.* MIKE *has moved back, the hood now in his hand.* ALICE, VAL, *and* DENNIS *are left.* BILL *is at center.* PETE *stands near lamp, a small timer in his hand.* GLORIA *has her hands on her neck.*) My ruby! My ruby is gone! (*Everyone gasps.*)

PETE: This timer on the wall outlet switched off the light.

BILL (*Realizing*): Then this was no accident!

GLORIA (*Hysterically*): Someone did it to steal my ruby. I felt hands around my neck and the pendant was pulled off! I felt the chain break!

VAL (*Pointing to* MIKE): Then he did it!

DENNIS: Why, you . . . (*Grabs* MIKE *by shoulders*)

MIKE: Believe me, I never touched her. Bill told me to fake the attack.

GLORIA: Dennis, stop! (*He and* MIKE *separate.*) I know who it was. I smelled her perfume when she reached for it. (*Points to* SUE) It was Sue Kelsey.

SUE: Don't be absurd. I did no such thing.

ALICE: Gloria, how can you be sure about the perfume?

GLORIA: Because I gave it to her—*Star Song.* I'm allergic to it, so I gave her what I had. She's wearing it now. (*Points at* SUE; *hysterically*) And there's the chain—in her pocket! (GLORIA *rushes at* SUE, *pulling end of chain that hangs out of* SUE's *side pocket.*)

SUE: But I didn't take it! I swear I didn't! (*Turns pockets inside out*)

ALICE (*To* VAL): Call the police. (VAL *exits right.*) Now, let's all stay exactly where we are. No one leaves until the police get here.

SUE (*Crying*): Oh, this is terrible!

ALICE: I've handled things like this in my books. Stay calm. I'm trying to think what Maude Fenwick would do. . . . (*Curtain*)

* * * * *

SCENE 2

TIME: *Several weeks later.*

SETTING: *Courtroom. Judge's bench is up center, with witness box to right of it. In front of bench is table for stenographer and clerk. Diagonally down left is table for defense, with chairs behind it for witnesses. Diagonally down right is prosecution table, with chairs for witnesses. Light timer is on table right.*

AT RISE: JUDGE FRASER *is on bench.* STENOGRAPHER *and* CLERK *are at their table.* SUE, JANE GREENWAY, *and* NANCY REDMOND *sit at table left, with* ALICE, MIKE, BILL, *and* MR. *and* MRS. KELSEY *in chairs behind them.* PETE, VAL, GLORIA, *and* DENNIS *sit in witness seats behind table right.* COURT OFFICERS *stand left.* HOWARD WRIGHT *is questioning* TOM ANDERSON, *who is in witness box. Throughout scene lawyers rise and come forward to question witnesses, then return to their seats.*

WRIGHT: Officer Anderson, do you identify the defendant, Susan Kelsey, as the young woman you arrested on Wednesday, February second?

ANDERSON: Yes, sir.

WRIGHT: Please tell the court the circumstances of the arrest.

ANDERSON: I received a call just before seven o'clock that evening and went to the TV studio. Miss Shepard was close to hysterics. She made the charge against Ms. Kelsey.

WRIGHT: Were there other people present?

ANDERSON: Yes, sir. Alice Martin, the script writer, seemed to have taken charge. She insisted that everyone be searched. We did that, but didn't find the ruby, although several witnesses saw the chain in Ms. Kelsey's pocket.

WRIGHT: Go on.

ANDERSON: Ms. Kelsey was booked at the station. Ms. Martin arranged for bail and called Ms. Kelsey's parents.

WRIGHT: No further questions. (*Turns to* JANE GREENWAY) Your witness. (*He sits at table right.* JANE GREENWAY *goes up to witness stand.*)

GREENWAY: Officer Anderson, have the police recovered the ruby?

ANDERSON: No. But we're still pursuing our investigation.

GREENWAY: No further questions.

JUDGE: The witness may step down. (ANDERSON *sits behind prosecution table.*)

WRIGHT: Miss Gloria Shepard. (GLORIA *comes forward.*)

CLERK: Do you swear to tell the truth, the whole truth, and nothing but the truth?

GLORIA: I do. (*Sits in witness chair*)

WRIGHT: Miss Shepard, tell the court your occupation, please.

GLORIA (*Loftily*): I'm a movie actress. I've always been in movies, but because so many of my fans kept urging me, I agreed to star in a TV series, *Maude Fenwick, Private Eye.* (*Laughs prettily*) So different from my movie roles, and it's a real challenge.

WRIGHT: On February second, you were in the TV studio rehearsing a scene, is that correct?

GLORIA: I was.

WRIGHT: Were you wearing the ruby pendant on a chain?

GLORIA: Of course. My fans expect it. They call it my trademark.

WRIGHT: Is it very valuable?

GLORIA: I love it. It was given to me by a dear friend years ago.

WRIGHT: I'm speaking of monetary value.

GLORIA: It's insured for half a million dollars.

WRIGHT: Tell us the circumstances under which it was stolen from you.

GLORIA: Our scene had barely started when all the lights went out. In the dark I felt hands around my neck and the ruby pendant was torn from my neck. Then I screamed. (*Shivers*) It was terrifying!

WRIGHT: When the lights came on again, did you accuse anybody?

GLORIA: Of course! Sue Kelsey!

WRIGHT: Why?

GLORIA: Because when the hands touched my neck, I smelled her perfume. (*Quickly*) It's an expensive and distinctive perfume called *Star Song*. A friend gave it to me as a gift, not knowing that I'm allergic to perfume. That's why I gave it to Sue. Then, when the ruby was stolen, I recognized the scent at once. I accused her of the theft, and then (*Sniffs dramatically into handkerchief*)—then when we saw the chain of my pendant hanging out of her pocket, I knew for certain she had done it.

WRIGHT: What did Ms. Kelsey say when you accused her?

GLORIA: She denied it. She said someone was trying to get her into trouble by planting the chain. But I am positive about the perfume, and the chain speaks for itself.

WRIGHT: Why, in your opinion, would Ms. Kelsey do such a thing?

GLORIA: For any number of reasons. She knew how much I treasured it. She wanted to hurt me—I think she hated me. I suppose she thought she could sell it—she probably dreamed of having the kind of luxurious life I have.

WRIGHT: Why do you think she hated you?

GREENWAY: Objection! Speculation!

JUDGE: Overruled.

GLORIA: I told Sue I wanted her out of my series. (*Earnestly*) I was sorry I had to do it. She seemed—at the time—such a sweet girl. But *so* inexperienced. Completely unsuitable for the part of my assistant.

WRIGHT: Did Ms. Kelsey object to losing the part?

GLORIA: She not only objected, she threatened me!

WRIGHT: Do you recall her exact words?

GLORIA: It wasn't so much her words as her tone of voice. She said (*Threateningly*) "I know what you're up to. Don't try it!"

WRIGHT: Did your director agree to drop Sue Kelsey from the show?

GLORIA: I really don't think he wanted to deal with it at all.

WRIGHT: And what about the writer, Alice Martin?

GLORIA: That woman had entirely too much to say. She acted as if she were the director.

WRIGHT: Now, about the series. Has it been canceled?

GLORIA: Certainly not. Merely postponed until this matter is settled.

WRIGHT: No further questions. (*To* GREENWAY) Your witness.

GREENWAY (*Coming forward*): Miss Shepard, you referred to yourself as a movie actress. Wouldn't it be more accurate to say *former* actress?

GLORIA (*Haughtily*): If you could see all the fan letters I get, and the way I'm pursued for autographs . . .

GREENWAY: How many years has it been since you made a picture?

GLORIA: Does it matter? Really, I don't remember.

GREENWAY: Then this series could be considered a comeback for you?

GLORIA: A comeback? Certainly not! I am an established star.

GREENWAY: You say you wanted Ms. Kelsey out of the part. Did you have anyone in mind to take her place?

GLORIA: I hadn't made any decision on that.

GREENWAY: One last question. You said the ruby is insured. Is it possible you'd prefer to have the insurance money instead of the ruby?

WRIGHT: Objection!

JUDGE: Sustained.

GREENWAY: I have no further questions, Your Honor.

JUDGE: The witness is excused. (GLORIA *returns to her seat.*)

WRIGHT: I call Peter Lansing to the stand. (PETE *comes forward, is sworn in by* CLERK, *and sits.*) Mr. Lansing, what is your occupation?

PETE: I'm a prop assistant at the TV studio.

WRIGHT: Were you present at the rehearsal the night of the theft?

PETE: Yes.

WRIGHT: At that time did you overhear a conversation between the defendant and someone else?

PETE: I heard Sue tell Alice Martin she was worried about her job.

WRIGHT: Were you on the set when the lights went out?

PETE: No, but I heard the director yelling, and I ran in.

WRIGHT: Were the lights supposed to go out as part of that scene?

PETE: They weren't supposed to go out at all. First thing I did was check the bulb in the lamp, then the wall outlet. That's where I found the light timer.

WRIGHT (*Picking up timer, showing it to* PETE): Is this the timer you're referring to?

PETE: That's the one. It's easy to set this to make a light go off or on at any time you want.

WRIGHT (*To* JUDGE): I ask that this be marked Exhibit A.

JUDGE: So ordered. (WRIGHT *puts timer on* JUDGE's *bench.*)

WRIGHT: Any idea who could have put it there?

PETE: Who knows? Any one of 'em, I suppose. Actors, they're kooky characters, y' know?

WRIGHT: Thank you, Mr. Lansing. (*To* GREENWAY) Your witness.

GREENWAY: Mr. Lansing, did you consider the ruby pendant one of the necessary props for the scene?

PETE: Are you kidding? That was no prop!

GREENWAY: You were aware how valuable it was?

PETE: Sure. I heard talk about it.

GREENWAY: Could you use that kind of money?

WRIGHT: Objection! Counsel is implying—

PETE (*Indignantly*): Hey, lady, what are you trying to do, blame *me?*

JUDGE (*Rapping gavel*): Order! Order in the court.

GREENWAY: No more questions. (*Glaring at* GREENWAY, PETE *returns to seat.*)

WRIGHT: I'd like to call Ms. Valerie Powers to the stand. (VAL *comes forward, is sworn in, sits.*) What work do you do, Ms. Powers?

VAL: I'm a reporter for *The Daily Bulletin*.

WRIGHT: You were at the TV studio before seven o'clock on the evening in question, weren't you?

VAL: Yes, sir.

WRIGHT: What was your purpose in going there?

VAL: I hoped to get an interview with Gloria Shepard.

WRIGHT: Did you get the interview?

VAL: No, but my story on what happened that night was sensational.

WRIGHT: Did you hear Ms. Kelsey threaten Gloria Shepard?

VAL: I heard what she said to Gloria, but I can't say whether or not it was a threat.

WRIGHT: Thank you, Ms. Powers. (*To* GREENWAY) Your witness.

GREENWAY: Were you on the rehearsal set at any time, Ms. Powers?

VAL: Why, yes. When the light went out, I went over in the dark to see what was going on.

GREENWAY: Did you see anything?

VAL: In the dark? (*Laughs*) Nobody could see anything.

GREENWAY: No more questions. (VAL *goes back to her seat.*)

WRIGHT: I now call Dennis Grant. (DENNIS *comes forward, is sworn in, takes witness chair.*) Mr. Grant, please tell us your occupation.

DENNIS: I'm an actor.

WRIGHT: Were you in the studio when the ruby was stolen?

DENNIS: Yes. I went there to pick up Miss Shepard for a dinner date, but the rehearsal was still going on.

WRIGHT: Would you say the rehearsal had been going smoothly?

DENNIS: Not very. Alice Martin was antagonistic to Miss Shepard, and the director was uncooperative. Ms. Kelsey was openly hostile.

GREENWAY: Objection! Interpretation by the witness.

JUDGE: Sustained. Mr. Wright, please confine your questions to what this witness saw and did.

DENNIS: I saw Mike Barstow enter in his role as a jewel thief. When the light came on again, I thought he had taken the ruby, but then Miss Shepard told us about Sue's perfume. Then, of course, we found the chain in Sue's pocket.

WRIGHT: Thank you, Mr. Grant. (*To* GREENWAY) Your witness.

GREENWAY: Mr. Grant, how much television experience have you had?

DENNIS: I've been in quite a few commercials.

GREENWAY: Ever do a TV series?

DENNIS: No.

GREENWAY: Would you like to?

DENNIS: Of course.

GREENWAY: How long have you known Miss Shepard?

DENNIS: Three months.

GREENWAY: Did she promise you the part of her assistant? Sue Kelsey's part?

DENNIS (*Vehemently*): Absolutely not!

GREENWAY: No more questions. (DENNIS *returns to his seat.*)

JUDGE: The defense may now call its first witness.

GREENWAY: Your Honor, I call Susan Kelsey. (SUE *comes forward, is sworn in, sits.*) Please tell us your occupation, Ms. Kelsey.

SUE: Television actress. Or I was, until Gloria Shepard accused me of something I didn't do!

GREENWAY: You deny taking the ruby?

SUE (*Spiritedly*): Yes, I deny it! Why would I do a thing like that?

GREENWAY: Did you feel resentment when Miss Shepard said she wanted you off the show?

SUE: Well, yes I did, because it just wasn't fair. But I never threatened her. When I said, "Don't try it!" I was, well, I guess I was really pleading with her.

GREENWAY: Is it true she gave you the perfume, *Star Song?*

SUE: Yes. She said she couldn't use it herself.

GREENWAY: Were you wearing it that night?

SUE: Yes, I was.

GREENWAY: Are you wearing it now?

SUE: No! I don't think I'll ever use it again!

GREENWAY: How do you think the chain from the pendant got into your pocket?

SUE: I don't know. I know I didn't put it there. The thief must have done it so I would be accused.

GREENWAY: Are you innocent of the charge against you, Ms. Kelsey?

SUE: I certainly am!

GREENWAY: Thank you. (*To* WRIGHT) Your witness.

WRIGHT: Ms. Kelsey, do you admit feeling resentment toward Gloria Shepard?

SUE: Mr. Wright, resentment is a whole lot different from stealing her ruby!

WRIGHT: Did you hope to sabotage the whole TV show if you couldn't be in it?

SUE: No! Of course not!

WRIGHT: Ms. Kelsey, would you know how to dispose of a valuable stolen jewel?

SUE: No. How would I know that?

WRIGHT: Would you please tell the court your father's occupation?

SUE (*Suddenly stunned*): Well . . . he's a jeweler.

WRIGHT (*Smugly*): I believe you have answered your own question.

MR. KELSEY (*Rising; angrily*): What are you trying to do to my daughter? And to me!

JUDGE (*Rapping gavel*): Order!

MR. KELSEY: This is an outrage!

JUDGE: I won't tolerate this disruption! (MR. KELSEY *sits.*)

WRIGHT: No more questions. (SUE *returns to seat.*)

GREENWAY: I ask the court's pardon for the interruption. (*Pause*) I now call Bill Taylor. (BILL *comes forward, is sworn in, sits.*) Mr. Taylor, what is your occupation?

BILL: I'm the director of *Maude Fenwick, Private Eye*. I was directing a rehearsal on the set the night of the theft.

GREENWAY: What is your opinion of Ms. Kelsey as an actress?

BILL: She's a fine actress. She was doing very well in her part and I saw no reason to replace her.

GREENWAY: Were you aware of friction between her and Miss Shepard?

BILL: Yes. Gloria Shepard was at odds with Alice Martin, too, but I felt confident I could handle things.

GREENWAY: Is it your opinion that the TV series will eventually be made?

BILL: Absolutely.

GREENWAY: Thank you. (*To* WRIGHT) Your witness.

WRIGHT: It's evident that Mr. Taylor is a loyal supporter of Ms. Kelsey's. No questions. (BILL *returns to his seat.*)

GREENWAY: I call Michael Barstow. (MIKE *comes forward, is sworn in, and sits.*) Mr. Barstow, what is your occupation?

MIKE: I'm an actor working on *Maude Fenwick, Private Eye*.

GREENWAY: And what is your role?

MIKE: I play the bad guy, a jewel thief. The night of the theft was just a rehearsal—the next day, at the taping, I was actually supposed to steal the ruby.

GREENWAY: You were standing very close to Ms. Shepard when the light went out. Did anyone else come closer?

MIKE: Obviously, someone did. I stepped back. The reporter seemed to think I really was the bad guy. She didn't know that Bill had told me to fake the attack at the rehearsal.

GREENWAY: Thanks, Mr. Barstow. (*To* WRIGHT) Your witness.

WRIGHT: Mr. Barstow, you and Ms. Kelsey are close friends, correct?

MIKE: Yes, that's right.

WRIGHT: Did you know that she was about to lose her part in the series?

MIKE: I knew she was afraid of losing it, but I hoped Alice Martin wouldn't let that happen.

WRIGHT: Why would Alice Martin care?

MIKE: Because she likes Sue and respects her work.

WRIGHT: Would you personally go to any length to keep Ms. Kelsey from losing her part?

MIKE: I can't reply to a hypothetical question like that.

WRIGHT: In rehearsal, when you played the bad guy, as you put it, and reached out your hands toward Miss Shepard, did it ever cross your mind to actually steal the pendant?

MIKE: You mean, for real? (*Laughs*) Well, I thought of how close I was to half a million dollars, sure. But grab it for myself? You've got the wrong guy, Mr. Wright.

WRIGHT: No further questions. (MIKE *returns to seat.*)

GREENWAY: I call my final witness, Alice Martin. (ALICE *comes forward, is sworn in, sits.*) Ms. Martin, what is your occupation?

ALICE: I'm the author of the Maude Fenwick books on which the series is based, and I've also written the TV script.

GREENWAY: Now, you and I have discussed this case at length, and I wonder if you would share your views with the court.

ALICE: Well, I've tried to concentrate on how Maude Fenwick, my detective character, would find out what really happened the night of the theft. As I have suggested to you, I think that if we recreate the rehearsal scene, it may help the judge to get a better understanding of the situation.

GREENWAY (*To* JUDGE): I want to thank Your Honor and the prosecutor for giving us permission to try what Ms. Martin has suggested.

WRIGHT (*Annoyed*): Courtroom trickery, in my opinion. But go ahead.

GREENWAY: Call it a demonstration, an instant replay. I have the necessary furnishings out in the hall. Will the court officers please help me set the scene?

JUDGE: They have been so instructed. (COURT OFFICERS, GREENWAY, *and* NANCY *exit right. Low murmurs start at each table.* COURT OFFICERS *carry in desk, place it up right.* GREENWAY *enters with desk chair, puts it in place.* NANCY *carries in telephone and plant, sets them on desk, exits. One* OFFICER *pushes in easy chair and the other puts floor lamp beside it.* NANCY *reenters with folding chair, which she places left.)*

GREENWAY: There. Now, I have the court's permission to allow Alice Martin to direct this operation. Will all who were present at the rehearsal, remembering that you are still under oath, please take your places as you were that night? (ALICE *sits in folding chair. Other witnesses rise, move up center.* NANCY *returns to table;* COURT OFFICERS *go to one side.)*

GLORIA (*Complaining*): I don't see what good this is going to do.

GREENWAY: It may clear up some misunderstanding. Now, where were you, Miss Shepard?

GLORIA: I was sitting behind the desk. (*Sits behind desk*) Sue was standing near me. (SUE *stands near.*)

DENNIS: I was standing beside Ms. Martin. (*He does so.* MIKE *crosses "set" and then goes off it, right. Meanwhile,* PETE *takes timer, plugs it in behind chair, then plugs lamp into it and lamp goes on.* BILL *stands left of center.* VAL *waits at side, ready to go on set.)*

GREENWAY: O.K. Now, is everything just as it was on the set? Is this the same furniture?

BILL: Yes, this is exactly the way it was.

PETE: And all the props were taken out of the storeroom at the studio.

ALICE: What about the pendant?

GREENWAY: We'll use a piece of costume jewelry as a substitute. (*Takes pendant from pocket, holds it up, then hands it to* GLORIA)

GLORIA (*Slipping pendant over her head; petulantly*): I don't like any of this one bit.

GREENWAY: May we have all the courtroom lights turned off, please? (1ST OFFICER *turns out courtroom lights, leaving set lighted only by lamp.)*

ALICE: Now, Sue, let's take it from your line about feeling worried.

SUE: O.K. (*In her part; to* GLORIA) Maude, I'm worried. Suppose he finds out that you know? (*Behind them* MIKE *approaches without gloves and hood, but with arms outstretched*)

GLORIA (*In her part*): Nonsense! He couldn't possibly find out. (MIKE's *hands almost reach her neck. Lamp goes out and stage is dark. There are gasps, cries, movements.*)

BILL: What happened to the light?

MIKE: Maybe the bulb burned out.

BILL: Check the light, somebody!

PETE: I'm checking, I'm checking. (VAL *joins group.*)

MIKE: Who bumped into me?

DENNIS: Hey, careful! (GLORIA *screams.*)

SUE: Gloria, what's wrong?

GLORIA: It happened again! The pendant is gone! And I smelled her perfume! (*Lights go on again and all are in same positions as in Scene 1.* PETE *holds timer.*)

ALICE: Well, Gloria, what happened?

GLORIA (*Upset*): Hands came around my neck. The new pendant is gone!

GREENWAY: *I* removed the pendant (*Pulling pendant from her pocket, holding it up*), although I didn't slip the chain into Sue's pocket as the thief did.

GLORIA: But the perfume! I smelled it again! I'm sure I did.

GREENWAY: Because I sprayed it near you. (*Takes spray bottle from pocket*) Same brand. *Star Song.*

GLORIA (*Confused*): *You* did it? But you weren't even there when—

DENNIS (*To* GREENWAY): You put those things in your pocket. Did you forget that we were searched the night of the theft? If someone had sprayed perfume, don't you think it would have been found when the police searched us?

GREENWAY (*Turning to* ALICE): Ms. Martin, would you please take over?

ALICE (*To* PETE): Pete, you're sure this is *exactly* the same set?

PETE: Exactly.

ALICE: Even the props? (PETE *nods.*) How about the plant?

PETE (*A bit sheepishly*): That's the same plant we used before. I'm sort of a plant freak, so I took it home with me and kept it watered.

ALICE: Then it's been in your apartment since the theft?

PETE: Right. I brought it here today. Anything wrong with that?

ALICE: No. (*Goes to plant*) Except that the thief must have felt very frustrated by what you did. (*Digs her fingers into dirt and takes out small bottle of spray perfume, holding it up.*) You see, the thief came prepared with the perfume. (*Reaches in again, taking out ruby*) And here's the ruby! (*Holds it up. All gasp in surprise, ad lib excited conversation.*)

GLORIA (*Stunned*): My ruby!

MIKE: It was in the plant all this time! (ALICE *gives perfume and pendant to* 2ND OFFICER, *who gives them to* JUDGE.)

ALICE: Gloria, you're positive you smelled the same perfume just now?

GLORIA: Of course I'm positive.

ALICE: Who knew the name of the perfume, besides you?

GLORIA: Sue did, because I gave it to her.

ALICE: Who gave the perfume to *you*?

GLORIA: Dennis gave it to me. (*Suddenly*) Dennis, you knew I gave it to Sue.

DENNIS (*Hotly*): I did not!

GLORIA: But I told you—I remember distinctly. (*Angrily*) You didn't do this to me, did you? (*Pauses; shocked*) You *did!*

DENNIS: That's a lie!

GLORIA (*Dramatically, her voice rising*): I was so good to you! Paid all your bills, promised to get you a part in the series, but that wasn't enough. You wanted more! You sprayed the perfume near me so I'd blame Sue and you'd get her part. And you stole the ruby to sell it!

ALICE (*To* DENNIS): You thought it would be easy to retrieve the ruby later, didn't you? You couldn't know that Pete would take the plant home.

GLORIA (*In broken voice*): Dennis, you didn't care anything about me at all! I tried to do so much for you!

DENNIS (*Scornfully*): Do you think I liked being treated like a pet dog on a leash? You acted as if you owned me, Gloria. That ruby was only an ornament to you, but to me, it would mean security. Yes, I took it! I took it!

JUDGE (*To* OFFICERS): Take Mr. Grant into custody and advise him of his rights. (OFFICERS *take* DENNIS *by the arm. He glares at* ALICE.)

DENNIS: You! Why didn't you stick to writing TV scripts? (OFFICERS *take him out left.*)

MIKE (*Putting arm around* SUE): Are you O.K.?

SUE (*Starting to cry*): Oh, Mike! (MR. *and* MRS. KELSEY *rush over to her, embrace her.*)

MR. *and* MRS. KELSEY (*Ad lib*): It's O.K., honey. It's all over now. (*Etc.* GREENWAY *and* WRIGHT *shake hands, ad lib quiet conversation.*)

ALICE (*Putting arm around* GLORIA): You'll be all right, too, Gloria. And so will the series. With Sue back in her old part. (*Smiles at* SUE) Well, Maude Fenwick just solved another case!

JUDGE: The case against Susan Kelsey is dismissed. (*Raps gavel as curtain closes.*)

THE END

Production Notes

THE COMEBACK CAPER

Characters: 8 male; 7 female; 4 male or female for Clerk, Stenographer, Officers.

Playing Time: 35 minutes.

Costumes: Modern everyday dress. In Scene 1, Sue wears jacket with chain in pocket. Gloria wears ruby pendant on chain. Anderson and Court Officers are in uniform. Judge wears black robe. Dennis has handkerchief in pocket.

Properties: Script, mug, two ruby pendants, timer, two small spray perfume bottles, plant in ornamental pot (small spray bottle and ruby are buried in dirt), handkerchief for Gloria in Scene 2, gavel.

Setting: Scene 1, TV studio. A few folding chairs are left, and rehearsal area, with floor lamp, easy chair, desk, chair, and telephone, is right. Exits are right and left. Scene 2, courtroom. Judge's bench with witness box to right is up center. Stenographer's table is in front of bench. Diagonally down right, defense table with chairs; down right, prosecution table with chairs. Later in scene, furniture from rehearsal scene is brought in.

Lighting: Lights go out in both scenes, as indicated.

❧The Secret Gifts

by Mary Satchell

African-Americans from the past inspire today's young people . . . .

Characters

TED
ESSIE
BILL } *Jefferson High students*
JERRY
ALICE
MS. REED, *teacher*
FREDERICK DOUGLASS
MARY MCLEOD BETHUNE
PHILLIS WHEATLEY
BOOKER T. WASHINGTON
TEACHER, *head of Hampton Institute*
MARTIN LUTHER KING, JR.

TIME: *Early afternoon; the present.*
SETTING: *High school newspaper workroom. Table and four chairs are center. Small bookcase with disorderly stacks of books, old newspapers, and yearbooks is up right; also chair and small, untidy desk with typewriter, phone, papers, etc. File cabinet and mail baskets are up left. Clock and bulletin board with notes pinned on it are on rear wall. Wooden bench is down left; old-fashioned desk with pen, and straight-back chair are down right. Broom is propped against wall near desk. Exit is left.*
AT RISE: TED *enters. He is neatly dressed, and wears campaign button reading* TED DAVIS FOR PRESIDENT. *He carries briefcase and several large printed posters, which he places on table.*

136

As he riffles through papers in briefcase, MS. REED *enters, carrying sheet of paper.*

MS. REED (*Cheerfully*): Hello, Ted. I made a list of suggestions for today's Black History Week committee meeting. (*Hands paper to* TED)

TED: Thanks, Ms. Reed. I didn't have time to put an agenda together. The campaign's been taking all my time.

MS. REED: How's it going?

TED: Right on target. I put all my posters up, and I'll finish writing my speech tonight.

MS. REED: Sounds as if you have everything under control.

TED: I've got to keep at it if I want to win. (*In determined tone*) And I mean to win.

MS. REED (*Seriously*): Being president of the student body isn't the most important thing in life, Ted. (*Glances at clock, and assumes lighter tone*) Well, I'm off to a faculty meeting. See you later. (*Exits*)

TED (*Tossing* MS. REED'*s paper onto table*): I don't understand why there's so much fuss over black history, anyway. All that's in the past. (*Ruefully*) It's today I'm worried about. (*Pacing*) I've just *got* to win! (*There is a noise offstage.* TED *stops pacing as* ESSIE, *weary and dejected, enters, carrying a pile of books.*)

ESSIE: Hi, Ted.

TED: You look really down, Essie. What's wrong? Was the physics test that bad?

ESSIE (*Dropping books heavily onto table*): That physics test is the least of my worries. (*Sinks wearily into chair at table*) The biggest problems in my life are at home.

TED (*Sitting and relaxing*): I know exactly how you feel. My parents are always on my case, too.

ESSIE (*Surprised*): *You* have problems with your folks? I can't believe that. What could they possibly find wrong about you?

TED: My dad gives me the same lecture over and over. (*Imitating*) Keep up the good work, son. I expect you to make top grades so you can get into a good college.

ESSIE (*Impatiently*): At least you'll be able to escape by going to college. I'd love to go to college—especially if it's far away from here. (BILL *and* JERRY *enter.* BILL *is outgoing, happy-go-lucky;* JERRY, *quiet, wears radio headphones.*)

BILL (*Pretending shock*): What's this, Essie? Did I hear you say you want to go to college? Now, you've got too much sense to do something like that. (*Turns chair around and sits in it backward, facing audience.* JERRY *sits at table, adjusts headset, still absorbed in music.*)

ESSIE (*Defiantly*): Not everybody is like you and hates school, Bill.

BILL (*Disregarding last remark*): How about getting this show on the road?

ESSIE: Fine with me. Everybody's here except Alice.

TED: She should be here soon. We might as well start. . . . O.K. We're here to come up with some special events for Black History Week. (*Pauses, then glances around table*) Any suggestions? (*No one answers. Suddenly* ALICE, *fashionably dressed, breezes in, carrying purse and portfolio.*)

ALICE (*Breathlessly*): Sorry I'm late. Mr. Collins asked me to hang some new pictures in the art lab. (*Pushes chair up to table and sits down*) I'll take notes. (*Takes pad and pen from purse*)

ESSIE (*Tugging at* JERRY's *headphones*): O.K., Jerry, let's get started. (JERRY *continues to look blank.*)

BILL: Leave Jerry to his music, Essie. (ESSIE *persists, pulls headphones off* JERRY's *head and holds one side up to her ear.*)

JERRY: Hey, Es, why don't you pick on somebody your own size? (ESSIE *listens a moment to headphones while looking at* JERRY, *puzzled.*)

ALICE: What's the matter?

ESSIE (*Hesitating*): Uh . . . nothing. (*Hands headphones back to* JERRY, *who quickly puts them back on.* ESSIE *continues to stare at* JERRY *as he settles back in his chair.*)

TED: All right, who's got some ideas? (*All look bored.*) Well, to tell the truth, I don't have any, either. (*Picks up paper*) Ms. Reed brought in this list of ideas to get us started.

BILL (*Impatiently*): What's the use in planning a lot of things that nobody's going to do anyway?

ESSIE: I say we just admit that we can't come up with any ideas and go home. Ms. Reed will just have to understand. (MS. REED *enters. Students turn sheepishly toward her.*)

MS. REED (*Pleasantly*): What will I have to understand?

TED (*Embarrassed*): Oh, nothing, really.

MS. REED (*Moving toward table*): Well, tell me what exciting ideas you've come up with for Black History Week.

ALICE (*Lamely*): We don't have any ideas, yet.

MS. REED (*Nodding*): Well, keep working at it. (*Looking at students*) I know you're busy, but I need someone to help me carry a few paintings to my car. Mr. Collins is donating some of his works to the school bazaar.

ALICE (*Dropping her pen and rising at once*): I'll help.

MS. REED: Thanks, Alice. (*She exits with* ALICE.)

ESSIE (*Eyeing* ALICE'*s portfolio*): I'm surprised Alice left that portfolio behind, even for a few minutes. She carries it with her everywhere. (*Rises, picks up portfolio*) I wonder what's in it? One little peek can't hurt. (*Tries to open portfolio and frowns*) It's locked!

TED: She probably has her artwork in it. (*Pauses*) Funny, though. I've never seen anything she painted. (*Students watch as* ESSIE *examines locks on portfolio.* ALICE *enters and sees* ESSIE *touching portfolio.*)

ALICE (*Moving quickly to table; angrily*): What are you doing, Essie?

ESSIE (*Guiltily*): I didn't open it, Alice. I only touched it.

ALICE (*Shouting, very upset*): You had no right! You're always meddling, Essie. Someday you'll go too far! (MS. REED *enters quickly.*)

MS. REED: Is everything O.K. in here?

BILL (*Covering, while* ALICE *glares at* ESSIE): We just got carried away with our enthusiasm for Black History Week.

ESSIE (*Glumly*): Actually, Ms. Reed, we haven't come up with anything yet. I guess we're just not interested.

MS. REED (*Disappointed; pausing before speaking seriously*): I chose each of you for this project because I thought you could do a good job. You'll just have to work on it until you've come up with some creative ideas. I'm counting on you. (*She exits.*)

ALICE (*Sighing*): This project is one big headache. (*Sits at table*)

TED (*With irritation*): My campaign plans for today are shot.

ESSIE (*Impatiently*): Ted, I'm tired of hearing about your campaign.

BILL: Yeah, me too. You act as if your whole life depends on that election. (*Others move closer together at table and talk softly.* TED *rises, moves down center, looking defeated. Lights fade upstage; spotlight shines on* TED.)

TED (*Defiantly*): My life *does* depend on this campaign. I've *got* to be somebody—and that's all I care about! (FREDERICK DOUGLASS, *carrying book, moves into spotlight.*)

FREDERICK DOUGLASS: Is that really all you care about, Ted? (TED *turns quickly, peers at* DOUGLASS.)

TED: Who are you?

DOUGLASS: I'm Frederick Douglass.

TED (*Stunned*): Frederick Douglass! (*Pauses, then laughs*) Aw, come off it! This is some kind of trick. . . . Hey, you must be in the drama club, right?

DOUGLASS (*Smiling*): I was just like you when I was young, Ted. I felt a great desire to succeed. I ran away from my slave master in Maryland and crossed the freedom line, where I knew I could accomplish anything I had the courage to do. My ambition brought me fame and success.

TED (*Smugly*): That's what I want, Mr. Douglass . . . or whoever you are.

DOUGLASS (*Thoughtfully*): But it didn't just happen, Ted. I realized early in my life as a free man that if I was going to succeed, I would have to care about other people.

TED (*Shrugging*): That *sounds* nice, but really, how can you take the time to help others when you're trying to make it to the top?

DOUGLASS (*Intensely*): You must make the time, Ted. My life would have been empty if I had lived only for myself.

TED (*Embarrassed*): Well, if you *are* Frederick Douglass, I have to admit that I don't know very much about your life.

DOUGLASS (*Offering book to* TED): This is my autobiography. Read it, and then perhaps you will understand what I've been trying to tell you.

TED (*Taking book; sincerely*): Thanks, Mr. Douglass.

DOUGLASS: Tell my story to your friends. (*He moves outside spotlight and exits, as* TED *opens book.*)

TED (*Nervously*): If I told anybody about meeting Frederick Douglass, I'd be laughed right out of school. (*Lights come up. Others are still sitting at table, talking quietly.* TED *turns and moves upstage.*)

BILL (*Pointing to book*): What's that?

TED: Oh, it's nothing you'd be interested in, Bill. (*Puts book inside briefcase, sits, and stares thoughtfully into space*)

ESSIE (*Rising*): You're acting weird all of a sudden, Ted.

ALICE: He's probably thinking about his campaign speech for tomorrow. (ESSIE *moves to exit.*)

JERRY (*Raising headphones*): Essie, if you're leaving now, I'm going with you. (*Starts to rise*) I'm tired of sitting here wasting time.

ESSIE (*Lowering voice*): I'm only going to peek into the hall to see if Ms. Reed's out there. (*Cautiously pokes her head outside door, then comes to stand beside* JERRY) And talk about wasting time! Jerry, you've spent your whole life daydreaming. (*To others*) Do you know that he's only pretending to listen to that music? When I listened through those headphones, there wasn't a sound. (JERRY, *embarrassed, takes off headphones.*)

BILL (*Defending* JERRY): What's wrong with dreaming?

ALICE: I guess you never have time for things like dreaming, Essie. (ESSIE *starts to retort, but pauses and moves left. Lights fade to soft spotlight on* ESSIE.)

ESSIE (*Wistfully*): I used to dream, but I stopped all that when I learned that dreams are useless. (*Moves slowly down center; pausing and assuming happy look, and calling into darkness outside spotlight*) Mama, I'm home! (*Takes a few steps to her right; spotlight follows her*) Where are you? (*Hesitates*) She must be in the kitchen. (*Walks farther right*) Oh, here you are. (*Eagerly*) Mama, guess what happened at school today? I joined the Journalism Club. Ms. Reed says I'll make a good reporter for the school newspaper. I think that's what I'd like to be, Mama, a journalist. Maybe I'll work for a TV station. (*Pause*) What? (*Pauses; crestfallen*) No, Mama. (*Sighs*) I forgot to take the rent money over to the landlord's office. . . . I'm sorry, Mama. It's just that—I was so excited to be on the newspaper, and we had a meeting after school today. . . . (*After a long pause, as if listening*) I know you can't do everything, and you're counting on me to help. (*Urgently*) Yes, I know you'll have to pay a ten-dollar late fee because I forgot. (*Hopelessly*) I know how tired you are from working so hard for me. (*Wrings her hands and moves left again*) I'm sorry, Mama. (ESSIE *covers her face with her hands.* MARY MCLEOD BETHUNE, *carrying scroll, enters spotlight.*)

MARY MCLEOD BETHUNE: Sometimes it's very difficult to be young, isn't it, Essie?

ESSIE (*Startled*): What's going on? Who are you? . . . (*Frowning*) How do you know my name?

BETHUNE (*Smiling*): I'm Mary McLeod Bethune.

ESSIE (*Dazed*): I don't believe this is happening.

BETHUNE: Believe? Essie, have you forgotten how to believe in anything?

ESSIE (*Morosely; folding her arms*): No one cares what I believe.

BETHUNE (*Earnestly*): I care. I spent my life helping young people like you to have faith in themselves, and in others. I established a school as a testimony of that faith. (*Holds out scroll*) This is my will, which shows how much I care about young people. (ESSIE *sits on bench;* BETHUNE *opens scroll, faces audience, and reads.*) Here is my legacy:

I leave you love.
I leave you hope.
I leave you a thirst for education.
I leave you faith.
I leave you racial dignity.
I leave you a desire to live harmoniously with your fellow human beings.
I leave you, finally, a responsibility to our young people.

(*Stops and turns to audience; earnestly*) Our children must never lose their zeal for building a better world. They must not be discouraged from aspiring toward greatness, for they are the leaders of tomorrow. Faith, courage, dignity, ambition, responsibility—these are needed today as never before. We must cultivate them and use them as tools for our task of completing the establishment of equality. (BETHUNE *rolls up scroll and gives it to* ESSIE.) I want you to have this, Essie. Keep it with you always as a reminder that someone cares about you very much. (BETHUNE *leaves spotlight, exits, and lights come up again.* ESSIE *returns to table and stands beside* ALICE.)

ESSIE: I'm sorry, Alice.

ALICE (*Puzzled*): What for?

ESSIE (*Pointing to portfolio*): I made fun of you for wanting to be an artist. You were right. I didn't believe in anything before, but that's not true now. (*Others look in bewilderment at* ESSIE.)

BILL (*Impatiently*): Es, you're not making any sense. Sit down and help us come up with some ideas. (ESSIE *sits, lights fade, and* ALICE *rises, turns to audience.*)

ALICE: It hurts so much when people laugh at you. (*Picks up portfolio, moves down right and sets portfolio on desk*) That's why I've never let anyone see my paintings—except Mr. Collins. (*Smiles*) He said my paintings are very good. (*Sobers*) But I don't know. My Aunt Mabel says I could never make a living just painting pictures to hang on somebody's wall. (*Pauses*) Sometimes I think she's right. Maybe I don't have enough talent. (*Opens portfolio and looks critically at a couple of her paintings;* PHILLIS WHEATLEY *enters and stands near desk, but* ALICE *does not see her.*) How do I know if I have what it takes to be a successful artist?

PHILLIS WHEATLEY: I asked myself that same question many times before I got the courage to write my first poem. (ALICE *is astonished, as* WHEATLEY *picks up a painting and studies it.*) This portrait of your father is very good, Alice.

ALICE (*In awe*): Why—I know who you are. You're Phillis Wheatley! Your picture's in my history book.

WHEATLEY (*Placing portrait on desk*): I hope you'll paint my portrait someday, Alice.

ALICE (*Shyly*): I don't know if I could do that.

WHEATLEY: You'll never know until you try. I was a young slave girl when I wrote my first poem. Many people believed

that slaves couldn't possibly have any creative talent. Suppose
I had listened to all the people who said a slave could never
become a poet?

ALICE (*Thoughtfully*): You'd never have written any poetry.

WHEATLEY (*Nodding*): That's right. And if *you* don't believe
in yourself, no one else will.

ALICE (*Slowly*): I see what you mean.

WHEATLEY (*Taking small scroll from apron pocket*): I wrote
this poem, "To the University of Cambridge in New England,"
when I was about your age, Alice. (*She hands scroll to
ALICE.*) I'd like you to have it—a gift from one artist to another.

ALICE: Thank you! . . . Miss Wheatley, do you really think I
could be a successful artist?

WHEATLEY: There are no guarantees in life, Alice, but you
must have confidence in yourself. In the future, if ever you
begin to feel that you cannot reach your goal, remember me,
Phillis Wheatley, a little slave girl who reached for the stars
and managed to gather a few of them in her hands. (*Exits*)

ALICE: So what if people laugh at my dreams? Phillis Wheatley
became a poet—so why can't I become a painter? (*Lights come
up.* BILL *turns to* ALICE.)

BILL (*To Alice*): Come on, Alice! You're supposed to be taking
notes of our meeting.

ALICE: I'm coming. (*Quickly puts scroll in portfolio and returns
to table*) Would you like to see my paintings? (*Others are
stunned.*)

ESSIE: We'd love to, Alice. (ALICE *takes out her paintings and
arranges them on table.*)

TED (*Looking at pictures appreciatively*): Hey, these are good!

BILL: You used to make such a big secret of your pictures, Alice.
What made you change your mind?

ALICE (*Smiling*): You wouldn't believe me if I told you, Bill.
(*Others admire paintings, as* BILL *moves away. Lights fade
on group;* BILL *walks down left.*)

BILL (*Rubbing his chin thoughtfully*): Alice used to be too scared
to let anybody know who she really is. I wish I could tell
somebody what I really want to do with my life, but I just

can't. (*Only downstage area is lighted.* TEACHER *enters and sits at desk. She writes for a few moments, then* BOOKER T. WASHINGTON, *rather shabbily dressed, enters and stands in front of desk.* BILL, *surprised and curious, steps forward and intently watches.*)

TEACHER (*Crisply, to* WASHINGTON): Well, young man, what can I do for you?

WASHINGTON (*Quietly*): I want to enroll in your school, ma'am.

TEACHER (*Studying* WASHINGTON *dubiously*): We're very particular about the students we enroll here at Hampton Institute. Tell me about yourself. What's your name?

WASHINGTON: My name is Booker T. Washington, and I'm from Malden, West Virginia.

TEACHER (*Surprised*): You came five hundred miles to Hampton, Virginia—a young boy like you?

WASHINGTON: I saved enough money to pay for part of my trip. When my money ran out in Richmond, I worked on the docks to earn my fare here.

TEACHER (*Sighing*): I suppose that explains your appearance.

WASHINGTON (*Pulling a coin from his pocket*): This fifty-cent piece is all the money I have, ma'am. (*Offers coin to* TEACHER, *who shakes her head and does not take it*)

TEACHER (*Rising*): Booker, I'm very sorry, but I don't think we have a place for you here. Hampton Institute is a teacher-training school . . . and you're so young. We're looking for older students who will make fine teachers someday. (*Moves from desk*) Excuse me, Booker. I have an important meeting with General Armstrong, our principal.

WASHINGTON (*Going quickly toward broom in corner*): Ma'am, please, I'll do any kind of work to pay for my schooling. (*Begins to sweep*)

TEACHER (*Turning back*): You really want an education badly, don't you? (WASHINGTON *stops sweeping.*)

WASHINGTON: I *will* get an education, ma'am.

TEACHER (*Relenting; with a smile*): How can I turn away someone as determined as you are? (*Decisively*) Very well. I believe we can make a place for you at Hampton. Something tells me to take a chance. (*Seriously*) Mind you now, you will have to prove yourself to be a good worker and student.

WASHINGTON (*Nodding eagerly*): Yes, ma'am. I won't let you down.

TEACHER: Please wait here, Booker. I must try to find a job for you. (*Exits*)

BILL (*Moving to* WASHINGTON): That teacher really gave you a hard time.

WASHINGTON: We can't give up just because things get hard, Bill.

BILL (*Surprised*): You know my name?

WASHINGTON: I know a lot more than that about you. (*Puts broom back against wall*) You want to go to college, but you're afraid to try.

BILL (*Uneasily*): I never told anybody that. People don't take me seriously, so I pretend I don't care.

WASHINGTON: It's what *you* think that's important, Bill.

BILL (*Sighing*): I guess you're right, but college seems like another world. It's a long way from home.

WASHINGTON: You didn't start life as a slave in a log cabin the way I did.

BILL (*Musing*): We read your autobiography *Up From Slavery* in class. I know you took many hard knocks in life, but you made it.

WASHINGTON: You can make it, too, Bill. (*Gives coin to* BILL) I began my education with this fifty-cent piece. Let's see what you can do with it.

BILL (*Peering closely at coin as* WASHINGTON *exits*): Booker T. Washington's fifty-cent piece! (*Glances up after* WASHINGTON *has gone*) Thanks a million—what? (*Stops in confusion; takes a few steps right and looks around*) Where'd he go? (*Lights come up; students sit in quiet discussion.* BILL *moves upstage as he tosses coin in air.*)

JERRY: Hey, Bill, I thought you didn't have any money. (*Puts out hand*) You owe me a dollar. Pay up.

BILL (*Pocketing coin*): Later, Jerry. This coin's going to help me get a college education.

JERRY (*Surprised*): I thought you always said college was a waste of time.

BILL (*Defensively*): A guy can change his mind, can't he? (*Sits at table*) Look, I've got some new ideas about a lot of things, including Black History Week. (*Students talk together quietly; lights fade upstage, leaving only* JERRY *in view.* JERRY *pulls on headphones; music to a popular song is suddenly heard;* JERRY *shakes his head, rises, and stumbles around stage, as if trying to escape loud music. Music stops abruptly.* JERRY *stands still, removes headphones.*)

JERRY (*Looking puzzled*): Where's the music coming from? These things aren't even turned on. (*Moving dejectedly to bench*) Essie's right. I hide behind my headphones while I daydream. If people think I'm listening to my radio, they leave me alone. (*Glancing furtively upstage*) They'd really get a laugh if they knew I dreamed of being an astronaut. (*Sits on bench, puts headphones on again, assumes rigid position*) O.K., Mission Control. (*Leans back*) Five, four, three, two, one—(*Raucous laughter is heard from group upstage.* JERRY *rises quickly. He shrugs.*) I must be crazy to dream of becoming an astronaut. (*Roughly pulls off headphones, tosses them on bench*) I'm through dreaming! Where did dreams ever get anyone? (JERRY *sits, shoulders drooping.* MARTIN LUTHER KING, *carrying scroll, enters, puts hand on* JERRY's *shoulder.*)

KING: A dream can be the first step toward changing an entire nation.

JERRY (*Rising; stammering*): You—you're Martin Luther King, Jr.!

KING (*Nodding and chuckling*): And you're Captain Jerry Baker. (*Shakes* JERRY's *hand*)

JERRY (*Embarrassed*): Aw, that's just a silly dream I used to have.

KING: Used to have? Having a dream and holding onto it—why, that's the first step to doing the impossible. A man can't live without a dream.

JERRY: Nobody would ever say you were just a dreamer, Dr. King.

KING: Jerry, I started out as a young man just like you.

JERRY (*Sincerely*): How did you make your dreams come true?

KING: I believed they were worth the hard work I knew it would take to make them come true.

JERRY: And you succeeded.

KING: Don't be ashamed of your dreams, Jerry. I told the whole world about mine, and many people found hope because I dared to dream. (*Stage darkens; spotlight on* KING, *leaving him alone as he faces audience.* KING *reads from scroll the following excerpt from "I Have a Dream" speech.*)

"I say to you today, my friends, that in spite of the difficulties and frustrations of the moment I still have a dream. It is a dream deeply rooted in the American dream.

"I have a dream that one day this nation will rise up and live out the true meaning of its creed: 'We hold these truths to be self-evident; that all men are created equal.'

"I have a dream today.

"I have a dream that one day every valley shall be exalted, every hill and mountain shall be made low, the rough places will be made plain, and the crooked places will be made straight. . . .

"This will be the day when all of God's children will be able to sing with new meaning 'My country 'tis of thee, sweet land of liberty, of thee I sing. Land where my fathers died, land of the pilgrims' pride, from every mountainside, let freedom ring.' . . .

"When we let freedom ring, when we let it ring from every village and every hamlet, from every state and every city, we will be able to speed up that day when . . . black men and white men, Jews and Gentiles, Protestants and Catholics, will be able to join hands and sing the words of the old Negro spiritual, 'Free at last! Free at last! Thank God Almighty, we are free at last!'" (JERRY *enters spotlight.*)

JERRY: Thanks, Dr. King. I needed to hear that. (KING *takes pen from pocket, signs scroll, then hands it to* JERRY.)

KING: Take this with you on your first rocket trip into space, Captain Baker.

JERRY (*Confidently*): I'll do just that, Dr. King. (KING *exits.*
JERRY *moves upstage, as lights come up.*)

ALICE (*Turning to* JERRY): Where are your headphones?

JERRY (*Laughing*): Oh, I don't need those anymore.

ESSIE: What have you got there? (*Grabs scroll from* JERRY)

JERRY: Come on, Es, give it back. (ESSIE *unrolls scroll.*)

ESSIE: It's a copy of Martin Luther King's "I Have a Dream"
speech. (*Looks up*) Where did you get this?

JERRY: Never mind.

ESSIE (*In awe*): It's signed by Martin Luther King. (*Touches
page; stunned*) The ink's wet! (*All stare at* JERRY.)

JERRY: O.K. Let me tell you where I got that speech, even
though you'll say I'm crazy, for sure.

ALICE: I think I know already, Jerry. (*Others watch as* ALICE
opens portfolio, takes out scroll, and unrolls it.) Phillis
Wheatley wrote this poem. She gave it to me as a gift.

BILL (*Putting his hand in his pocket*): Guess I might as well
show you my secret, too. (*Holds out coin*) When Booker T.
Washington first went to Hampton Institute, this coin is all
the money he had. He gave it to me.

JERRY (*Moving closer*): Wow! That old coin must be worth a
fortune now.

BILL (*Pocketing coin again*): I wouldn't give it up for anything.

ESSIE: Your coin's priceless, Bill, (*Takes out scroll, opens it*) and
so is *this*. Mary McLeod Bethune left me her will—a legacy
to encourage us to do our best with our lives.

JERRY: What about that book in your briefcase, Ted?

TED (*Nervously*): Look, if any of this gets out . . . well, that
would be the end of my campaign.

ESSIE: We won't tell your secret, Ted, if you don't tell ours.

BILL (*Shrugging*): Who'd believe us, anyway?

ALICE: I really don't care if people laugh.

TED: If you agree to keep it a secret, I'll let you see the book
Frederick Douglass gave me.

OTHERS (*Ad lib*): Frederick Douglass! Wow! Let's see. (*Etc.
They gather around to admire book.*)

BILL: What did he say to you, Ted?

TED: He wants me to tell his story to others. Frederick Douglass's goal in life was to help black people.

ALICE (*Taking book*): We can't keep any of this a secret, then.

JERRY: But how can we let people know what we've learned today?

ESSIE: Maybe we don't have to say it with words.

BILL: Essie's right. We can *show* how we feel about the importance of our black heritage.

TED: The best way to do that is to plan a Black History Week that the students at Jefferson High School will never forget.

ESSIE: Well, let's get on with it! (*All return to their seats. ALICE picks up writing pad; MS. REED enters.*)

MS. REED (*Surprised and pleased*): You're still here? I never expected you to stay this late. (*Goes to peer over ALICE's shoulder*) Why, you've got a whole page full of activities. That's wonderful!

ALICE (*Holding up notepad*): This is only the beginning.

TED: Our Black History program won't be just for one week, Ms. Reed. We'll have special events all year long.

MS. REED (*Beaming*): A little while ago, you couldn't have cared less about your committee work. What made you change your attitudes? (*Students exchange knowing looks.*)

BILL: Sorry, Ms. Reed, but we can't tell you that.

JERRY (*Smiling*): Just say it's a secret, Ms. Reed. (*Winks at others*) *Our* little secret. (*Curtain*)

THE END

Production Notes

THE SECRET GIFTS

Characters: 6 male; 6 female.

Playing Time: 25 minutes.

Costumes: Students wear modern, everyday dress. Ted wears button reading, TED DAVIS FOR PRESIDENT. Douglass, Bethune, Wheatley, Washington, Teacher, and King all wear costumes appropriate to their period. Wheatley wears apron with scroll in pocket; King has pen in jacket pocket.

Properties: Briefcase; posters; sheet of paper; pile of books; headphones; purse containing pad and pen; portfolio containing paintings; book; three scrolls; coin.

Setting: High school newspaper workroom. Table and four chairs are center. Small bookcase with stacks of books, old newspapers, and yearbooks is up right. Chair and small, untidy desk with typewriter, phone, papers, etc., are also upstage. File cabinet and mail baskets are up left. Bulletin board filled with notes is on rear wall; clock hangs beside it. Wooden bench is down left; old-fashioned desk with pen, and straight-back chair are down right. Broom is propped against wall near desk downstage. Exit is left.

Lighting: Lights fade and spotlighting, as indicated in text.

∼Landslide for Shakespeare

by Earl J. Dias

Whiz kid saves a stadium with a little help from the Bard . . . .

Characters

MIMI WATSON
MRS. CLEMENS
MR. CLEMENS
BEN KRAMER
LILY BANKS
DIZZY GREEN
HENRY OLDHAM
SALLY ROWE
EIGHT STUDENTS, *extras*

SCENE 1

TIME: *Early afternoon, the present.*
SETTING: *The End Zone, a restaurant hangout for Benson High
    School students. Up center is long counter holding glasses,
    doughnuts, candy, etc. Small tables, each with four chairs, are
    scattered about. At left is exit to street; windows on either side
    have* THE END ZONE *stenciled on them. On right wall is banner
    reading* BENSON HIGH SCHOOL.
AT RISE: MR. *and* MRS. CLEMENS, *proprietors of The End
    Zone, are busy behind the counter.* MRS. CLEMENS *is drying
    glasses.* MR. CLEMENS *is putting out a new supply of candy
    bars. At one of the tables,* MIMI WATSON *sips coffee.*

MIMI: It's so nice and quiet in here! (*Looking at watch*) How much longer do I have before the brat pack arrives?

MRS. CLEMENS (*Unenthusiastically*): They'll be here soon. And when they get here, the place will sound like an amusement park. (*Sighing*) My head is aching already just thinking of the din.

MR. CLEMENS: Now, Grace, just remember. If it weren't for the kids, we'd probably starve to death.

MRS. CLEMENS (*Patting her stomach; dryly*): There's not much chance of *that,* I'm afraid.

MIMI: And what do you and your husband think of our new local hero?

MR. CLEMENS: You mean Henry Oldham?

MIMI: Sure! The celebrated game show wizard!

MR. CLEMENS (*Coming from behind counter to stand by MIMI's table*): I'll tell you, Mimi, we haven't had as much excitement around here since Benson High became the state football champs. The place has been frantic.

MRS. CLEMENS: You never heard so much fuss about Shakespeare in all your life. (*Importantly*) He's a pretty famous playwright, you know.

MR. CLEMENS: If he wasn't, he certainly is now. All the kids go around quoting *Hamlet* and *Macbeth*.

MRS. CLEMENS: Most of the time this place sounds like the Globe Theatre on a day with standing room only.

MIMI: You know, I've never seen Henry, except on television. He looks like a quiet, harmless kid.

MR. CLEMENS: He always has been. But he's a killer on that quiz show. I never knew he was so smart.

MIMI: Well, I have to interview him for the paper. (*Sips coffee, then takes notepad from bag*) You folks know as much about the situation as anyone in Benson. Do I have the facts straight? (*Reads from notepad*) Henry has now appeared for three weeks in a row on "Jam the Jackpot." His category is Shakespeare. He's up to $7,000 in winnings, and if he wins tonight, he gets the $15,000 jackpot.

MRS. CLEMENS: That's about it, except that the sponsor of the program will also donate $5,000 to any enterprise that the winning contestant chooses.

MIMI (*Impressed; laughing*): I wish I could be the enterprise that he chooses.

MR. CLEMENS: I don't know how he can lose—that boy is a genius. You should hear the questions he's answered. He knows more about Shakespeare than Shakespeare himself. It's uncanny. (*Voices are heard. LILY BANKS, BEN KRA-MER, and other high school STUDENTS enter chatting noisily. STUDENTS sit at tables, order food and drink, and continue chatting. LILY and BEN sit at one table together. Their conversation is heard above the murmurs and laughter of the others.*) Orders! Orders!

STUDENTS (*Calling out, ad lib*): Ginger ale. Iced tea. Root beer. (*Etc.*)

BEN: What'll you have, Lily?

LILY (*Indifferently*): I don't care. After that French test today, I probably should have a cup of hemlock.

BEN (*Calling to* MR. CLEMENS): Make it two root beers, Mr. Clemens.

MR. CLEMENS: Coming up.

BEN (*Dryly*): I suppose the great Henry Oldham will be in soon with his parade of admirers.

LILY: Don't be bitter, Ben. (*Gushing*) Henry is sweet—and so brilliant.

BEN: He's brilliant, but I'll bet he doesn't have any common sense.

LILY: He knows Shakespeare, and that seems to be worth a lot of money these days.

BEN: I notice *you've* been paying plenty of attention to him. It's pathetic the way all you girls hang on his every word as though he were an oracle or something.

LILY (*Scolding*): Ben Kramer, there comes a time in a girl's life when she realizes brains may be more important than brawn. You may be the football captain, but there are other things in life besides chasing a pigskin up and down a field.

BEN: What's wrong with football? You used to think it was just great.

LILY (*Dismissively*): Let's not talk about muscles, Ben. It's the mind that counts. Just think what Henry has accomplished.

BEN: I've got nothing against brains. After all, I can read without moving my lips. Didn't I get all "B's" on my report card?

LILY: Henry got all "A's."

BEN: Henry again! What's the use?

LILY: I don't know why you're being so negative about Henry. He likes you. In fact, he really admires you. He says he's always wanted to play football himself, but he doesn't weigh enough.

BEN: That's a laugh! (LILY *glares at him; he shrugs.*) Oh, I suppose he's all right in his way, but he certainly isn't the football type. Anyway, as far as football goes, we'll be lucky if we even have a team next season.

LILY (*Looking toward the door; distractedly*): Really?

BEN (*Irritated*): You sound all broken up about it.

LILY: I'm positively shattered.

BEN: We need new bleachers. In fact, the whole field needs to be resurfaced. The town can't spend the money this year, because they're building the new junior high, and the teachers have just been given a raise.

LILY: Teachers have to eat, too.

BEN: I know that—but the team ought to have a decent field just the same.

MIMI (*Rising and crossing to their table*): Excuse me, but I couldn't help overhearing you. I'm Mimi Watson of the *Evening Blade*.

LILY: Hi, how are you? I'm Lily Banks, and this is Ben Kramer.

MIMI (*To* BEN): You're Benson High's football captain, aren't you?

BEN (*Gloomily*): I'm the only football captain in the nation whose team probably won't have a field to play on next season.

MIMI: Yes, I know about that. On the other hand, Benson High's certainly in the spotlight because of Henry Oldham. Do you know him?

LILY (*Enthusiastically*): Yes!

BEN (*Gloomily*): Yeah.

MIMI: Then I wonder if you'd do me a favor. When Henry comes in, will you introduce me to him? I have to interview him for the paper.

BEN: You'd better see Dizzy Green, then.

MIMI: Dizzy Green?

LILY: He's Henry's self-appointed manager.

BEN (*Grumpily*): Henry needs somebody to lead him around.

LILY: Don't mind Ben, Ms. Watson. He's just jealous. (*Sound of voices again. DIZZY GREEN enters, carrying books in his arms, and small notebook and pencil in his shirt pocket. He is followed by HENRY OLDHAM, bespectacled and rather meek in appearance, and SALLY ROWE, also bespectacled and carrying books. The three go to sit at an empty table.*)

DIZZY (*Loudly*): Hear ye! Hear ye! Henry Oldham, the pride of Benson and the world's greatest authority on William Shakespeare, has arrived!

STUDENTS (*Ad lib*): Hi, Henry! Hey, Dizzy! (*Etc. DIZZY opens one of his books.*)

DIZZY: O.K., Henry, here's another one: To whom was the First Folio of 1623 dedicated?

HENRY (*Quietly*): To the Earl of Pembroke and the Earl of Montgomery. Both were Knights of the Garter.

SALLY (*Admiringly*): That's wonderful, Henry.

HENRY (*Sniffing slightly*): Thank you, Sally. (MR. CLEMENS *goes quickly to their table.*)

MR. CLEMENS: Say, was that a sniff I heard, Henry? You're not getting a cold, are you? You've got to be in shape for tonight.

HENRY: Just a little hay fever, Mr. Clemens.

DIZZY: Fear not! All is well. Dizzy Green is on the job. I've already given Henry his vitamins for the day, Mr. Clemens, and I supervised his nap during study period.

MR. CLEMENS: Sodas all around?

SALLY: Sure, thanks, Mr. Clemens. (*To* HENRY) Who spoke the following: "Blanch and Sweetheart, see, they bark at me"?

HENRY: King Lear said it—Act 2, Scene 6.

SALLY: Good. That $15,000 is practically in your pocket now.

DIZZY: How beautiful those crisp, green bills will feel!

HENRY: Please! There's plenty about Shakespeare I don't know.
    (LILY *comes to table, followed by* BEN *and* MIMI.)

LILY (*Sweetly*): Hello, Henry.

HENRY (*Shyly*): H-hello, Lily.

LILY: I've been listening to you, Henry. It's just super to hear how much you know.

DIZZY: The boy is fantastic, simply fantastic. He's got a mind like a steel trap. If I do say so myself, I've been training him expertly.

BEN: Give me a break, Dizzy! A week ago, you didn't know Shakespeare from Stephen King.

DIZZY: Those are fighting words, but you're bigger than I am. Therefore, I forgive you.

LILY: You're going to the dance tomorrow night, aren't you, Henry?

HENRY: I—I'm not much for tripping the light fantastic.

LILY: But it will be a wonderful opportunity for you to celebrate winning the jackpot.

HENRY (*Firmly*): I haven't won yet.

LILY: You will. You must know more about Shakespeare than anybody in the world.

HENRY (*Protesting*): N-no, really, I don't. There's Professor Kincaid of Harvard, and Professor Tallman of Oxford, and Professor—

LILY: Don't be so modest, Henry. Anyway, I'm giving a little party before the dance, and I'd like you to come. I thought that afterward, we could go to the dance together.

BEN (*Bristling*): I thought you were going with me.

LILY (*Flippantly*): I never said that. How about it, Henry?

SALLY (*Timidly*): Henry and I were planning to work on our play tomorrow night.

LILY: What play?

HENRY: We're writing a play for the talent show.

LILY: That's a couple of months away. Please, Henry.

BEN (*Clapping* HENRY *on the back*): You go right ahead and write that play, Henry. The school needs you.

LILY (*Through clenched teeth*): You keep out of this, Ben.

MIMI: At the risk of being a spoilsport, may I interrupt? Lily, you promised to introduce me.

LILY (*Exasperated*): Oh, I'm sorry. Henry, this is Mimi Watson from the *Blade*. She wants to interview you. (HENRY *rises politely and shakes hands with* MIMI.)

DIZZY (*Importantly*): Ah, a member of the press. (*He takes a small notebook from his shirt pocket.*) Let me see; we're just about snowed under with engagements. (*Leafing through book*) We could give you ten minutes two weeks from today.

MIMI (*Wryly*): Listen, kid, my editor is not the sort of guy who will wait two weeks for an interview. He'd have my scalp—and yours, too.

DIZZY (*Rechecking his book; quickly*): Let me see. How about one week from today?

MIMI (*Brashly*): How about right now?

HENRY: Ms. Watson, I'd be happy to answer any questions you care to ask.

MIMI: Thanks a lot, Henry. (*She and* HENRY *sit.*) Now, how did you become so interested in Shakespeare?

HENRY: My mother is a professor of English, and I've been reading Shakespeare since I was seven years old. (MIMI *begins to take notes. She continues the interview in a low voice, while* BEN *and* LILY *return to their table and sit.*)

BEN: You certainly threw yourself at that poor guy. Can't you see that Sally Rowe is more his type? They're both interested in playwriting.

LILY (*Defensively*): I could write a play, too.

BEN: Yeah, right. I saw your last essay. You got a "C" on it.

LILY: That's only because I wrote it in a hurry.

BEN: He doesn't even know how to dance. What kind of a time would you have with him?

LILY: Dancing isn't that important. We could talk—about intellectual things. You wouldn't understand that.

BEN (*Agitated*): I understand that Henry is happy just the way he is. And I'm happy the way I am. You ought to be happy the way you are. It sure was different when you accepted my class ring.

LILY: So that's what's bothering you. Well, you can take your old ring back right now. (LILY *attempts to remove the ring from her finger, but it won't budge. She pulls vigorously.*)

BEN (*Smirking*): See, Fate wants to keep us together.

LILY (*Desperately*): I'll cut my finger off first. (*She pulls again and the ring comes off.*) There. Fate just changed her mind. (*She gives ring to* BEN.)

BEN (*Sadly*): I don't really want this, Lily. You know how I feel about you.

LILY: I just don't like your insinuations. Goodbye. (*She rises and goes to* HENRY's *table.*) How's the interview coming, Ms. Watson?

MIMI: Great! Henry makes wonderful copy. We're just about finished. (*She rises.*) I want to thank you, Henry. (*Dryly*) And, of course, your brilliant manager here.

DIZZY: Think nothing of it, Ms. Watson. We always cooperate with the press. If there's anything else we can do for you, just give me a ring. Dizzy Green—always at your service.

MIMI (*Sarcastically*): You're the soul of chivalry, Dizzy. Henry, I want to wish you good luck for tonight.

HENRY: Thank you, Ms. Watson. I'll try my best.

DIZZY: The whole thing's in the bag. This boy has the greatest brain since Leonardo da Vinci.

SALLY (*Proudly*): Henry has been studying very hard, Ms. Watson. I know he'll do well.

LILY: Of course he will. We'll all celebrate his victory at the dance tomorrow night.

SALLY (*Timidly*): W-well, I'm not sure—

MIMI: And I also want to say, Henry, that I think you're very generous. What you've told me is a credit to you.

HENRY: Please, Ms. Watson, don't say anything about that until your interview appears in tomorrow's paper. Only Dizzy and Sally know about it.

MIMI: My lips are sealed. Goodbye—and again, good luck. (MIMI *exits.*)

SALLY: She's very nice, isn't she?

HENRY: A most genteel young woman.

DIZZY: O.K., Henry, social hour is over. Back to work. The zero hour approaches.

SALLY (*Looking at her book*): Who was the first man to play the role of Hamlet?

DIZZY: Child's play. Child's play. Henry can answer that one with both hands tied behind his back.

LILY: I suppose you know the answer, Dizzy.

MRS. CLEMENS (*Coming to table with tray of sodas*): What Dizzy doesn't know, he'll make up. (*Puts sodas on table*) I've never heard such a smooth talker.

DIZZY: Thank you, friends. Thank you. Only my great modesty forbids my answering the question. It would be unfair to outshine my great and good friend, Henry Oldham.

MRS. CLEMENS: Some people kiss the Blarney Stone, but I think you swallowed it.

HENRY: The first man to play the role of Hamlet was Richard Burbage of Shakespeare's own acting company.

DIZZY: You took the words right out of my mouth.

MR. CLEMENS (*Coming to table*): How's he doing, Grace?

MRS. CLEMENS (*Dryly*): With Dizzy's help, I think he'll manage to squeak by.

MR. CLEMENS: Good. We're banking on you, boy. (*Smugly*) Ah, the theater. I used to act a bit myself. (*Dramatically*)
"To be, or not to be—that is the question.
Whether 'tis nobler in the mind to suffer
The slings and arrows of outrageous fortune—" (*Suddenly DIZZY interrupts.*)

DIZZY: I hate to break in on all this cultural stuff, but my man, Henry, needs to relax now. (*Checking his watch*) Yes, sir, Henry, time to go home and rest up for tonight's great triumph.

SALLY: Dizzy's right, Henry. You ought to rest for a while.

MR. CLEMENS: Absolutely. We all want you to be fresh as a daisy tonight. Good luck, Henry.

OTHERS (*Shouting ad lib*): Good luck, Henry! Bring home the bacon! (*Etc.*)

HENRY (*Rising*): Thank you. I appreciate it. (*To* BEN) By the way, Ben, could I see you a minute outside? It's important.

BEN: Uh, sure.

LILY: I'll come, too.

HENRY: I'm sorry, Lily—the fact is, this is rather confidential.

LILY (*Deflated*): Oh.

BEN (*Grinning*): You heard what the man said. (HENRY *and* BEN *exit.*)

LILY: I can't imagine what business Henry has with Ben.

SALLY (*Feigning ignorance*): Maybe it's just a guy thing, Lily. Who knows?

DIZZY: Lily, I see you're not wearing Ben's ring.

LILY (*Snapping*): That's none of your business, Dizzy.

SALLY (*Concerned*): I hope nothing's happened between you, Lily. I've always thought you and Ben made a nice couple.

LILY (*Melting a bit*): Thanks, Sally. But that's life.

DIZZY: Come on, Sally. Time to take our champ home.

LILY: Do you think Henry will come to my party, Dizzy?

DIZZY: He's a busy man—a busy man. Could be—could not be.

LILY: You're a big help.

DIZZY: Henry just isn't the gadfly. His mind is on bigger and better things. Come on, Sally. (DIZZY *and* SALLY *exit.* LILY *looks very gloomy.*)

MRS. CLEMENS: You look as though you'd failed all your final exams.

LILY: And I feel just the way I look.

MR. CLEMENS: Well, cheer up, everyone. Let's hope that Henry will hit the jackpot tonight. The great Shakespeare! What a man he was! (*He recites.*) "To be, or not to be—that is the question—" (*All others join in happily, except* LILY, *who exits dejectedly. Curtain*)

* * * * *

SCENE 2

TIME: *Early the next afternoon.*

SETTING: *Same as Scene 1. On counter is a newspaper.*

AT RISE: MR. *and* MRS. CLEMENS *are working behind counter. Both are in happy moods, whistling and singing to themselves.* STUDENTS *are seated at tables, talking excitedly in low tones.*

MR. CLEMENS: Last night was terrific! I never saw anything like it! Henry whipped through those questions like a hurricane. Just think of how many sodas he could buy with that $15,000 he won.

MRS. CLEMENS: Don't forget the $5,000 he's donating to the high school to fix up the football field. He did himself proud, all right.

MR. CLEMENS: It was generous of him to have Ben Kramer on the program, too. After Henry won, and Ben appeared on the screen with him, you could have knocked me over with a feather. (*Picks up newspaper from counter*) Mimi knew everything before it happened. Henry must've tipped her off yesterday.

MRS. CLEMENS: The town ought to be pleased. Henry is saving them a heap of money. (MIMI *enters*.) Hello, Mimi.

MIMI: Hi, Mrs. Clemens. Hasn't the toast of Benson arrived yet?

MR. CLEMENS: Not yet. All the kids are waiting for him. (LILY *enters*.)

LILY: Hello, Ms. Watson.

MIMI: How are you, Lily? Say, did you see your boyfriend on TV last night? He made an excellent little speech.

LILY (*Downcast*): I saw him, all right.

MIMI: You don't sound very enthusiastic.

LILY: I'm not. I'm glad that Henry won, and I think he's very generous.

MIMI: What about Ben?

LILY: I'd rather not talk about him, if you don't mind.

MIMI (*Taken aback*): No problem. I'm sorry if I said the wrong thing.

LILY (*Going to table and sitting alone*): That's all right.

MRS. CLEMENS (*Going to LILY's table*): What'll you have, Miss Lonelyhearts?

LILY (*Glumly*): Any old thing. It really doesn't matter.

MRS. CLEMENS: I'll squeeze you some fresh orange juice. You look as though you could use the vitamins. (DIZZY *enters, followed by* HENRY, SALLY, *and* BEN.)

DIZZY (*Grandly*): Make way for the pride of Benson—a gentleman, a scholar, and a man of culture and refinement! (*All students rise from their tables and go over to congratulate*

HENRY, *who beams modestly. After students return to their seats,* HENRY, DIZZY, SALLY, *and* BEN *sit at a table.*)

BEN: I can't thank you enough for what you've done, Henry.

HENRY: I was glad to do it, Ben. I really love football.

BEN: So as matters stand, I've gained a football field and lost my girlfriend.

HENRY (*Thoughtfully*): I feel bad about Lily, Ben. But you know something? I think I can help you there.

BEN (*Surprised*): You can?

HENRY: I'll give it a try. (*Speaking as though he has a bad cold*) Hey, Lily, why don't you join us?

LILY (*Hesitantly*): Well—I—

SALLY: Please, Lily.

LILY: Well—all right. (*She joins them.*) Henry, you did a wonderful job last night, and I wanted to thank you for your donation to the school.

HENRY: It was the least I could do. (*Sniffing violently*) I've always wanted to play football myself.

LILY: Have you got a cold?

HENRY: Not really. It's just my hay fever. It's terrible at this time of year. That's why I can't play football—that and the fact that I can't seem to gain weight and—(*He moves his right arm painfully*)—the fact that I'm plagued by these funny pains in my arms.

LILY (*Apprehensively*): Pains?

HENRY: The doctor says they'll probably get worse as I get older. Could be arthritis. That's one of the reasons I don't dance much. I get it in my back, too. A form of lumbago.

LILY (*Warily*): That all sounds pretty painful.

HENRY (*Shrugging*): So, I've had to devote myself to the intellectual life. Still, I did want to do my bit for the football team.

BEN: You did more than your bit, Henry. Inviting me to accept that check on TV was pretty exciting.

HENRY (*Sneezing*): The stadium will now be called the Shakespeare Memorial Field.

LILY: Shakespeare Memorial—

BEN: After all, it's the least we can do for the man who made all this possible.

HENRY (*Sneezing again and blowing his nose*): Whoops! Excuse me. I should be home in bed with a hot water bottle. I use one every night. As I was saying, I think there's plenty of room for cooperation between brains and brawn. They ought to work together. That's why I did what I did. (*To* BEN) I don't mean that you're just a mass of muscle, Ben. I know that your grades are good.

BEN: Thanks, Henry. I understand perfectly. There's room in the world for intellectuals and those of us who are average—not stupid, but not brilliant, either.

DIZZY: Well-spoken, my man—well-spoken.

MR. CLEMENS (*Coming to table*): Henry, you're a man in a million.

HENRY (*Croaking*): Thank you, Mr. Clemens.

MR. CLEMENS: Say, your throat sounds as though it's been treated with sandpaper. Can I get you some tea?

HENRY: No, thanks. I'll be all right when the weather changes.

MR. CLEMENS: Let's hope so. You're too valuable a man to be on the sick list. You kids all want sodas?

HENRY: Yes, and I'm treating. (*Smiling*) I can afford it today.

DIZZY: I'll say you can! (MR. CLEMENS *returns to counter.*)

HENRY: If I can stop sneezing long enough and if my leg doesn't hurt too much, I'll come to your party tonight, Lily.

LILY: Your leg, Henry? I thought the pains were in your arms and your back.

HENRY (*Stumbling a bit*): Yes, well—they're all connected, you know.

LILY (*Graciously*): At any rate, I hope you feel well enough to make it, Henry. But I understand perfectly if you can't come.

HENRY: I'll see. I think I really ought to get out more. My social life has been rather limited. (*Sneezes*) I don't want to seem inhospitable, but I don't want you to catch anything I've got. Why don't you and Ben sit by yourselves at another table?

DIZZY: Good idea. Don't worry about Sally and me. We're immune.

BEN: If you say so, Henry. Coming, Lily?

LILY (*Rising*): Maybe I'd better. (LILY *goes to next table and sits.* BEN *exchanges grins with* HENRY *and follows her.*)

BEN: Henry is a really great guy.

LILY: Yes, he is. (*Laughs*) But he's a terrible actor.

BEN (*Shocked*): You mean, you saw through that act just now?

LILY (*Ruefully*): Well, I must admit he had me going for a while. (*Guffaws*) But *lumbago?* Honestly, Ben!

BEN (*Grinning*): So, if you knew he was putting us on, why'd you go along with it?

LILY (*Shrugging*): I don't want to stay where I'm not wanted. Besides, I wanted to ask you to the dance tonight.

BEN (*Surprised*): You mean you still want to go out with me?

LILY (*Apologetically*): I never *stopped* liking you, Ben. I think I must've had a case of temporary insanity. (*Clutching forehead, dramatically*) My doctor says it will go away if you let me wear your class ring again.

BEN (*Examining ring on his finger; teasingly*): Well, I don't know. I kind of like the way it looks on my finger. (*Pulls ring off*) But, in the interest of medical science, I'm willing to part with it. (*Puts it on* LILY's *finger, gives her quick kiss. They laugh.*)

MRS. CLEMENS (*Appearing at table with sodas*): All this romance must be making you two thirsty.

BEN (*Raising his glass*): I'll say. (LILY *drinks her soda.*)

LILY: I just remembered. I've got to get a book at the library before it closes.

BEN (*Finishing his soda*): I'll walk down with you. (*They move toward exit.* BEN *stops at* HENRY's *table and holds out his hand.*) Henry, you're a prince. Thanks for everything. (*They shake hands.*)

HENRY: Remember what I said—people like us should cooperate, each using his particular talents for the benefit of all.

BEN: I'll remember that. (BEN *and* LILY *exit hand in hand.* HENRY *suddenly jumps to his feet, lets out a whoop, and does a brief jig.*)

DIZZY: Hey, I thought you were sick. I was all set to order flowers.

SALLY (*Suspiciously*): Come clean, Henry Oldham. You haven't got a really bad case of hay fever, and you obviously don't have arthritis.

DIZZY (*Suddenly realizing*): I've got it! You were just doing Ben a favor.

SALLY: He sure was!

DIZZY (*Boasting*): I knew it all along. I saw right through it.

SALLY: It was very decent of you, Henry.

HENRY: It was nothing, really. After all, I don't care much for dances, and I do want to write that play with you.

SALLY (*Firmly*): We're going to the dance, anyway.

HENRY (*Surprised*): We are?

SALLY: Yes. A little social life will be good for both of us.

DIZZY (*Laughing*): That is, if your lumbago can stand it.

HENRY (*Grinning*): I'll bring the hot water bottle.

MR. CLEMENS (*Coming to table with sodas*): Here you go, root beers all around. Compliments of Henry Oldham—*and* William Shakespeare.

DIZZY (*Rising; dramatically*): You said it! (*Raising his glass*) Friends, a toast to Shakespeare: A gentleman, a scholar, and a great fan of football. (*All respond enthusiastically, raising their glasses and cheering*) Here, here! To Shakespeare! (*All laugh and cheer. Curtain*)

THE END

Production Notes

LANDSLIDE FOR SHAKESPEARE

Characters: 4 male; 4 female; 8 male or female extras for Students.

Playing Time: 30 minutes.

Costumes: Everyday school clothes for students. Mrs. Clemens, dress and apron. Mr. Clemens, dark trousers, white shirt, apron. Mimi, business clothes.

Properties: Napkins, candy bars, reporter's notebook, pen, books, pocket-sized notebook, pencil, handkerchief, class ring.

Setting: The End Zone, a Benson High School dining hangout. Up center is long counter holding glass case of doughnuts, glasses, candy, etc. On stage are four or five small tables, at each of which are four chairs. At left is exit to the street, with windows on either side on which are stenciled THE END ZONE. On right wall is banner reading BENSON HIGH SCHOOL.

Lighting: No special effects.

∾Shoo Fly Pudding

by Elbert M. Hoppenstedt

Students cause trouble with a half-baked protest . . . .

Characters

DAN WILKINS, *high school senior*
BRIAN, *a freshman*
MARY LOU, *a senior*
TANYA, *a senior*
PETE ⎫
GLENN ⎬ *students*
STEVE ⎭
STUDENTS, *extras*
DRUMMER
MRS. MOORE ⎫
MRS. JOHNSON ⎬ *cafeteria cooks*
MRS. O'HARA ⎭
MR. EDWARDS, *high school principal*

SCENE 1

TIME: *Late morning; the present.*
SETTING: *Conference room of Big Valley High School. Long table with chairs around it stands center.*
AT RISE: DAN WILKINS *enters carrying briefcase and three signs on poles. He moves to head of table, places signs on floor, opens case, and takes out papers. He looks at his watch and then paces.*
BRIAN (*Entering; hesitantly*): Is this where the Watchdog Committee is meeting?
DAN (*In booming voice*): You have reached your destination, my

168

boy. You must be Brian. (*Bowing*) Dan Wilkins at your service, Chairman of Big Valley High School's Watchdog Committee. We are the guardians of student rights, preservers of democracy for the American high school—and arch enemies of the administration and the establishment. Come on in and have a seat.

BRIAN (*Doubtfully*): You sure make the committee sound important.

DAN: Have you any doubt about that? If you do, it's because you're a freshman, and of course freshmen aren't expected to know anything. Our committee has worked miracles for this school.

BRIAN (*Sitting at table*): Like what?

DAN (*Importantly*): Two years ago we won senior privileges from those tyrants, the administration.

BRIAN: What are senior privileges?

DAN (*Indignantly*): You don't know? Why do you think you lesser creatures stand up when we seniors enter assemblies? Why do we have a special area in the cafeteria? And why don't we have to take any exams at the end of our senior year?

BRIAN (*Uncertainly*): Well, I guess that's pretty impressive. But what has the committee done for us lower classmen?

DAN (*Slapping forehead*): How can anyone be so ignorant? We must start a publicity drive instantly to educate our freshmen. I'll tell you what we've won for you. (*Dramatically*) A salted nut machine!

BRIAN (*In awe*): A salted nut machine! Where is it?

DAN (*Embarrassed*): Well ... uh ... it seems some students scattered nuts all over the building, which in turn attracted mice, so the administration took it out. (*Quickly*) It was all a set-up by the principal and the vice-principal, of course. (*Proudly*) But what about the juke box we got for the cafeteria?

BRIAN: Oh, so that's where it came from.

DAN: Of course! Don't you like it?

BRIAN (*Haltingly*): Well—to tell you the truth—I find it kind of hard to talk to my friends at lunch with that music playing all the time. It is a little loud, Dan—just a little, of course.

DAN (*In disgust*): Just like a freshman. You don't appreciate anything that's done for you. (MARY LOU *enters with* TANYA.)

MARY LOU (*With sarcasm*): Ah, I see that Dan Wilkins, friend to all students, has already arrived. (*With exaggerated gestures*) Hail, O glorious leader.

TANYA (*To* DAN): I suppose you came early to make up for all the meetings you failed to call this year.

DAN (*Coldly*): I have more important things to do than sit around at meetings. Besides, results are what count—as you and the rest of this school will soon find out!

MARY LOU (*Sarcastically*): I can hardly wait!

DAN: We've wasted enough time. I want all of you to gather round. I have something important to show you.

MARY LOU: Yes, my lord and master! (*She and* TANYA *sit.* DAN *picks up papers from table.*)

DAN: I have here the results of the questionnaire we distributed to the homerooms yesterday.

MARY LOU: How did it turn out?

DAN (*Embarrassed*): Well, it seems that a few students—barely a majority—feel we haven't been doing very much so far this year.

BRIAN (*Innocently*): Maybe that's because you haven't met all year.

DAN (*Ignoring remark*): Most of the students feel that we should do something to remedy the horrible conditions in our cafeteria.

TANYA: They *are* bad.

MARY LOU: Sometimes I wait in line until my lunch period is almost over.

TANYA: And the food is often cold.

BRIAN: I'm on the last lunch shift and a lot of times there's nothing left.

DAN (*Excitedly*): Exactly! The situation is an outrage. We must take action!

TANYA: Have you talked to Mr. Edwards about it?

DAN (*Astonished*): Talk to the principal? You've got to be kidding, Tanya. Who talks to the establishment these days? The

only thing they listen to is action. And that's exactly what
I propose.

TANYA: I still say we should talk to Mr. Edwards before we
do anything.

DAN: Nonsense! We need action, not talk. (*Paces in agitation*)
What we have to do is create an incident that will arouse the
student body and catch the administration off guard. Then
they'll be forced to meet our demands. And I know just how
to do it!

TANYA: Dan, this is making me very nervous.

DAN (*Ignoring her*): Not only do I have a plan, but I am ready
to put it into effect. (*Takes envelope from briefcase and empties
contents onto table*) I've been down in Little Bog Swamp for
days collecting these.

MARY LOU (*Aghast*): Flies! Ick! Get them out of here!

TANYA: Dead flies! Really, Dan, you must be cracking up!

DAN: No, just using the old noodle. These little rascals will do
the job for us. I can hear the uproar now!

BRIAN (*Confused*): What uproar?

DAN (*Smiling broadly at him*): The uproar that you will create,
Brian. I have selected you to play a key role in this incident.
You may well go down in history as the hero of Big Valley
High School.

BRIAN (*Flattered*): Me? You mean it?

DAN: Sure do! It isn't often that a freshman gets such a chance.
(*Looks at watch*) The second lunch shift will be starting soon,
so you'd better get moving. (*Brushes flies back into envelope*)

BRIAN (*Perplexed*): What am I supposed to do?

DAN: Well, Brian, today is rice pudding day. Have you forgotten?

BRIAN (*Confused*): Yes . . . no . . .

DAN: Here, take the envelope. (*Hands him envelope*)

TANYA (*Horrified*): Dan! You couldn't possibly . . .

BRIAN: But I still don't know what I'm supposed to do.

DAN: Add more *raisins*—ha-ha—to the pudding! What else?

BRIAN (*Appalled*): You mean—the flies?

TANYA: Dan, this is awful!

MARY LOU (*Grinning*): Wow! What a fantastic idea!

DAN (*Motioning for silence, impatiently*): Just scatter them lightly on top of each serving. And don't miss any.

BRIAN: But if I'm caught, I might get suspended!

DAN (*Annoyed*): All great leaders take risks, Brian. Now get going.

BRIAN (*Unhappily*): I don't think I like this. (*Exits grumbling*)

TANYA (*Upset*): I don't like it, either. It's all wrong!

DAN (*Cheerfully*): Nonsense! The only time anybody listens to the younger generation these days is when they make enough noise.

MARY LOU (*Admiringly*): You're absolutely right, Dan. This will really stir up a fuss!

TANYA (*Vehemently*): Mary Lou! He's absolutely wrong! Sure, conditions in the cafeteria need to be improved, but there has to be another way!

DAN (*Pompously*): Then let's hear it.

TANYA: I—I can't come up with anything at the moment. But give me some time to think about it.

DAN: By the time you finish thinking, it will be the end of the year. Besides, the student body wants action, so I'm giving them action. (*Grinning*) Cheer up, Tanya. You'll be a hero in a little while. When you walk down the halls, you'll be cheered.

TANYA (*Angrily*): Don't be so silly! I don't want to be a hero. I just want to solve this lunchroom problem in a sensible, logical way!

DAN: Which is just what we're doing. (*Looks at watch*) By now the die is cast. The flies are planted. So we must move into phase two. You're with me, aren't you, Mary Lou?

MARY LOU: You bet I am. I think this is exciting. What comes next?

DAN: The clincher. (*He holds up protest signs reading:* RAISINS YES—FLIES NO; NO MEAT IN OUR DESSERTS!; STUDENTS UPRISE AGAINST FLIES) We parade up and down the aisles in the cafeteria holding these signs. (*Hands signs to* MARY LOU *and* TANYA. MARY LOU *and* DAN *march around room, laughing and chanting slogans on signs.* TANYA *stands silently watching them.*) O.K., girls. It's time for the real thing. Oh, boy! For two nights I've been dreaming about this.

MARY LOU: Really, Dan? What happened in your dream?

DAN (*Dramatically*): Mr. Edwards comes in and finds the lunchroom in an uproar. He tries to tell everyone to calm down, but nobody will listen to him. Then everybody falls into our protest line, and we march up and down the halls chanting our slogans.

MARY LOU (*Excitedly*): Yes, yes, then what?

TANYA (*In disgust*): Yes, tell us. What is done to improve conditions in the cafeteria?

DAN (*Lamely*): Well—that's where my dream ended.

MARY LOU: Just when you were getting to the good part. Oh, well, pretty soon we'll know what really happens!

DAN: Right! Let's go! (TANYA *hangs back*.) Come on, Tanya.

TANYA (*Stubbornly*): I'm not going. (*Hands him sign*)

DAN (*Shrugging*): O.K., do what you want. We'll take all the credit for defeating the administration.

TANYA: And I'm resigning from this committee, too. Goodbye! (*Exits*)

DAN: So, who needs her? Right, Mary Lou? Wow! Is this going to be a scene! Something this school will never forget! (*They march off.*)

* * * * *

SCENE 2

SETTING: *Cafeteria. Sign at rear lists the day's menu, including* RICE PUDDING. *Rows of long tables and chairs or benches are at center.*

AT RISE: PETE, GLENN, STEVE, *and* STUDENTS *sit at tables, eating, talking, laughing. Part of the serving line may also be seen.*

PETE (*Getting to his feet suddenly with a yell*): Now this is really too much! This is the last straw! Hey, everyone! Quiet! Quiet! (*He climbs onto a chair. Others stop talking and listen.*) You want to see what they're putting in the food today? Take a look at this! (*Holds up fly*) A fly in my rice pudding! What do you think of that? Cute little fellow, isn't he?

GLENN (*Also rising*): I have one, too! A green one, with beautiful eyes. (*Students squeal.*)

STEVE (*Climbing onto chair*): Mine has purple stripes, but I think he's cross-eyed! Anyhow, only one eye's looking at me.

STUDENTS (*Rising, ad lib*): Me, too! I have two—do I get a prize? You have two? I have three! (*Etc.*)

PETE (*Calling for silence*): Listen, everybody, quiet! I ask you, are we going to take any more of this? (*While he speaks,* GLENN *and* STEVE *move about showing flies to everyone.*) It's time we did something about this cafeteria. We stand in line for hours. The hot lunches are cold. Now we find flies in the rice pudding. Are we going to stand for any more?

STUDENTS (*Shouting, pounding tables; ad lib*): No way! Let's show 'em! We have rights! (*Etc.*)

PETE: And what's our Watchdog Committee doing? Nothing. They're asleep at the wheel.

1ST STUDENT: You said it! They've gone over to the establishment.

PETE: So we have to take matters into our own hands.

2ND STUDENT: A boycott!

3RD STUDENT: Yes, a boycott! Force 'em out of business.

PETE: That's what I like to hear! Action! We'll boycott the food until changes are made. (*Climbs up on table*) Enough is enough—flies are too much!

STUDENTS (*Picking up chant*): Enough is enough—flies are too much! Enough is enough—flies are too much! (*They pound floor with feet in rhythm to chant.* DAN, MARY LOU, *and* BRIAN *enter, holding protest signs, followed by* DRUMMER *in band uniform, beating a drum. They march up and down between tables.* STUDENTS *cheer and whistle.* PETE *cheers them on. Some* STUDENTS *fall in behind* DAN *and* DRUMMER, *chanting.*) Enough is enough—flies are too much! (MRS. O'HARA, MRS. MOORE, *and* MRS. JOHNSON *enter from behind serving line.*)

MRS. MOORE (*Shouting*): Stop this! Stop it this instant! (STUDENTS *grow quiet.*) What are you doing? What is going on here?

PETE (*Still on table, holding up fly*): You should know, Mrs. Moore—flies, that's what! Flies in the rice pudding.

MRS. MOORE: Well, I never! The idea! Are you insinuating that we put flies in our rice pudding?

PETE (*Coolly*): We're not insinuating anything, Mrs. Moore. We're saying that there are flies in the pudding. And enough is enough!

STUDENTS (*Chanting, ad lib*): Enough is enough—flies are too much! (*Etc.*)

MRS. JOHNSON (*Furiously*): That's right. Enough is enough! Come on, ladies. These smart alecks can get their own meals!

MRS. O'HARA: That's right. (*They take off aprons.*) The years we've worked to give them hot lunches, and this is the thanks we get! (MRS. O'HARA, MRS. MOORE, *and* MRS. JOHNSON *stomp off angrily.* MR. EDWARDS *enters, stands watching for a moment, and then moves to where* PETE *is standing on table. He casually climbs up on table beside* PETE, *raising one hand for quiet.*)

MR. EDWARDS (*To* PETE, *but loud enough for all to hear*): You don't mind, do you, Pete? This is the first time I've ever had the opportunity to speak from on top of a lunchroom table. I hope the superintendent doesn't catch me here. (*Laughter*) Now, Pete, what's going on here?

PETE: Flies, Mr. Edwards, that's what's going on.

GLENN: That's right. Flies in our rice pudding.

STEVE: Swarms of 'em. Everybody's got 'em.

MR. EDWARDS (*Examining pudding*): I see. Flies in the rice pudding.

PETE: Yes, sir. Just another example of the mess this cafeteria's in, and we've had it.

STUDENTS (*Ad lib*): That's right! We've had it! This is too much (*Etc.*)

MR. EDWARDS (*Motioning for silence*): Funny! All of a sudden—just like that—swarms of flies appear in this cafeteria. Are they all dead?

PETE: Yes, sir. All dead.

MR. EDWARDS: Hm-m. No signs of any live ones?

PETE (*Suddenly dubious*): No—no, sir.

MR. EDWARDS: Doesn't that strike you as odd? Not a single
fly at the first lunch shift. Then suddenly hundreds appear
for the second shift—all dead. How do you explain that, Pete?

PETE (*Slowly*): I—I don't really know.

MR. EDWARDS: And how do you explain those placards, Pete?
All printed up, arriving just at the right time, and each one
mentioning *flies*. Tell me, Pete, do you suppose these flies
tipped off someone in our school that they were planning an
invasion? (*Laughter*)

PETE: I—I think I see what you're driving at. Those signs would
have to have been painted ahead of time.

STUDENTS (*Ad lib*): Yeah. How could they know? Good question! Something fishy's going on! (DAN *puts sign down quietly
and tries to edge out of room.* MARY LOU *and* BRIAN *hide
behind other* STUDENTS.)

MR. EDWARDS: Maybe we should ask Dan Wilkins to explain.
The Watchdog Committee seem to be the only ones who
have signs.

DAN (*Stopping short, turning, with a bright smile*): What's that,
Mr. Edwards? Can I be of service?

MR. EDWARDS: I just thought you might explain how you and
the other committee members were able to predict this sudden
invasion of flies, and how these placards were made so quickly.

DAN (*Shuffling his feet*): Well—uh—you see, sir, it's just another example of our uncanny intuition.

MR. EDWARDS: I see. Your uncanny intuition informed you
ahead of time that we would be infested with flies.

DAN: Yes, sir! That's it exactly.

MR. EDWARDS: Then why didn't you tell me, so we could prevent it? Surely you didn't want your fellow students to have
flies in their lunches?

DAN (*Feigning shock*): Oh, no, not that! Heaven forbid!

MR. EDWARDS: And just one more thing. As a former biology
teacher, I'm mystified about how these flies got here.

DAN (*Arrogantly*): Flies do have wings, sir.

MR. EDWARDS: I'm well aware of that—a dipterous insect of
the family *Muscidae*. Yes, they have wings. But this particular species is indigenous only to marshlands.

DAN: Indigenous to marshlands. That's very interesting, Mr. Edwards. (*Laughs nervously*) You certainly do know a lot . . .

MR. EDWARDS (*Interrupting him*): Never found more than a few hundred feet from wetlands.

DAN (*Unhappily*): A few hundred feet . . .

MR. EDWARDS: And I believe that the nearest marshland is Little Bog Swamp, which is at least two miles from here. Now, how could so many of those flies come such a long distance?

STUDENTS (*Ad lib*): Yeah, how? That's funny. Answer that one, Dan. (*Etc.*)

DAN (*Desperately*): Well, sir. You see, it's like this—(*Stalling*) There's a very strong wind today, and it's blowing directly from Little Bog Swamp.

MR. EDWARDS: Actually, the wind today is very light, and it happens to be blowing from the east. (*To* STUDENTS) I don't believe I need to say more. I think the situation is pretty clear.

PETE (*Nodding vigorously*): It sure is! I see the whole thing now! (STUDENTS *murmur assent.*)

MR. EDWARDS: Your Watchdog Committee spotted a real and important problem—and they tried to solve it in a very illogical way. Dan, Mary Lou, Brian, go back to your committee room now and take those signs with you. I'll come down to talk with you shortly. (*Dejectedly,* DAN, MARY LOU, *and* BRIAN *start to exit, dragging signs behind them.*)

PETE (*Calling out*): Enough's enough—Dan's too much! (*Others take up chant as curtain closes.*)

* * * * *

SCENE 3

SETTING: *The same as Scene 1.*

AT RISE: DAN, MARY LOU, *and* BRIAN *enter gloomily, and sit at table.*

DAN (*Striking table with fist*): Mr. Edwards just doesn't play fair!

BRIAN: He saw through your plan as if you'd written it out and given him a copy.

MARY LOU (*Sarcastically*): What do we do now, most resourceful leader?

DAN (*Crossly*): Quiet, both of you. I have to think of a way that I can retreat and still save face.

MARY LOU: Just don't forget about us, Dan. We were the ones that were right behind you with those signs.

BRIAN: Yeah, that's right. You took advantage of an ignorant, defenseless, naïve freshman—namely me.

DAN (*Irritably*): Be quiet, so I can think.

MARY LOU: Why don't we just face the music and admit we were wrong?

DAN: That's the coward's way out. Besides, it's against my principles.

BRIAN: Mr. Edwards is your principal—ha! ha!

DAN (*Glaring at* BRIAN): Typical freshman humor. (*Gets up from table and paces around, musing*) Maybe I could tell Mr. Edwards I'm interested in ecology, and that's why I collected those flies.

MARY LOU: And then you can explain how ecology got the flies into the pudding. (MRS. O'HARA, MRS. MOORE, *and* MRS. JOHNSON *enter, each carrying a wooden spoon.*)

MRS. O'HARA (*Pointing at* DAN *threateningly with spoon*): That's the ringleader! He's the one who ruined our pudding! (DAN *dodges behind table, and* BRIAN *and* MARY LOU *cower.*)

MRS. MOORE: That's him, all right. Him and his signs and fancy slogans! Rabble-rouser! Just let me at him.

MRS. JOHNSON: We'll tell him about our rights!

MRS. O'HARA: You think you're the only ones with rights— like the right to put flies in food. (*Waves spoon angrily*)

DAN (*Nervously*): Ladies, please. Put down those—those weapons, before somebody gets hurt. Like maybe me.

MRS. MOORE (*Waving spoon*): No maybes about it. When we're through with you, you'll really have something to protest about! And don't think we don't have plenty of support!

MRS. JOHNSON: Like a couple of hundred hungry kids who won't get anything to eat until we reopen the cafeteria.

DAN: But that—that's unfair!

MRS. MOORE (*Indignantly*): Unfair, he says!

MRS. O'HARA: We closed it down for health reasons, that's what. Can't be selling food with flies in it, now can we?

DAN (*Desperately*): There won't be any more flies. I promise. The wind has shifted. Look, where's your sense of humor?

MRS. MOORE: Oh, now we have no sense of humor, ladies. Did you ever hear of anything so funny—ha-ha—putting flies in our rice pudding?

MRS. JOHNSON: Come on. It's no use talking to him. I can tell he's not one bit sorry for what he did. Now it's our turn to protest. Dottie, go get the signs. (MRS. MOORE *exits*.) Now you'll see some protesting, because we really have something to complain about! (MRS. MOORE *reenters with signs reading:* ADULTS HAVE RIGHTS; NO LUNCH, NO JOKE; COOKS PROTEST. *Each woman takes one. They parade around stage, then march off.*)

DAN (*Starting after them*): Wait, please. You don't understand—oh, what's the use?

MARY LOU: You just can't admit we were wrong, can you, Dan? Honestly, I think that's what's the matter with the world today. Nobody can back down when they're wrong—kids and grownups both.

DAN (*Crossly*): I don't need any moralizing from you. And I don't think we were wrong. The cafeteria is a problem, isn't it?

MARY LOU: Sure it is. But I think Tanya was right. There has to be a better way. (TANYA *enters*.)

DAN (*To* TANYA): Don't say it! I don't want to hear a word from you. No I-told-you-so's.

TANYA: I don't have to say a word. Mr. Edwards is on his way, and he'll say it a lot better than I could.

DAN: The moment of truth! (*Melodramatically*) Here goes Dan Wilkins on a week's unexpected vacation.

BRIAN: That probably goes for all of us. (MR. EDWARDS *enters*.)

MR. EDWARDS: I got down here just as soon as I could. I was afraid you'd hatch some hideous new scheme if I was delayed.

DAN (*Coming forward*): Go ahead, Mr. Edwards. (*Holds his hands out*) Put on the handcuffs. I'm resigned to my fate.

MR. EDWARDS (*Wryly*): Judging from your tone, Dan, I'd say you weren't resigned to anything. And that's really too bad. I thought that somehow I might have reached you when I spoke in the cafeteria.

DAN: Sure you reached me, Mr. Edwards. The next time I'll use another species of fly. (*Guffaws*)

MR. EDWARDS (*Sternly*): I thought you might have noticed that most of the students weren't impressed with your scheme.

DAN (*Airily*): Oh, I think they'll come around.

MR. EDWARDS: I wouldn't count on that. You see, Dan, the next lunch shift has arrived in the cafeteria, and they are very, *very* hungry. And when they heard why the cafeteria was closed—well, I don't think they were too pleased with you and your Watchdog Committee.

BRIAN: Won't the cooks open the cafeteria?

MR. EDWARDS: No, they're picketing with their own protest signs.

DAN: Couldn't you make them stop?

MR. EDWARDS: That wouldn't be very democratic, would it? They have a right to protest, just the same as you do.

DAN: Then you admit what we did was O.K.?

MR. EDWARDS: I didn't say that. I said you have rights. Everyone has rights. How you use them is another question.

MARY LOU: Then, you're questioning our methods, Mr. Edwards.

MR. EDWARDS: Exactly. Right now I'm interested in whether you've learned anything constructive from what has happened. Have you?

DAN (*Impertinently*): Yes, sir. I have. I've learned never to prepare picket signs in advance and to gather only local flies.

MR. EDWARDS: Dan, can we talk seriously for *once?* Just once? Sit down—all of you. (*They take chairs.*) Now. The easiest thing for me to do is suspend all of you for a week, and let it go at that. But I'm more interested in making sure that you learn something from this experience.

DAN: I'm sorry, Mr. Edwards, but I just can't agree with you that we were wrong. The cafeteria situation is deplorable.

MR. EDWARDS: I agree. It *is* deplorable.

DAN (*Taken aback*): Then, you agree we had every right to protest?

MR. EDWARDS: I already said you had the *right* to protest, but against *whom?*

DAN: The system, of course, the establishment . . .

MR. EDWARDS: Let me ask a few questions. (*Pause*) Question number one: Why are the hot lunches often cold?

DAN: Probably because the ladies don't care. Or maybe they're lazy.

MR. EDWARDS: Wrong. The correct answer is: The steam tables are twenty-five years old, and they're continually breaking down. Now, question number two: Why do they run out of food for the last lunch shift?

DAN (*Confidently*): That's easy. Poor planning. Somebody doesn't figure well.

MR. EDWARDS: Wrong again. There hasn't been a new stove, mixer, oven, or blender purchased in the past fifteen years. In that time, our school population has doubled. Question number three: Why are the lines so long?

DAN (*Squirming*): Maybe for the reasons you already gave?

MR. EDWARDS: Partly. But in addition, let me say that there are only three cafeteria workers to take care of 1,000 students. That's the same number of workers we had ten years ago. (*Pause*) And now—aside from the health issues, which I won't even address—the most important question: Can you tell me how putting flies in the rice pudding called attention to the real issues?

DAN (*Embarrassed*): It didn't, I guess.

MR. EDWARDS: In fact, it was directed against the very people who are working overtime to try to improve the situation.

DAN (*Uncomfortably*): I see that now.

MR. EDWARDS: How long do you think we've been petitioning the Board of Education for new equipment and more cafeteria staff?

DAN: A long time, I guess.

MR. EDWARDS: For five years. And each year they're cut from the budget. (*Sighs*) So, we continue to make do.

MARY LOU: I never realized it was like that. I just assumed it was carelessness or plain negligence. I guess we didn't think it through.

BRIAN: It all seemed so logical at the time. Almost, anyway.

DAN: I'm the one who's really to blame, Mr. Edwards. The flies and the protest signs were my idea. (*To others*) I don't know about the rest of you, but I'm going to write a letter of apology to Mrs. O'Hara and the other cafeteria workers. If I'd only known how hard things were for them, I'd never have used the methods I did.

MR. EDWARDS: That's the point I'm trying to make, Dan. Protests are a legitimate American method of calling attention to problems. But the protesters must always realize that they have a very powerful weapon in their hands. They must be sure they know all the facts, and that they are aiming their protest against the right people. And they should be sure they won't cause more problems than they solve.

DAN: Yes. I see that now.

MR. EDWARDS: If you really mean it, Dan—and all of you— then I'm satisfied.

BRIAN (*Hopefully*): You mean—no week's vacation, all by ourselves?

MR. EDWARDS: Right. Instead of a week out of school, I'm assigning you three to a week in the cafeteria. You'll work during your activity periods helping the lunch staff. It may give you a chance to learn what the problems really are.

DAN: That seems fair, Mr. Edwards.

MARY LOU: Thank you, Mr. Edwards.

MR. EDWARDS (*Wryly*): Even in school, there are many ways of learning.

BRIAN: Can the Watchdog Committee continue to function?

MR. EDWARDS: Of course. We need a committee like this so there's communication between the student body and the— er—establishment.

DAN: Then I suggest we continue our meeting right now and study the lunchroom problem in greater depth.

MR. EDWARDS: A very good idea. (*Exits*)

DAN: Well, that didn't turn out so bad after all, did it?

TANYA: Not after you finally admitted that you were wrong.

MARY LOU: He wasn't the only one. It was our fault as well as Dan's. I should have put a stop to it, but I thought it was exciting.

TANYA: And I should have done something besides walking out, too.

DAN: Well, now that the Mutual Condolence Society has finished weeping on one another's shoulders, shall we get down to business? (*All turn to* DAN.) I now call the Big Valley High School Watchdog Committee back into session. Our first order of business is to draft a letter of apology to the cafeteria workers which we will all sign. All in favor?

OTHERS (*In unison*): Aye.

DAN: Our next piece of business is to consider suggestions for dealing with the lunchroom situation. Do I hear any? (*Long silence, as* DAN *looks from one to another.*) Well, how about sending an avalanche of anonymous letters to the Board of Education?

TANYA (*Exasperated*): Dan! Haven't you learned anything?

DAN: Then how about buying all the equipment the cafeteria needs and sending the bill to the Board of Education?

OTHERS (*In unison*): *Dan!*

DAN: No good?

MARY LOU: You know it! (DAN *thinks deeply for a moment. Others look anxious.* DAN *suddenly snaps his fingers and smiles.*)

DAN: Say! How about writing up a petition protesting conditions in the cafeteria, circulating it among the student body, and then sending it to the Board of Education? And a letter home to our parents, too?

TANYA (*Sighing in relief*): Now you're talking! (*All smile and shake hands. Curtain*)

THE END

Production Notes

SHOO FLY PUDDING

Characters: 6 male; 5 female; male or female for Drummer; male and female extras for Students.

Playing Time: 30 minutes.

Costumes: Modern dress for students. White kitchen uniforms, hair nets, and aprons for cafeteria workers. Suit and tie for Mr. Edwards.

Properties: Brief case and papers; protest signs that read: RAISINS YES—FLIES NO; NO MEAT IN OUR DESSERTS; STUDENTS UPRISE AGAINST FLIES; ADULTS HAVE RIGHTS; NO LUNCH, NO JOKE; COOKS PROTEST; envelope with "flies"; three large wooden spoons; drum.

Setting: Scenes 1 and 3: A conference room in Big Valley High School. Table, center stage, with several chairs around it, perhaps a pitcher and glasses. Scene 2: A section of the cafeteria with several rows of long tables and folding chairs, or benches. A menu sign hangs on rear wall, listing RICE PUDDING. Cafeteria trays, dishes and food are on tables, including small dishes of pudding. Section of serving line may be shown.

Lighting: No special effects.

Middle and Lower Grades

✦Face Value

by *Christina Hamlett*

Brave Sir Steven discovers the answer to the most puzzling riddle of all . . . .

Characters

THREE NARRATORS
FOUR PEASANTS
SIR STEVEN, *a knight*
NINIAN, *his squire*
BRAGGENWULFF, *a wizard*
ROXILAINE, *a mysterious hag*

SCENE 1

TIME: *Long ago.*
SETTING: *A pleasant kingdom. Painted backdrop of castle on a hill in background and rolling green meadows in foreground.*
AT RISE: THREE NARRATORS *enter, wearing troubadour costumes, and stand down center.*
1ST NARRATOR: Once upon a time in a land of castles and dragons, there stood a kingdom whose valleys were always green, its weather always perfect, and its subjects blissfully content.
2ND NARRATOR: And in this kingdom were assembled the highest order of wizards and the finest circle of knights to keep it safe.
3RD NARRATOR: If there was a single knight admired most for his valor and honesty, it would be our hero, Sir Steven. (NARRATORS *move aside and stand down right as* FOUR PEASANTS *enter, chattering excitedly.*)

185

1ST PEASANT: He made short work of that last dragon, with only two swipes of his sword!

2ND PEASANT: And did you hear that he swam against the fiercest current to save the miller's son?

3RD PEASANT: With no thought of danger to himself! (PEASANTS *ad lib admiration as* SIR STEVEN *enters. He waves greetings to* PEASANTS.)

SIR STEVEN (*Modestly*): Really, it was nothing. Anyone else would have done the same.

1ST NARRATOR: There came a day, however, when Sir Steven's mettle was put to the most difficult test. He had to make a journey that was to take him through an enchanted forest. (NINIAN *enters, carrying two stick horses.*)

SIR STEVEN (*Indicating* NINIAN): Ah, here is my squire with my horse. We must be off if we are going to make it through the forest and back in the daylight.

4TH PEASANT: Shouldn't you take another route, Sir Steven?

2ND PEASANT: We fear for your safety!

SIR STEVEN (*Soothingly*): Dear friends, it is only a forest. Just trees and flowers and rocks . . .

3RD PEASANT: And evil, Sir Steven. No one's ever come back.

SIR STEVEN: And why would that be?

1ST PEASANT: It's a curse even to talk about it, Sir Steven.

4TH PEASANT: They say *he* lives there. (*Lowers his voice*) Braggenwulff. (NINIAN *gasps.*)

SIR STEVEN (*With curiosity*): Braggenwulff, the wizard?

3RD PEASANT (*Flustered*): Sh-h-h! You mustn't speak his name so loudly. It's dangerous.

NINIAN (*Uneasily*): Perhaps they have a point, good sir. Couldn't we consider another path?

SIR STEVEN: Come now, Ninian. It is the shortest route between our kingdom and our destination. We'll go through the forest and be back by supper, none the worse for the journey. (SIR STEVEN *and* NINIAN *mount horses and exit right as* PEASANTS *wave goodbye. Blackout, as backdrop is changed to that of the enchanted forest, depicting the eerie eyes of forest animals peering from huge, gnarled trees. Spotlight on* NARRATORS, *down right.*)

1ST NARRATOR: How the evil wizard, Braggenwulff, came to enchant the forest was the source of much gossip in the kingdom.

2ND NARRATOR: It is said that the King had insulted Braggenwulff by refusing to invite him into his royal order of wizards. Infuriated, Braggenwulff stormed into the woods to carry out his revenge, proclaiming the kingdom would suffer for the insult.

3RD NARRATOR: Brave Sir Steven, however, was not one to let such matters stand in his way. (NARRATORS *exit. Lights up as* SIR STEVEN *and* NINIAN *enter right on stick horses.*)

NINIAN (*Tremulously*): It grows dark, Sir Steven, and I don't like the looks of this forest.

SIR STEVEN (*Calmly*): It's only a forest, Ninian, and just like any other. You're letting your imagination run wild. (*Roar of thunder is heard.*)

NINIAN (*Nervously*): What was that?

SIR STEVEN: Just a storm, Ninian. It will pass soon enough.

NINIAN (*Pointing off; alarmed*): Look! Over there!

SIR STEVEN (*Looking off*): Come now, Ninian. It is only the shadow of our horses. (*Screeching sound is heard.*)

NINIAN (*In surprise*): Ah-h! Watch out!

SIR STEVEN (*Chuckling*): It's just an owl, Ninian, probably more frightened of us than we are of it.

NINIAN (*Pointing off nervously*): Then what about *him*? (*Crash of thunder is heard, as* BRAGGENWULFF *enters. He is hunched over, has huge ears, warts on face, and wears rumpled black cape covered with half-moons and stars.* NINIAN *rears back, terrified.*) It's the wizard, Sir. Braggenwulff! (*More thunder*)

SIR STEVEN (*Quietly*): We mustn't show our fear, Ninian. After all, we've done nothing to offend him. Perhaps he'll let us pass.

BRAGGENWULFF (*Roaring*): Who goes there?

SIR STEVEN (*Clearing his throat*): Sir Steven, and my trusted squire, Ninian. (NINIAN *cowers behind him.*)

BRAGGENWULFF: And from what kingdom do you come?

SIR STEVEN (*Fondly*): The kingdom of green valleys, perfect

weather, and blissful contentment. (*Kindly*) We are on a journey of peace.

BRAGGENWULFF (*Angrily*): There is no peace for any citizen
of that realm. You shall die! (*More thunder*)

NINIAN (*Drawing back; terrified*): Oh, no!

SIR STEVEN (*Boldly*): And for what offense, wizard?

BRAGGENWULFF: For trespassing in my forest!

SIR STEVEN (*Calmly*): Sir, I question any claim you might have
to this forest, short of the right to enjoy it, though perhaps
you might tell us what sort of toll would guarantee our safe
passage?

BRAGGENWULFF (*Furiously*): Nothing short of your very
lives!

NINIAN (*Under his breath, to* SIR STEVEN): I *told* you we
should have taken that path.

SIR STEVEN (*Pleasantly*): Now certainly, wizard, a man as reasonable as you can see that such a payment well exceeds the
right to pass through the forest. Perhaps we might compromise.

BRAGGENWULFF (*Scornfully*): Compromise? Why should I?
It is you who are trespassing, not I.

SIR STEVEN: Why, in the spirit of fairness, of course. Perhaps
we might settle this with a wager, a test of skill, a riddle . . .

BRAGGENWULFF (*Intrigued*): A riddle, hm-m-m. Very well,
let me see . . .

NINIAN (*Under his breath*): You can't trust him, Sir Steven.
The man's a wizard!

BRAGGENWULFF (*Craftily*): I have it! Answer this riddle, and
I shall allow you and your squire to go free.

SIR STEVEN: And what of future knights who pass this way?
Will you grant them safe passage as well?

BRAGGENWULFF (*Offended*): Of course not! How dare you
make such a demand!

SIR STEVEN: It is a reasonable one, I think. If I can answer
the riddle correctly, you must give me your word that others
will come to no harm in this forest.

BRAGGENWULFF (*Laughing evilly*): Oh, you have my word
on it.

NINIAN (*Stepping forward*): What are you laughing about?

BRAGGENWULFF: I am laughing, squire, because the riddle is impossible to answer.

SIR STEVEN (*Firmly*): Ask your riddle, then.

BRAGGENWULFF (*Pausing; then slyly*): What do women want? (*Crash of thunder is heard.*)

SIR STEVEN (*Puzzled*): What do women want? Is that the riddle?

BRAGGENWULFF: You shall have until the sun rises to find the answer. If when I return you cannot answer it correctly, you shall pay with your lives. (*Laughs evilly as he exits*)

SIR STEVEN (*Pondering*): Hm-m-m. What do women want?

NINIAN (*Shaking his head*): It's a ridiculous riddle if you ask me, sir. Why, the maidens in our own kingdom are content enough with sweets and flowers and dancing! Why should he think it's impossible to answer?

SIR STEVEN (*Seriously*): Because, Ninian, I'm afraid the answer to his riddle goes much deeper than that.

NINIAN: What, then, is the answer?

SIR STEVEN: Regrettably, Ninian, I don't know. It's a question that men have pondered long before our own kingdom ever came into being.

NINIAN (*Panicked*): But there *has* to be an answer, Sir Steven! And we have to discover what it is by dawn or pay with our lives! (ROXILAINE *enters unnoticed, wearing hooded cloak. Her hood is off, revealing greatly disheveled silver hair. She has a long, hooked nose and walks stooped over a gnarled cane.*)

ROXILAINE (*In croaking voice*): Perhaps *I* might help you. (SIR STEVEN *and* NINIAN *turn, startled, and stare at her in amazement.*)

SIR STEVEN: Did you address us, my good woman?

NINIAN (*Aside*): Careful, Sir Steven, she might be a witch!

ROXILAINE: Yes, I could not help but overhear your conversation with the wizard.

NINIAN (*To* SIR STEVEN): Don't listen to her. She probably works for Braggenwulff.

ROXILAINE: That could not be farther from the truth, sir. For ten years past, I have been a prisoner in this forest, and I have seen many knights meet their death at his hands.

SIR STEVEN: And have you tried to save them as well?

ROXILAINE: You are the first, sir, to whom a riddle has been posed for which I know the answer. That answer will win your freedom.

NINIAN (*Anxiously*): Then will you tell us what it is?

ROXILAINE: Not just yet, squire, for my own answer does not come without a price.

NINIAN (*Annoyed*): I *knew* there was a trick to it, sir.

SIR STEVEN (*To* NINIAN): It is a foolish person, Ninian, who expects something for nothing. (*To* ROXILAINE) Name your price, good woman, and I'll do all in my power to grant it.

ROXILAINE: It is a simple thing, Sir Steven, but one that may distress you.

SIR STEVEN: Whatever it is, I will keep my word to you as a knight of the realm.

NINIAN: Don't you think you'd better hear what she wants first, sir?

ROXILAINE: In exchange for the correct answer, Sir Steven, I would like you to take me back to your kingdom when you leave this forest.

SIR STEVEN (*Quickly*): Done! My king will want to meet you to thank you personally for your deed.

ROXILAINE: You spoke in haste, sir. I hadn't finished my request of you.

SIR STEVEN (*Bowing slightly*): One thousand pardons. Please continue.

ROXILAINE: Have you a sweetheart who waits for you? A bride who wears your ring?

SIR STEVEN: None, my lady, never having found the one with whom I wished to spend the rest of my days.

ROXILAINE (*Happily*): Then you must take *me* as your wife within three days of our return.

NINIAN (*Aside*): If you take that old crone back and marry her, you'll be the laughing stock of the kingdom.

SIR STEVEN (*Uncomfortably*): Certainly there must be some-

thing else you would accept instead, my good woman. Fine
clothes? Jewelry? Your own castle and servants?

ROXILAINE (*Insistently*): I have told you what I require, Sir
Steven. Nothing less will do. (NINIAN *sighs heavily.*)

SIR STEVEN: Very well, I accept your bargain.

NINIAN (*Shocked*): Sir Steven! How can you even dream of
such a thing! Why, any maiden in the village would gladly be
your bride!

SIR STEVEN (*Firmly*): I have decided, Ninian. And I shall keep
my promise.

ROXILAINE: Thank you, sir. Now, lean close and I shall whisper the answer that the wizard seeks. (SIR STEVEN *leans
close to her and she whispers to him. Blackout to indicate the
passage of time, during which* ROXILAINE *exits and* BRAG-
GENWULFF *enters. When lights come up* SIR STEVEN, NIN-
IAN, *and* BRAGGENWULFF *are in heated discussion.*)

BRAGGENWULFF (*Angrily*): Curses! That old hag gave you
the answer, didn't she? You've cheated!

SIR STEVEN: I have played fairly, wizard. The conditions were
only that I give you the answer, not that I discover the answer
on my own.

BRAGGENWULFF (*Grumbling*): I am a wizard of his word. Sir
Steven, you and your squire shall go free, and all who venture
this way in the future shall find safe passage. (SIR STEVEN
and NINIAN *exit left as he exits right, grumbling as he
goes. Curtain*)

* * * * *

SCENE 2

TIME: *A short while later.*

BEFORE RISE: SIR STEVEN *and* NINIAN *enter left on horse-
back, conversing as they ride.*

NINIAN (*Impatiently*): You'd think if she was coming with us,
she would have shown up by now.

SIR STEVEN (*Pointing right*): I think I see her waiting on the
path just ahead. (ROXILAINE *enters right.*)

NINIAN (*Hopefully*): Perhaps if we ride quickly and pretend not to see her, she won't be able to catch up.

SIR STEVEN (*Firmly*): No, Ninian. I gave her my word as a knight of the realm, and I shall honor it. (*They approach* ROXILAINE.)

ROXILAINE: I see the wizard has granted your freedom, Sir Steven.

SIR STEVEN: My gratitude to you for that, my good woman. (*Dismounts his stick horse and offers it to her*) It is a long journey back to our kingdom, my lady. I shall not have my bride making that journey on foot.

ROXILAINE (*Accepting horse*): You are most kind, Sir Steven. (*They exit right*.)

* * *

TIME: *A short time later.*

SETTING: *The kingdom. Backdrop of castle as in Scene 1.*

AT RISE: PEASANTS *enter left, excitedly pointing right, as* SIR STEVEN *walks on, followed by* NINIAN *and* ROXILAINE *on horses.* ROXILAINE's *hood covers her head.*

PEASANTS (*Rushing to meet them, ad libbing greetings*): Welcome home, sir! The bravest of all knights! Thank goodness you're safe! (*Etc. Suddenly,* ROXILAINE *throws back her hood and* PEASANTS *gasp in horror and back away*.)

NINIAN (*To* SIR STEVEN): Couldn't you just have the king throw her in the dungeon, sir? See how the very sight of her frightens the peasants?

SIR STEVEN (*Firmly*): Enough, Ninian. You speak unkindly of my betrothed and I'll hear no more of it. (*He offers his hand to* ROXILAINE, *as she dismounts her stick horse.* NINIAN *takes horse*.) Come, my lady. We are home. (*He escorts her off left.* NINIAN *follows dejectedly. Curtain*)

* * * * *

SCENE 3

TIME: *The night of the wedding.*

BEFORE RISE: NARRATORS *enter and stand down right.*

1ST NARRATOR: Three days later, there was great feasting in the kingdom to celebrate Sir Steven's marriage to the old crone.

2ND NARRATOR: No one could understand why a man as handsome and brave as Sir Steven would take for his bride so ugly a creature as the woman from the enchanted forest. (NARRATORS *remain down right*.)

* * *

SETTING: *Sir Steven's bedchamber. Backdrop may be black. There is a chair down right, and a settee down center.*

AT RISE: SIR STEVEN *sits alone.*

SIR STEVEN (*Sighing, to himself*): What have I done? Was it really the wise thing to do? (*Suddenly, he looks up in astonishment as* ROXILAINE, *now a beautiful woman, enters left. She wears flowing white gown and has long silver hair.* SIR STEVEN *jumps to his feet.*)

ROXILAINE (*Standing before him*): Sir Steven, my husband.

SIR STEVEN (*In amazement*): What sorcery is this? Could you be the old woman that I married?

ROXILAINE: She and I are the same, Sir Steven. Braggenwulff's sorcery made me into an old hag. He forbade me ever to mention it until I had one day been taken as a bride. (*Curtseying*) Because of your goodness, I am now my true self. My name is Roxilaine.

SIR STEVEN (*Delighted*): Roxilaine! A fitting name for my beautiful wife. (*Takes her hands, gazes at her.* ROXILAINE *smiles sadly.*) Something is troubling you, my love.

ROXILAINE: The spell is not yet broken, sir, for there still remains a choice that you must make.

SIR STEVEN: A choice? I don't understand.

ROXILAINE: What you see before you, gentle knight, is the way I looked before the wizard's evil spell.

SIR STEVEN: But isn't that spell broken?

ROXILAINE (*Tearfully*): I am doomed, Sir Steven, to live half my days as the crone you first met, and half as the lady you see before you now.

SIR STEVEN: Half your days? But which half?

ROXILAINE (*Miserably*): You must choose, my love, whether you wish for me to look as I do now when we are alone and to show my face as the crone's when we are among others. Or whether you wish to present me to the world as your beautiful wife . . . and to see me as an old crone each night. (SIR STEVEN *pulls her into his arms.*)

SIR STEVEN (*Groaning*): I would rather slay a dozen dragons than answer a question such as this.

ROXILAINE: Come, my love. We will rest, and in the morning, you must tell me your answer. (*Lights dim as she walks to settee and lies down on it.* SIR STEVEN *sits on floor beside it, gazing at her.*)

3RD NARRATOR: It was an agonizing night for Sir Steven, and sleep did not come easily to him.

2ND NARRATOR: As he gazed upon fair Roxilaine in the moonlight and remembered her kindness in Braggenwulff's forest, he realized that the answer he sought could be found in the very riddle she herself had answered for him. (*Lights fade to black, then come up on* ROXILAINE, *sitting on settee, and watching* SIR STEVEN, *now asleep on the floor.* ROXILAINE *is once again dressed as old hag.* [*See Production Notes.*] *Her hood is raised to hide her face from audience.* SIR STEVEN *awakens.*)

ROXILAINE (*In croaking voice*): What have you decided, Sir Steven? How shall I look to the world, and to you? (SIR STEVEN *takes her hand and looks into her eyes.*)

SIR STEVEN (*Compassionately*): For many years, my lady, you've lived with a horrible curse. And yet in spite of the frightening reflection you saw in the lakes and ponds of that accursed forest, it did not change the kindness in your heart or your goodness to strangers.

ROXILAINE: Your words are sweet, but they puzzle me.

SIR STEVEN: My answer is the only one I can give, Lady Roxilaine. I must defer to whatever it is that *you* wish for yourself, and I shall be content with that choice. As much as I adore the beautiful face I saw last night, it is your soul I have come to love the most. (*A great rush of wind is heard, followed by*

a flickering of lights and a brief blackout. During blackout,
ROXILAINE *throws off her cloak, and when lights come up,*
she is wearing white gown and long silver hair. SIR STEVEN
gasps and stares at her in wonder.)

ROXILAINE (*Happily*): Oh, Sir Steven, you have broken the
wizard's curse for good!

SIR STEVEN (*Confused*): Can this be? What have I done?

ROXILAINE: You have allowed the answer to the riddle to
guide your own heart, and in doing so, you have set me free.

SIR STEVEN (*Wondrously*): It is true, then. That what women
want—indeed, what anyone wants—is the freedom to make
her own choices . . . and to be loved for whatever those choices
may be.

ROXILAINE: And in that choosing, there shall never be anything less than the happiest ending for all. (*They kiss.*
Curtain)

THE END

Production Notes

FACE VALUE

Characters: 2 male; 1 female; 8 male or female for Narrators, Peasants, and Braggenwulff.

Playing Time: 25 minutes.

Costumes: Medieval troubadour costumes for Narrators. Ornate tunic and tights for Sir Steven, plain tunic and tights for Ninian. When dressed as old hag, Roxilaine wears frizzy silver wig, hooked nose piece, and black cloak with hood big enough to cover her face, as indicated in text. When dressed as beautiful lady, she wears flowing white dressing gown and long silver wig. During first blackout in Scene 4, she puts on hag's cloak and hood over dress, then removes cloak during second blackout. Cloak may be stored behind settee for easy access. Braggenwulff is dressed as an ugly wizard, with warts, large ears, and a dark cape decorated with half-moons and stars.

Properties: Stick horses, gnarled cane.

Setting: Scene 1: Pleasant kingdom, as depicted on painted backdrop. Castle on hill is in background, with rolling green meadows in foreground. Setting changes to enchanted forest, as depicted on painted backdrop. Huge, gnarled trees and the glowing eyes of forest animals may be shown. Scene 2: First part of scene is played before curtain, which opens on pleasant kingdom, as in Scene 1. Scene 3: Sir Steven's bedchamber. There is a black backdrop. A chair is up right, and a settee is down center.

Lighting: Spotlight, dimming, and blackouts, as noted in text.

Sound: Thunder, screech of owl, rush of wind, as noted in text.

❧Pied Piper's Land

by E. Blanche Norcross

What ever happened to the lost children of Hamelin? . . .

Characters

HELGA
KARL
STEFAN
CHRISTOPHER
JOHANN   } *children of Hamelin, various ages*
KRISTI
MELINDA
ANNA
PETERKIN
OTHER CHILDREN, *extras*
MAYOR
TWO ALDERMEN
TWO BURGHERS
PIED PIPER
ARAMINDA, *a wicked witch*

SCENE 1

TIME: *July 22, 1376.*

SETTING: *Town square of Hamelin. There is a round well house in center of square with a visible rope and bucket hanging inside. Backdrop depicts fronts of medieval houses, with usable steps in front of house right. Town Hall with working door is center.*

AT RISE: HELGA, CHRISTOPHER, JOHANN, KRISTI, ME-LINDA, ANNA, PETERKIN, *who is lame, and* OTHER

197

CHILDREN *are around well, holding pails.* HELGA *is filling her pail from bucket.* KARL *and* STEFAN *enter left,* STEFAN *carrying two fishing rods.* KARL *is holding a pipe (recorder) or small flute to his lips, pretending to play it.*

KARL: Toot-toot, toot-a-toot, toot! (*He skips around group at well.*)

HELGA (*Disapprovingly*): Why are you so cheerful, Karl? What is there to be happy about when we have so much trouble here in Hamelin town? Rats—a plague of them—everywhere we go.

KRISTI: I don't know why they aren't nipping at our heels, even here.

KARL (*Snatching two pails and banging them together*): Hear ye! Hear ye! Good news! Everybody listen! (*Children turn to him and fall silent.*) The best thing that's ever happened in Hamelin happened this morning! Stefan and I saw it! (*Pauses*)

HELGA (*Impatiently*): Well, what was it?

KARL: Just this, Helga. We started out early to go fishing— and we saw an odd man come into the square. He was wearing a long cloak, half yellow, half red, and he was holding a long pipe. He started to play the strangest music you ever heard.

STEFAN (*Eagerly*): And the rats came tumbling out of the houses—big rats, small rats, lean rats, fat rats—grave old plodders, gay young friskers—

KARL: Fathers, mothers, families by tens and dozens, and all of them followed the Piper as he played. We followed them right to the River Weser.

STEFAN: And there we saw the rats plunge into the water and perish.

KRISTI (*Excitedly*): The rats—gone! It's too good to believe. Imagine Hamelin without any rats! They fought the dogs and killed the cats and bit the babies in their cradles . . .

KARL: S-sh! Listen! There's the Piper's music now! (*Sound of a pipe playing is heard from back of auditorium.*)

CHRISTOPHER: I can't see him. (*They run to house at right, and* CHRISTOPHER *and* KARL *climb to top step, peering over audience. Other children also stand on steps, peering into audience. Sound of the pipe gets louder, and* PIPER *comes down the center aisle through the audience, with a skipping step, piping a tune.* MAYOR *and* TWO ALDERMEN *enter from Town Hall. All watch and listen with amazement.*)

1ST ALDERMAN: That looks like the beggar we talked to yesterday.

MAYOR: Well, if it is, we shall get rid of him quickly.

1ST ALDERMAN (*With a laugh*): Yes, as quickly as he got rid of the rats.

2ND ALDERMAN: *If* he got rid of them . . .

MAYOR: Oh, he got rid of them, all right. My house used to be quite overrun, and I didn't hear even a scratch of one this morning.

PIPER (*Going to stage, addressing men*): Good morning, masters. I have done the job I promised—there's not a rat left in Hamelin town. So, give me my thousand guilders, please. (*Holds out hand*)

1ST ALDERMAN (*Scornfully*): A thousand guilders! Did you hear that? He wants a thousand guilders for getting rid of a few rats! (MAYOR *and* ALDERMEN *laugh.*)

MAYOR (*To* PIPER): Do you take us for fools? A thousand guilders to a wandering piper with a coat of red and yellow? You are joking, of course. But we'll be fair with you. You have rid us of the rats, so I'll give you fifty guilders. (*He pulls out coins and offers them to* PIPER.)

PIPER (*Angrily*): I am no bargain-driver. I'll not take a penny less than you promised me. (*In threatening tone*) Be warned! Folks who put me in a passion will find me pipe to a different fashion!

MAYOR (*Raising voice*): You dare to threaten us, fellow? Do your worst! Blow your pipe there till you burst! (*He throws coins at* PIPER, *then he and* ALDERMEN *exit left.* PIPER *stalks off, right, ignoring the coins.* CHILDREN *chatter quietly, dejected. Sound of pipe is heard from off, softly.* PIPER *reenters right, crosses slowly to well, and sits on edge, piping.* CHILDREN *move to* PIPER. *They listen to music in growing enchantment, in a semicircle around* PIPER, *who ignores them.*)

PIPER (*Holding pipe in front of him*): Well, little pipe, I told the aldermen I would punish all Hamelin for cheating me, but these are good children—I don't want to punish them, too. It wouldn't be right, though, to let them grow up here and learn to be deceitful like their parents. (*Muses briefly*) Hm-m. Perhaps there's a way to punish the town of Hamelin—but save the children. (*He jumps up.*) Now, my little pipe, it is your turn. (*He starts piping again, circling the well, and* CHILDREN *rise and fall in behind him, moving as if in a trance. Curtains close. Music continues.*)

* * * * *

SCENE 2

SETTING: *House fronts and well have been removed revealing a backdrop of trees and grass. There is a large boulder down right.*

AT RISE: PIPER *enters left, playing faster music.* CHILDREN *follow, skipping, smiling, and laughing.* PIPER *leads them across stage and off, right, but* PETERKIN, *limping, is left behind. He tries to keep up, then stops.*)

PETERKIN (*Upset*): Wait! Wait for me! (KRISTI *runs back to him.*)

KRISTI: I'll help you, Peterkin. (*She puts an arm around his shoulders and tries to lead him off with her.*)

PETERKIN: No, no. You go on, Kristi. I'll rest a bit and try to catch up later. (KRISTI *runs off right.* PETERKIN *gazes after her, then takes a few steps; alarmed*) Wait! Wait! I want to come, too! (*Music stops. Sadly*) Oh—it's too late. (PETERKIN *limps to boulder and sits, resting his head in his hands.* TWO BURGHERS *enter left.*)

1ST BURGHER: What are you doing here, my Peterkin?

2ND BURGHER: And where are all your playmates?

1ST BURGHER: We stood there like blocks of wood, unable to move a step, while the Piper's charmed music led them skipping away.

PETERKIN: It was a charm—we had to follow. And oh, Father! If you could have heard what he promised! He was leading us to a land where the fruit trees and flowers were much fairer than ours, the birds sang more sweetly, and even the sparrows were brighter than peacocks.

2ND BURGHER: But where are the children now? We must fetch them back.

PETERKIN (*Sadly*): We shall never see them again. A door opened in Koppelberg Hill and they passed through. With my lame foot, I couldn't keep up and was left behind. (*Tearfully*) Then the door shut fast, and now I'll never hear of that country again . . .

1ST BURGHER: Come, Peterkin. Come home. (*They go off left,* 1ST BURGHER *with his arm around* PETERKIN. *Curtains close.*)

* * * * *

SCENE 3

SETTING: *A clearing in a wood. There are bushes near right and left exits, and a cherry tree near center rear. Down left is a bench with a grass mat in front of it.*

AT RISE: PIPER, *playing his pipe, leads* CHILDREN *through audience and onto stage.* CHILDREN *laugh and skip gaily behind him.* PIPER *leads them across stage, then circles around to back, and stops center. He turns and faces* CHILDREN.

PIPER (*With an expansive gesture*): Boys and girls, you can rest and play here, for this morning, anyway.

KRISTI: May we go anywhere we like?

PIPER: Not quite, Kristi. You must not go beyond the river over there. (*Gesturing to back of stage*) The river is swift and dangerous. You must promise not to go near it.

CHILDREN: We promise! (*They run about, exploring.* PIPER *sits on bench.*)

ANNA: Look, Helga! Roses!

HELGA: Aren't they lovely, Anna! (KARL *pulls her hair ribbon and runs out of reach.*) Oh, Karl!

JOHANN: Let's go and see the river.

STEFAN: All right. Come on, Karl.

KARL: No, thanks. You can run around getting blisters, if you like. I'm going to sleep. (JOHANN *and* STEFAN *run off right. Others exit.* KARL *steps behind bush near right exit, stretches sleepily, then goes to sleep.*)

ARAMINDA (*Entering left, carrying scepter; angrily*) Well, Piper, what does this mean?

PIPER (*Rising, turning to her, surprised*): Araminda! The wicked witch! What brings you here?

ARAMINDA: This is my domain. What are *you* doing here?

PIPER: I am taking the children of Hamelin to Krythia before they become greedy, like their parents.

ARAMINDA (*Scornfully*): Don't waste your time, Piper. These children will grow up to be just as evil as the burghers of Hamelin.

PIPER (*Obstinately*): They will grow up to be like the Krythians—good, honest, kind-hearted people.

ARAMINDA (*Laughing meanly*): The poor naïve Piper! (*She moves to bench and sits.* PIPER *sits on grass in front of her.*) I'll make a bargain with you. I have a kingdom with no subjects. If I prove that these children are too wicked to belong in Krythia, you must give me your pipe so that I may lead them where I will.

PIPER: And what will be your part of the bargain when you lose?

ARAMINDA: If I lose, I'll give up my magic scepter and all my evil powers forever! What do you say, Piper?

PIPER (*Rising*): I trust these children, but I don't trust you, Araminda. How will you prove these children are wicked?

ARAMINDA (*Rising*): If one of these boys and girls does something cruel, I have won. If one of them lies, I have won. (*Considering*) And third—third—I know! If one of them breaks a promise, I have won! Those are my terms, Piper. Is it a bargain? Or perhaps after all you don't trust them.

PIPER (*Firmly*): I do trust them! And when you lose, there will be one less bad witch in the world. I give you until noon.

ARAMINDA: It's a bargain, Piper! (PIPER *exits left.* KARL *wakes up, rises, and walks center.*)

KARL (*To* ARAMINDA): Who are you?

ARAMINDA (*With an evil laugh*): You will learn who I am—in good time! (*She makes a sweeping gesture with her scepter in front of* KARL. *He starts back, frightened.* ARAMINDA *exits quickly.*)

KARL: Whew! She was scary! She must be a witch! I wish Kristi were here. (*Calling*) Kristi! Where are you?

KRISTI (*Entering*): Isn't it lovely here, Karl? (*Points right*) See that trail through the mountains? That's where I want to explore. Come on!

KARL: No. You go if you like, but don't go too far or that old witch will find you.

KRISTI: What old witch? Karl are you making up stories again?

KARL (*Earnestly*): No, I really think I saw a witch.

KRISTI (*Laughing*): Oh, Karl! Are you sure you don't want to explore? (*He nods.*) O.K. Bye then. (*She starts right.*)

KARL: Come back soon. (*To himself*) I'm going to find the others. (*Exits*)

MELINDA (*Running on*): Kristi! Kristi! My ribbon's untied. Fix it for me, please.

KRISTI (*Turning back*): All right, Melinda. (*She ties ribbon.*) Now, go back and play with the others. (*She starts right.*)

CHRISTOPHER (*Entering and hopping up and down trying to reach cherries on tree*): Kristi, Kristi, I can't reach these cherries. Help me! (CHILDREN *enter at rear and try unsuccessfully to reach cherries.*)

MELINDA: Kristi, come and help us! (KRISTI *hesitates.* ARAMINDA *enters left front.*)

ARAMINDA (*Under her breath*): Go on, go on, Kristi! Forget about these children.

KRISTI: Oh, dear, I'm the only one tall enough. I'll have to help. (*Crosses stage to* CHILDREN)

ARAMINDA (*Aside*): That stupid girl!

PIPER (*Entering at left; with mock sympathy*): Too bad, Araminda!

ARAMINDA: I'm not beaten yet, Piper. (*She exits left.* PIPER *remains, watching* CHILDREN. KRISTI *pantomimes picking cherries and handing them around.*)

KRISTI (*To* CHILDREN): That's enough. I'm going to explore that trail. You think of a game to play. Just don't go near the river. (*She walks right.*)

KARL: We'll play "Go, go, stop." (CHILDREN *line up and walk on command to back of stage.*) Go—go—STOP! (*Game continues.* CHILDREN *start to exit, still playing. Suddenly, JOHANN runs after KRISTI.*)

JOHANN: Kristi, Kristi, I pricked my finger!

KRISTI (*Looking at finger, crossly*): Oh, Johann, that's nothing. You're just a baby.

JOHANN (*Crying*): But it hurts! (KRISTI *turns her back.* PIPER *watches her intently.* KRISTI *turns back to* JOHANN.)

KRISTI: Don't cry, Johann. We'll tie your finger up in my handkerchief. (*Tying handkerchief*) There! How's that?

JOHANN: It's better already. (PIPER *smiles happily and exits.*) Thank you, Kristi. (*Runs off stage rear.* KRISTI *turns right once more.* CHRISTOPHER *and* STEFAN *enter rear, quarreling.*)

STEFAN: We're too far away, Christopher.

CHRISTOPHER: No, we're not. I'll bet I can hit it from here! (*He raises his hand to throw.* ARAMINDA *enters left front and smiles triumphantly.* KRISTI *turns back.*)

KRISTI: Stefan! Christopher! What are you up to?

CHRISTOPHER: There's a bird down there that has something wrong with its wing, and it can't fly.

STEFAN (*Interrupting*): And Christopher and I are having a contest to see who can hit it with a rock.

KRISTI: Oh, no! You mustn't. The poor little bird! (CHILDREN *enter.*)

CHRISTOPHER: If it can't fly, a hawk or something will get it. We might as well have some fun using it as a target.

KRISTI: Christopher, that's cruel! You mustn't do it.

CHRISTOPHER (*Defiantly*): You're not my mother, Kristi. You can't tell me what to do.

KRISTI (*Reasonably*): Look, Christopher, if you had a lame foot, would you think it was fair if a stronger boy beat you?

CHRISTOPHER (*Shrugging*): I guess not.

STEFAN (*Eagerly*): I have some crumbs in my pocket. We'll give them to the bird. (*He and* CHRISTOPHER *run off stage, rear.*)

KRISTI: The rest of you go on with your game. And do try to stay out of mischief. (CHILDREN *exit at rear.*) Oh, dear. I'm so tired, and the children are such a worry! I think I'll rest before I climb that trail. (*She lies down and sleeps.* ARAMINDA *shakes her scepter at* KRISTI.)

ARAMINDA (*Angrily*): Every time the children are on the point of doing something bad, Kristi stops them. No one has lied, no one has been cruel. I must get them all to do something bad, but what shall it be? (*With a cry of triumph*) I know! I know what to do—and Kristi shall tell them to do it—ha! ha! (*She exits left.* KRISTI *wakes up, frightened.*)

KRISTI: What was that? I feel as if something terrible had happened. (*She jumps up.*) Where is everybody? (*Calling*) Helga! Johann! Children! (CHILDREN *reenter, rear.*)

CHILDREN (*Ad lib*): What's the matter, Kristi? What's happened, Kristi? You look upset. (*Etc.*)

KRISTI: I must have had a bad dream. I thought something dreadful had happened. I'm all right now. The Piper will be back soon and will lead us on to the beautiful land beyond the mountains.

ARAMINDA (*Entering, disguised as an old woman, hobbling and leaning on scepter*): I thought I heard someone cry out. Oh, you poor, lost children! How lucky it is I have found you! I am Mother Huben.

KRISTI: We aren't lost. The Piper is coming to take us to Krythia.

ARAMINDA: While you are waiting for him, you must come to my house and have something to eat. I have some lovely chicken pies in the oven.

JOHANN *and* STEFAN: Oh, Kristi, let's go! We are hungry!

KRISTI: Is your house nearby, Mother Huben? We can't go far or we'll miss the Piper.

ARAMINDA: It's very near—just on the other side of that little stream. (*Points to river at rear*)

HELGA (*Doubtfully*): It is not a little stream—it's the river.

KRISTI: We promised the Piper we wouldn't cross the river.

ARAMINDA: That was only because he was afraid you might get hurt. I know where there are steppingstones, so I can lead you across safely. (*Coaxingly*) You are all so hungry. You must come with me and have something to eat.

CHILDREN (*Ad lib*): Oh yes, Kristi. We'll be safe. Let's go. (*Etc.*)

KRISTI (*Doubtfully*): Well, perhaps ... (*Suddenly*) No! We promised.

ARAMINDA (*Looking at sky; furiously*): It's almost noon! (*Recovering; sweetly*) I mean, the pies will burn if we don't hurry. You must come quickly! I'll take your hand, little girl. (*She reaches for* MELINDA's *hand and drops her scepter.* KARL *picks it up and steps back.*)

KARL: I've seen this before! (*Alarmed*) It's the wicked witch's scepter. (ARAMINDA *darts at him, but* KARL *jumps out of reach.*) You're not an old woman! You're the wicked witch!

ARAMINDA (*In a rage*): Give that scepter back to me, you miserable boy! (*She rushes at* KARL, *and knocks* MELINDA *down. There is general confusion, then the sound of the pipe is heard.* PIPER *enters. All turn to face him.*)

PIPER: Too late, Araminda. The morning is over, and you have lost. Now you must keep your promise to give up your scepter and all your wicked powers forever.

ARAMINDA (*Screaming*): Promises? Who cares about promises? The are just for stupid Hamelin children. I'll never give up my wicked powers. I'll get even with you yet, Piper. You'll see! (*She snatches her scepter from* KARL *and rushes off, rear.*)

ANNA (*Scared*): What will she do now, Piper? (*A splash and a scream are heard.* PIPER *hurries to rear and peers off.*)

PIPER: She slipped off her steppingstones and fell into the river. (*Crossing center*) We are well rid of her.

CHILDREN: Hurrah!

PIPER (*Turning*): And now, come! We are going on to Krythia. (*He leads them off right, piping a tune.* CHILDREN *hop and skip off behind.*)

CHILDREN (*As they skip off*): Krythia! Krythia! On to Krythia! (*Curtain*)

THE END

Production Notes

PIED PIPER'S LAND

Characters: 11 male; 5 female; as many male and female extras as desired for Other Children.

Playing Time: 20 minutes.

Costumes: Appropriate dress of the middle ages. Piper wears red and yellow cloak and scarf. Araminda enters in a witch's costume and later reenters disguised as an old woman, in shawl, etc. Kristi has handkerchief in her pocket.

Properties: Pails, fishing rods, two "pipes" (flutes or recorders may be used), purse full of coins, scepter.

Setting: Scene 1: Town square of Hamelin. Backdrop depicts fronts of medieval houses, with usable steps in front of house right. Town Hall is center; there is an opening at Hall door. There is a round well house at center stage, with a rope and bucket inside it. A second backdrop of a rural scene, with trees and grass, is revealed when town square is pulled away. Large boulder is at center of rural scene. Scene 2: A clearing in a wood, giving glimpses of a river in gaps between trees. There are bushes near right and left exits and a cherry tree near center rear (may be painted on backdrop). Down center is a bench with grass mat in front of it. Exits are right, left, and through aisles of auditorium.

Lighting: No special effects.

Sound: Recorded music for Piper's playing, loud splash, as indicated in text.

❧A Better Mousetrap

by Colleen Neuman

Wanted: state-of-the-art pest control for clever rodent . . .

Characters

MOUSE
WOMAN
MAN
FOUR CORNERS
METAL
BAR
CATCH ONE
CATCH TWO
WIDER
LONGER
HIGHER

TIME: *Now.*

SETTING: *There are two chairs onstage: one far left, one up center.*

AT RISE: *All performers sit in line on floor upstage, facing audience. MOUSE crouches at end of line, far right; WOMAN sits at end of line, far left, MAN sits in middle of line, center. All sit and hold same position until they get up to take part in the action. All but WOMAN and MAN wear character name signs pinned to costumes; signs are folded and taped up so that the audience can't read them.*

MOUSE (*Stands, crossing to center*): Welcome to "A Better Mousetrap." Once there was a mouse (*Untapes and turns down sign, showing* MOUSE *to audience*) and a woman

(WOMAN *stands, comes forward.* MOUSE *goes right.*) who was afraid of the mouse.

WOMAN (*Seeing* MOUSE): Eek! Eek! A mouse! A mouse! Oh, help, help! (*Jumps up onto chair, left*) Ooh, ooh, ooh!!!

MAN (*Standing and coming over to* WOMAN): What's wrong, my dear?

WOMAN (*Hiding her face in her hands*): A mouse! I saw a mouse!

MAN (*Crossing center, looking carefully at* MOUSE): So it is. (*Politely; tips hat*) Morning, to you.

MOUSE (*Tipping hat*): Morning, sir.

MAN: You would seem to be a mouse.

MOUSE: I am, indeed. And you are?

MAN: I am Richard Esquith, Esquire, Sr., the Third. I own this house.

MOUSE: And a charming abode it is.

MAN: How kind of you to say.

WOMAN: Eek, eek!

MAN: Oh, where are my manners? This is Dorothea Esquith, Esquire, Sr., the Third, my lovely wife.

WOMAN (*Crooking finger; through clenched teeth*): Richard, dear.

MAN (*Going back to* WOMAN): Yes, dear?

WOMAN (*Icily, deliberately*): You-are-talking-to-the-mouse!

MAN: Actually, it was more of an introduction than a talk . . .

WOMAN (*Shrieking*): Kill it!

MAN: Oh, yes, of course, I was getting to that. Let's see— (*Checking pockets*) slingshot, hatchet, MTV, rap music—no, I don't seem to have anything lethal on me.

WOMAN (*Seething*): Set a mousetrap!

MAN: A mousetrap! (*Hits forehead with hand*) Of course! A mousetrap! Obviously a mousetrap! (*Checking pockets*) I don't seem to have a mousetrap, so I'll have to build one.

MOUSE (*Sighing heavily*): Here we go.

MAN: A mousetrap is a rectangle, so I'll need four corners. (CORNERS *turn down their signs.* MAN *notices them.*) Ah, there you are. Come right over here. Yes, that's right—(MAN *puts them in sitting or lying positions where corners of mouse-*

trap will be, then arranges their arms and legs at right angles to form corners.) here, and here, and here, and here. And a mousetrap has a metal bar. (METAL *and* BAR *turn down their signs.*) Yes, you two will do. Right over here. (MAN *moves them to bend at waist, in center of trap, with out-stretched arms touching. Then, as though with great effort,* MAN *pushes them into an erect position.*) And I need a catch (CATCH ONE *and* CATCH TWO *turn over their signs.*) to hold back the bar. Yes! You two! Over here! Quickly! (*They run over, kneel, reach up and hold arms of* METAL BAR. MAN *lets go.*) Whew! And, of course, no mousetrap would be complete without a one-pound block of the finest cheddar . . . (*Takes cheese out of pocket*)

MOUSE *and* TRAP: Mm-m-m.

MAN: . . . cheese. (*Sets cheese on floor in middle of trap*) Ah. There we are, my dear. All done. You may come down now.

WOMAN: Not until that disgusting rodent is dead.

MAN: Well, I've built a very fine trap that will no doubt do the job sometime during the night.

WOMAN (*In relief*): I certainly hope so, dear. I'll look forward to it.

MAN: Good night. See you in the morning.

WOMAN: Nighty-night. (MAN *stands just right of* WOMAN's *chair. They both tilt heads to one side, rest cheeks on folded hands, close eyes, as if asleep.*)

MOUSE: *That* was the first night.

HIGHER (*Raising alarm clock high above head, giving it a good shake*): R-r-r-ring!

MAN: Good morning, Duck.

WOMAN: Morning, Cupcake.

MAN (*Offering hand*): Let me help you down.

WOMAN: How splendid of you. (*Sees* MOUSE *and screams*) Eek, eek!

MAN: Is it the same disgusting rodent?

WOMAN (*Covering eyes, pointing at* MOUSE): I can't bear to look!

MAN (*Turning toward center*): The trap didn't work, I suppose?

MOUSE *and* TRAP (*Shaking heads, in unison*): Trap didn't work.

MOUSE: It isn't that it's not a fine mousetrap. It's a very fine mousetrap. I just find it a bit small for me.

MAN: Of course! (*Hits forehead with hand*) Why didn't I see that? It should be wider (WIDER *turns over sign.*) and longer (LONGER *turns over sign.*) and higher. (HIGHER *turns over sign.*) Yes, yes, all of you—over here and here and here. (WIDER *lies along end of trap*, LONGER *lies along the front*, HIGHER *stands on chair center.*) And the metal bar should have teeth! (METAL BAR *looks at audience, bares teeth.*) Ah, much better. (*Goes back to* WOMAN)

WOMAN: Well done, dear.

MAN: Tonight will be the night, my sweet. Never fear.

MAN *and* WOMAN: Nighty-night. (*They assume sleep positions again.*)

MOUSE: *That* was the second night.

HIGHER (*Raising clock, shaking it*): R-r-r-ring!

MAN: Morning, Petunia.

WOMAN: Morning, Muffin. (*Notices* MOUSE; *screams*) Eek, eek!

MAN (*Turning to center stage*): So, once again, the trap didn't work?

MOUSE *and* TRAP: Trap didn't work.

MOUSE (*Matter-of-factly*): It's the noise, you know.

MAN: The noise? But there isn't any noise. It's as silent as a stone here.

MOUSE: That's the problem. A mouse *likes* a noisy trap.

MAN: Of course! (*Hits forehead with hand*) Noise! I should have thought of noise! (*To* TRAP) Well, go ahead. Make some noise.

CORNERS: Wubba wubba.

MAN (*To audience*): Wubba wubba? (*To* METAL BAR) And you?

METAL BAR: Woosh woosh.

MAN (*To* CATCHES): And you?

CATCHES: Wibba wibba.

MAN (*To* WIDER, LONGER, HIGHER): And you?

WIDER, LONGER, HIGHER (*Together*): Ugh!

MAN (*Worried*): Hm-m-m. Again. (*Points to each of them in turn*)

CORNERS: Wubba wubba.

METAL BAR: Woosh woosh.

CATCHES: Wibba wibba.

WIDER, LONGER, HIGHER: Ugh!

MAN (*Pleased*): Hm-m-m. Not bad. Again. (*He conducts. Performers in trap make their noises with even more rhythm this time, looking pleased with themselves.*)

TRAP: Wubba wubba, woosh woosh, wibba wibba, ugh! Wubba wubba, woosh woosh, wibba wibba, ugh! Wubba wubba, woosh woosh, wibba wibba, ugh! (MAN *stops conducting. Trap continues "noise" to end of play, though not so loudly that actors have to shout.*)

MAN: Very good. Keep it up until tomorrow. (*To* WOMAN) Nighty-night, dear.

WOMAN: How will we sleep with all this noise?

MAN: Probably not very well. Nighty-night. (*They assume sleep positions again.*)

MOUSE: *That* was the third night.

HIGHER (*Raising clock, shaking it*): R-r-r-ring!

MAN: Morning, Dumpling.

WOMAN (*Annoyed*): What?

MAN (*Louder*): I said: Morning, Dumpling.

WOMAN (*Screeching as she sees* MOUSE): Yikes!

MAN (*Turning center*): Don't tell me. Trap didn't work?

MOUSE *and* TRAP: Trap didn't work.

MOUSE: You see, it doesn't move. And a trap that doesn't move is always such a disappointment.

MAN: Well, you're in luck. Movement happens to be my specialty. Let me see. . . . (*Goes to each performer in trap and "starts" a movement—feet twitch back and forth, head nods, arm goes in circle, etc.—while ad libbing. Actions must be simple enough for actors to continue through end of play.*) This arm can do this. This leg can bend back. That's good. (*Etc. Stands next to* WOMAN) There we are! Isn't that just perfect? Who could resist a trap like that? Good night, Gumdrop.

WOMAN (*Wearily*): Of course, right, whatever. (*They take sleep position.*)

MOUSE: *That* was the fourth night.

HIGHER (*Raising clock, shaking it*): R-r-r-ring!

MAN: Good morning, my little Peppermint Drop.

WOMAN: Well, did it work? (MAN *looks center;* MOUSE *waves.*)

MAN: Trap didn't work? (*Trap stops noise briefly to speak next line with* MOUSE.)

MOUSE *and* TRAP: Trap didn't work.

MOUSE: May I make just one final suggestion?

MAN: I would most appreciate it.

WOMAN: You're going to listen to that miserable rodent *again?* Every time you do, things just get worse.

MAN: The way I see it is, who better to give advice on mouse-traps, than a mouse? Besides, if I hadn't listened to him so far I wouldn't have made this lovely trap. (*To* MOUSE) Now, you were saying?

MOUSE: Though it is indeed a wonderful mousetrap, a marvelous mousetrap, it would be perfect if it were louder.

MAN: Louder?

MOUSE: Louder. And faster.

MAN: Faster?

MOUSE: *Much* faster. (TRAP *looks worried.*)

MAN: Louder . . . (*Turns "knob"—perhaps the ear or nose of a player—on* TRAP. TRAP *gets louder.*) . . . and faster. (*Pulls a lever—perhaps the arm or leg of another player—and* TRAP *starts moving very fast. Actors' lines now have to be bellowed.*) Nighty-night, Sweet Pea.

WOMAN: As if anybody could sleep standing on a chair in the middle of all this racket and commotion! (*They sleep.* WOMAN *tosses and turns.*)

MOUSE: And *this* is the fifth night. (TRAP *works frantically for a few more seconds, and then collapses into a big heap of bodies.*)

TRAP: Boom!!! (*Actors lie very still after "explosion." They should not land on cheese.*)

HIGHER (*Raising arm out of pile, shaking clock*): R-r-ring!

MAN: Good morning, Lambiecakes.

WOMAN (*Testily*): It is not a good morning, it wasn't a good night, and I'm not your lambiecakes! (*Thundering*) *Did it work?*

MAN (*Looking over and gasping*): It collapsed! No more trap?

MOUSE *and* TRAP: No more trap.

MAN: Oh, my beautiful, clever, wonderful trap! Gone!

WOMAN: You fool! Five days and five nights I've stood on this chair. (*Gets down*) I'm hungry and tired and suffering from nervous exhaustion and all you care about is that ridiculous mousetrap! I can't take it anymore! I'm going to my sister's house to eat and sleep and take a bath—not necessarily in that order! (*Stomps off*)

MAN: Oh. Well, if she's leaving, (*To* MOUSE) I suppose you can stay.

MOUSE: Why, thank you.

MAN: And I guess I won't be needing a trap.

MOUSE: How kind of you. It was a marvelous mousetrap, though, the best I've ever seen. (*Picks up cheese*) You wouldn't happen to have any crackers, would you? (*Comes center*)

MAN (*Moving center*): Why, yes, I believe I do. (*Takes crackers and plate from pocket, arranges crackers on plate*)

MOUSE (*To audience, while taking slice of cheese from package*): You see, while they did build a better mousetrap, what they didn't realize is they were dealing with . . . (*Turns down second sign*) a slightly better mouse (*Second sign reads* SLIGHTLY BETTER MOUSE) . . . who wasn't hungry . . . (*Takes cracker, puts cheese on it*) until now. (*Takes bite. Quick curtain*)

THE END

Production Notes

A BETTER MOUSETRAP

Characters: 14 or more male or female. You could, for example, have any number of actors play Wider, Longer, and Higher to expand size of mousetrap. The more performers added, the larger and more elaborate the mousetrap will be, and the bigger the explosion.

Playing Time: 10 minutes.

Costumes: Performers who are part of the mousetrap need only a sign, and may wear matching t-shirts and pants. Mouse wears gray baseball cap with gray felt or paper ears stapled to it, and also has a sign. Woman wears hat, long skirt, stole, jewelry. Man wears hat, suit coat, tie. All performers should have identical circles of red rouge on cheeks.

Properties: Cardboard signs pinned to front of costumes should read: MOUSE, CORNER (four of them), METAL, BAR, CATCH (two of them), WIDER, LONGER, HIGHER. Signs are folded in half and taped up to be concealed from audience, until tape is removed at appropriate moment, and sign unfolds. The words SLIGHTLY BETTER are written on separate piece of paper, folded and taped in space above mouse sign; when indicated, the second sign is untaped to reveal new message reading: SLIGHTLY BETTER MOUSE. Man has package of sliced cheese in one pocket, a small packet of crackers, and a small plate in another pocket. Higher holds an old-fashioned alarm clock.

Setting: There are two chairs onstage: one far left, one up center.

Lighting: No special effects.

Sound: Higher holds an alarm clock and "rings" it at various times during the play.

⁓Peter Salem, Minuteman

by Mark Keats

A slave's heroism at Bunker Hill leads to freedom . . . .

Characters

JENNIFER ⎫
TOMMY ⎬ *children*

PETER SALEM, *a former slave*
ISAAC BELKNAP, *a farmer*
CRISPUS ATTUCKS
SAMUEL MAVERICK
JAMES CALDWELL
SAMUEL GRAY
PATRICK CARR
SAMUEL ADAMS
CAPTAIN SIMON EDGEL
MRS. BELKNAP
MRS. WRIGHT
MRS. FAIRCHILD
MRS. CRAIGMILE
FOUR NARRATORS
MINUTEMEN, *extras*
OFFSTAGE VOICES

TIME: *About ten years after the American Revolution.*
SETTING: *The stage is bare except for a stool down left.*
AT RISE: JENNIFER *and* TOMMY *run on playing and laughing.*
SALEM (*Offstage*): Whoa, George, you ornery old horse.

216

(TOMMY *and* JENNIFER *stop playing and look off right.*)
You'll get fed soon enough. Whoa, boy!

TOMMY (*Pointing*): Hey, that's Peter Salem. He fought at Bunker Hill under Captain Simon Edgel's command.

JENNIFER (*Skeptically, looking off*): That man?

TOMMY: Yes, he's a hero! And before that he was a slave.

JENNIFER: Oh, you're teasing.

TOMMY: It's true. Here he comes. Ask him yourself. (JENNIFER *shakes her head shyly, as* SALEM *enters wiping his face with kerchief.*) Mr. Salem, Jennifer didn't believe me when I said you fought at Bunker Hill. (*Eagerly*) Tell her about fighting with the Minutemen!

SALEM (*Laughing*): Let a man catch his breath, Tommy. I just finished plowing a whole acre, stones, stubble, and all.

TOMMY (*Eagerly*): Tell us about the Battle of Bunker Hill!

SALEM (*Slowly, thinking*): The Battle of Bunker Hill—that was ten long years ago.

JENNIFER: Were you really a slave?

SALEM: Yes, indeed I was. My master was Isaac Belknap, a good man as masters go. He owned a farm in Framingham, Massachusetts.

JENNIFER: But why would a slave join up to fight?

SALEM: You want to know what stirred me to join the fight? It was a man, Crispus Attucks. He was a slave like me. I was just a little boy when I heard about Crispus Attucks. He came from Framingham. One day he ran away on a whaling ship. He was free! A sailor, like the white men! His master, William Brown, posted handbills offering a ten-pound reward for the capture of Attucks, but no one turned him in. He owned himself. Free to come and go as he wanted. From then on he was my hero. I never met Crispus Attucks, but I felt him here. (*Puts his hand to his heart; sadly*) Poor Crispus. (*They walk left.* SALEM *sits on stool. Children sit cross-legged on floor.*)

JENNIFER: Why? What happened to him?

SALEM: Years later, when I was twenty, fights broke out nearly every day between the citizens of Boston and the Redcoats. The citizens were getting angrier and angrier. (1ST NARRATOR *enters right. Lights dim as* SALEM's *voice trails off.*)

Then one night—(*Spotlight shines on* 1ST NARRATOR, *who stands down right.*)

1ST NARRATOR: The snow was packed hard in the streets of Boston that bitter cold Monday night of March 5, 1770. It was about nine o'clock. Crispus Attucks and some friends were gathered at Dock Square in Boston where the ships moored. That afternoon, a Redcoat had struck a boy with his rifle butt. Feelings ran high. Attucks led an angry crowd up to the brick Customs House. (1ST NARRATOR *steps back. Lights come up. Loud shouting is heard offstage. Five men enter:* CRISPUS ATTUCKS, *brandishing a club, rushes on followed by* SAMUEL MAVERICK, JAMES CALDWELL, SAMUEL GRAY, PATRICK CARR.)

MEN (*Shouting, ad lib*): We're not afraid of you lobsterbacks. Make way you British swine. Down with tyranny! (*Etc.*)

VOICE (*From offstage*): Disperse or we'll fire!

ATTUCKS: Attack the guard! Strike for freedom! (*Shots are heard offstage.* ATTUCKS *falls dead, then* MAVERICK, CALDWELL, GRAY, *and* CARR *fall one by one. Lights dim; spotlight comes up on* 1ST NARRATOR.)

1ST NARRATOR: Crispus Attucks was the first to fall. Then Samuel Maverick . . . James Caldwell, only nineteen . . Samuel Gray . . . Patrick Carr, from Ireland. The day of the burial, the funeral procession stretched for miles. (*Bell tolls.*) They were buried in a common grave. (1ST NARRATOR *and* MEN *exit. Lights come up.* SALEM *rises.*)

SALEM (*Pacing, sadly*): When I heard the news I cried. Crispus Attucks was dead. (*Long pause*) I began to shake. Anger ran through me. Out in the woods that day, hauling logs for firewood, I shouted, "Down with King George!" The woods cried back, "Down with King George!" I was crazy mad. (*Shaking his head; quietly*) Crispus Attucks, my hero was dead.

JENNIFER (*Gently*): Please tell us more, Mr. Salem.

SALEM: My master hated King George. You should have heard Master Belknap when the King put a stamp tax on everything the citizens bought. He was enraged! I remember one night he spoke up at a meeting at the Framingham Town Hall.

(*Lights dim as* ISAAC BELKNAP *enters and stands center. Spotlight up on* BELKNAP.)

BELKNAP (*Pacing angrily, counting on fingers*): Tax on newspapers, playing cards, college diplomas, glass, paint, wood, paper, sugar, molasses, tea! (*Stops; furiously*) Tax on the air we breathe ... on our freedom! When do we fight? (*Exits; lights up*)

SALEM: I didn't understand all his talk about taxes, but when he talked of freedom, that made me think of Crispus Attucks. It wasn't right—my master talking about freedom and me a slave! It made me mad.

TOMMY (*Enthusiastically*): Tell us the part about the Minutemen.

SALEM (*Sighs deeply*): All the colonials were hurt by the Stamp Act—all except the Royalists, of course. But did King George listen to the angry citizens fussing, quarreling, and grumbling? (*Scornfully*) Like a fox promises not to steal chickens. He ordered more Redcoats to Boston to protect his tax agents. King George was making the colonists madder and madder. Master Belknap rode to Boston about twice a week to keep up with what was going on. One day, he sent me to Boston with a wagonload of field corn to sell. (BELKNAP *enters and walks to* SALEM.)

BELKNAP: Peter, keep your eyes and ears open. Trouble's brewing faster'n greased lightning. If you see lobsterbacks coming your way, avoid them. They spell trouble.

SALEM: Lobsterbacks?

BELKNAP: Lobsterbacks, redbacks. That's the name we give the Redcoats. If you see them coming, just head the other way. (BELKNAP *exits.* SALEM *moves left and sits again.*)

SALEM: So I hauled the load to Boston. After I delivered the corn, I saw all the citizens rushing one way, fast, talking mad, shaking their fists. I followed them to a big building—it was the Old South Meetinghouse. (*Gesturing widely*) It was the biggest hall I'd ever seen, and it was packed tight with citizens. I saw Samuel Adams get up on the stage. He was a fiery Boston patriot. A leader of the resistance. (*Lights dim;*

spotlight on SAMUEL ADAMS, *who enters and addresses audience.*)

ADAMS (*Hotly*): Countrymen! We have no alternative to independence, except the most ignominious and galling servitude. The British soldiers are drunkards and cutthroats recruited from the dregs of London. They harass our citizens, insult our women. The King demands without consent taxes that impoverish us, idle our mills and fleets. The families of workers and sailors are starving. We are forced to house the insulting Redcoats. Our privacy is destroyed. Our homes are searched without warrants. For years King George has turned a deaf ear to our protest and petitions. Countrymen, the conflict that is brewing will be long and hard. Tyranny is not conquered by words, nor always by arms. But we must fight! Now! Freedom or death! Our cause is just! Fight!

VOICES (*Offstage, cheering and shouting, ad lib*): Hurrah for Sam Adams! Freedom or death! Down with King George. (*Etc.* ADAMS *exits. Lights up.* SALEM *rises.*)

SALEM (*Striding back and forth*): Adams' talk about freedom beat on me like a whip. I could feel the blood pumping in my throat! I saw men on the road, running, carrying rifles, muskets, blunderbusses. I even saw Negroes like me with rifles! I couldn't believe my eyes. The men were cheering, whistling, shouting. (*Pauses a moment, thinking*) When I rode into the farmyard, Master Belknap came running. (BELKNAP *runs in.*)

BELKNAP: What happened in Boston, Peter?

SALEM (*Excitedly*): Master Belknap, I heard Sam Adams talk. They're going to fight! The men are marching on the road to Lexington with rifles.

BELKNAP (*Punching fist into hand*): Glory be. At last! (*Starts to exit*) I'll get my rifle, powder horn, and shot.

SALEM (*Agitated*): Master Belknap, I want to fight the lobsterbacks, too. (BELKNAP *stops, turns.*) I want to fight. (*Clenches fists*) I've got to fight.

BELKNAP (*Puzzled*): You? Fight? But you're a slave, Peter.

SALEM: Master Belknap, you know how I can shoot. I can hit a rabbit's eye at a hundred paces. Let me fight, Master Belknap.

(*Pauses. Sadly, proudly*) Crispus Attucks was the first to die. For freedom.

BELKNAP: Yes, poor Attucks. But Attucks was a free man, Peter.

SALEM (*Stubbornly*): I want to fight against King George for my freedom. (*They stare at each other for a moment.*) Master Belknap, give me a rifle. I want to join the Minutemen.

BELKNAP (*Stroking his chin, nodding*): So be it, Peter. We'll need all the men we can muster. (*He looks off right and calls.*) Emily! (MRS. BELKNAP *runs on.*)

MRS. BELKNAP (*Worriedly*): Isaac, what's happened?

BELKNAP: Men are marching to Lexington.

MRS. BELKNAP (*Solemnly*): So, it has finally begun. You'll be headed off to fight?

BELKNAP: Yes, Emily. Peter is going with me. (SALEM *straightens proudly.*) I'll get the rifles and powder, and we'll be off. Take care of the children. The Redcoats may pass this way.

MRS. BELKNAP (*Bravely*): I'll alert the neighbors, too. There will be much to do. Take care, Isaac, and you, too, Peter.

SALEM: Thank you, Mistress Belknap.

BELKNAP (*As he and* SALEM *exit left*): Don't worry, Emily. I'll be back for the plowing. (*Lights dim. Spotlight on* 2ND NARRATOR, *who enters right. As he speaks, a table and three chairs are placed down center.* MRS. WRIGHT, MRS. CRAIG-MILE, *and* MRS. FAIRCHILD *enter and sit. Throughout scene* MRS. BELKNAP *stands at table folding cloth,* MRS. WRIGHT *spins at a spinning wheel,* MRS. CRAIGMILE *weaves at a loom, and* MRS. FAIRCHILD *stirs a pot as if at a fireplace. These actions may be pantomimed or props may be used.*)

2ND NARRATOR: As the men fought the British, the women fought to keep their homes and farms together. They worked hard for the war, too, making bandages, uniforms, and ammunition for the soldiers. The price of freedom was high, but the spirit of the colonials was strong. (*Exits. Lights come up.*)

MRS. FAIRCHILD (*Making a face*): The awful smell of melting pewter!

MRS. BELKNAP: This old linen cloth you brought, Mrs.

Wright, is just what's needed for bandages. Supplies ran out after the Battle of Lexington.

MRS. WRIGHT: Oh, that linen's been in our attic since Grandma died. (*Turning back to her work at spinning wheel*) This is a fine bunch of flax.

MRS. BELKNAP: What a lot of work it was, washing and combing the flax so many times.

MRS. WRIGHT: It should weave into beautiful cloth for the uniforms.

MRS. CRAIGMILE (*Absently*): Beautiful uniforms.

MRS. BELKNAP: With our men gone we'd never make it if we didn't help each other.

MRS. WRIGHT (*To* MRS. BELKNAP): How is Mr. Belknap doing?

MRS. BELKNAP: His wound healed nicely, and he's back in camp. He owes his life to Peter Salem. Peter dragged Isaac behind a stone fence after he was shot. (*Shaking her head*) Isaac feels the war will be long.

MRS. WRIGHT: Those barbarians! Burning down houses and barns!

MRS. CRAIGMILE: Yes, barbarians. You never know when they will sneak up and search your home.

MRS. BELKNAP: Our dog, Gabriel, can smell strangers a mile off, so if he starts to bark you know where to hide everything. Mrs. Fairchild, you hide the pewter melting pot—

MRS. FAIRCHILD: Under the hearth flagstone in the pit. I'll throw chicken feathers on the fire to cover the smell of melted pewter.

MRS. BELKNAP: Fine! The quilting frame is on the table. All four of us can work on it together.

MRS. FAIRCHILD (*Stirring*): There goes my beautiful pewter bowl. (*Sighs*) It's been in our family for generations.

MRS. WRIGHT (*Brightly*): There's nothing like good old-fashioned woodenware. I guess that's what we'll all be using—at least until this war is over.

MRS. FAIRCHILD (*Coughing and fanning her face with her hand*): At least we won't smell the pewter when it's a cold bullet.

MRS. CRAIGMILE (*Stopping her weaving*): A cold bullet . . . I worry so about my husband and my son, Robert. (*Other women exchange glances.*) Robert is hardly fourteen. But how could I keep him at home? (*Proudly and sadly*) What does the boy say? "I'm big enough to plow, run the mill, hunt. I'm going with Father." What could I say? (*Sound of baby crying is heard offstage.*) Oh, that's my Esther. Poor baby, she must be hungry. (*She exits.*)

MRS. WRIGHT (*Whispering, shocked*): She hasn't heard that Robert was killed in a skirmish? (*They look at each other sadly, shake their heads, and resume their tasks. Lights dim. 3RD NARRATOR enters and spotlight comes up. As he speaks, the women exit, taking with them the table and chairs.*)

3RD NARRATOR: The embattled farmers, unlike the well-trained British, were not accustomed to army discipline. They were ready to fight for liberty and independence, but they worried about their farms, and desertions were frequent. Independent by nature, they resisted and scoffed at army orders, and had difficulty even marching together. (*Lights up as 3RD NARRATOR exits. CAPTAIN SIMON EDGEL marches on, followed by a disorganized troop of MINUTEMEN. They stop center stage.*)

EDGEL (*Exasperated*): This is "right face"! (*Executes a perfect right face*) This is "left face"! (*Exaggerates turning on left foot*) This is "to the rear, march"! (*Performs action. To MINUTEMEN*) Right face! (*MINUTEMEN turn awkwardly, some one way, some the other, bumping into each other.*) Left face! (*Again they do it wrong*) Halt! (*They stop and face him.*) We're not going to win this war by fighting behind fences and trees as we did at Lexington. We are facing great generals and well-drilled troops. Do you men want to defeat King George and his army, or do you want to remain colonial tax slaves? (*There is a moment of silence.*) What's your answer, men?

1ST MINUTEMAN (*Weakly*): We want liberty.

EDGEL: Shall we beat King George?

MINUTEMEN (*With growing enthusiasm, ad lib*): Yes! Down with King George! Liberty! (*Etc.*)

EDGEL: All right, then. Do you know hay from straw?

MINUTEMEN (*Shouting*): Yes! (EDGEL *takes some hay out of one pocket and some straw out of another.*)

EDGEL (*Passing out hay and straw to* MINUTEMEN): I want each of you to stick a stalk of straw in this shoe. (*Points to right foot*), and a stalk of hay in that shoe. (*Points to left foot.* MINUTEMEN *do so.*) All right, fall in. Attention! Hay foot, turn! (MINUTEMEN *turn left.*) Straw foot, turn! (*They turn right.*) Good! By two's, march! Hay foot, straw foot! (*They fall in line and march out. Lights dim; spotlight up on* 4TH NARRATOR, *who enters right.*)

4TH NARRATOR: The morning of June 17, 1775, Captain Edgel and his Minutemen were busy digging trenches on Breed's Hill, close to Boston Harbor. Behind Breed's Hill is Bunker Hill. (MINUTEMEN *and* SALEM, *each carrying rifle, take places on stage, as* NARRATOR *continues.*) British General Gage was surprised to see the colonials fortifying the hills— he had considered them a bunch of Yankee yokels. So he ordered his troops to attack at once. Colonel Pitcairn, the same officer who had raided Concord in search of Sam Adams and John Hancock, led the charge. (4TH NARRATOR *exits. Lights come up on* MINUTEMEN *and* SALEM *"digging." They pant and pause now and then to wipe their brows. After a moment, the sounds of cannons firing and cannon balls whistling are heard off.* EDGEL *runs on right.*)

EDGEL (*Shouting*): Take cover, men!

SALEM: Captain Edgel, sir. These fortifications are not high enough if the British attack. We must keep digging.

EDGEL: They're laying a heavy barrage. I order you to take cover. (*All flatten out on ground, facing left. Sound of cannon balls whistling close is heard. Then firing stops.* EDGEL *rises.*) They haven't found the range. Up, men. (MINUTEMEN *rise.*) Keep digging. (*They do so.*) They're loading for the next round. (*Pointing off left*) Ha, that ball bounced off those rocks and fences you raised, Peter. It could have killed half a dozen men. (*Claps* SALEM *on shoulder*) Good work, Peter.

SALEM (*Heatedly*): We'll show them! (*Shouting*) Fire away, you lobsterbacks.

EDGEL (*Suddenly*): Take cover, here comes the second round.

(*Cannon fire is heard.* MINUTEMEN *crouch, as if behind fortifications.*)

VOICES (*Offstage, shouting, ad lib*): Charge! At them, men! Clear out those rebels! (*Etc.*)

EDGEL: Look at those stupid Redcoats. They think they're at a dress parade before King George. Don't waste your fire, men. Shoot when I give the order. (*Fife and drum and marching feet are heard off, growing louder.* MINUTEMEN *stare off left.*) Prepare to fire! (*They raise rifles, aim off left.*) Get ready. Don't shoot yet. Ready, fire! (*They fire as heavy fusillade of shots is heard.*) They're retreating! Good work, men!

SALEM (*Shaking his head*): They're so young. Those Redcoats don't even know what they're fighting for. (*Sound of cannon is heard.*)

EDGEL (*Shouting*): Here they come again. Ready, aim, fire! (MINUTEMEN *do so. Sound of shots is heard.*) Look at them run. They're dropping their packs!

2ND MINUTEMAN: Captain, we're out of powder and shot.

EDGEL: Oh, no and they're preparing a third charge. Are you sure all the powder is gone?

SALEM: I have one shot left, Captain.

EDGEL: Use it well, Peter. (*Shouting*) You men use rifle butts, shovels, stones, anything. Then retreat to Bunker Hill. Here they come. That's Colonel Pitcairn leading the charge!

VOICE (*Offstage*): Charge, men! The day is ours! (SALEM *stands, aims rifle, and shoots.*)

EDGEL: Peter, you hit him! Colonel Pitcairn is down! His men are in confusion. Good work, brave lad. (*Shots are heard offstage.*) Retreat, men. Back to Bunker Hill. Peter Salem has saved us! (*Blackout as* MINUTEMEN *and* EDGEL *exit.* SALEM *returns to his seat down left. Lights come up.* TOMMY *and* JENNIFER *stare at* SALEM *wide-eyed.*)

SALEM: That was ten long years ago, my friends. The Battle of Bunker Hill. Now (*Rises*), if you'll excuse me, I have to go feed my horses. When Mr. Belknap gave me my freedom, he gave me two horses, too—George and Queenie. Old George is still George, only he's named for George Washington now. (*Laughs*) And do you know what I call Queenie?

TOMMY: Martha!

SALEM (*Clapping his hands*): Right. Now, if I'm going to start my planting tomorrow, I best finish my chores and get to bed. The town gave me this farm for fighting in the war, and I take pride in keeping it up.

JENNIFER (*Solemnly*): Mr. Salem, how many men are left from Captain Edgel's company?

SALEM (*After a pause, soberly*): Not enough, I'm afraid. Not nearly enough. (*Pauses*) Anyway, I won my freedom, and my country won its freedom. (*Seriously*) I hope you'll never forget our fight for independence. The struggle for freedom never ends. (SALEM *slowly walks to right exit as stage slowly darkens. Curtain.*)

THE END

Production Notes

PETER SALEM, MINUTEMAN

Characters: 10 male; 5 female; 4 male or female for narrators; male extras for minutemen; male and female extras for offstage voices.

Playing Time: 35 minutes.

Costumes: All wear appropriate colonial clothes. Captain Edgel has wisps of hay in one pocket, straw in another.

Properties: Kerchief, table and three chairs, cloth, rifles. Spinning wheel, loom, and pot with paddle may be used or actions may be pantomimed.

Setting: Bare stage except for stool down left.

Lighting: Lights dim; spotlight, as indicated in text.

Sound: Bells; cannon and rifle shots; baby crying; cannon balls whistling; fife and drums; marching.

❧Melodrama at Mayfair Meadows

by Roberta Olsen Major

With heroes and heroines in danger, who is left to save them? . . .

Characters

MILLIE, *housemaid*
FREDDY, *footman*
MARIGOLD MAYFAIR, *wealthy young lady*
FLORIMOND FLOOTE, *music master*
MADAME DIAMANTE GLITTERATA, *Marigold's aunt*
MIMOSA MEADOWS, *Marigold's country cousin*
FLOYD BRIGHT, *yokel hero*
DUNSTON DARKSTORM, *villain*
QUARTET, *singers*
CHORUS, *singing furniture*
DIRECTOR

SCENE 1

TIME: *Spring of yesteryear.*
SETTING: *The parlor at Mayfair Meadows. At center, two rows of chorus members create "piano": back row, dressed in black, stands; front row, dressed alternately in black or white to give the impression of piano keys, sits on low stools; a stool is in front of piano. Four jump ropes lie on floor behind piano. Two chorus members hold curtain rod with ruffled curtains to give impression of open bay window up right. Other chorus members represent various pieces of furniture, such as lamps, by standing with lampshade on head; chairs, by sitting on floor*

with throw pillows in lap; and potted plants, by squatting and holding greenery. Quartet, dressed in matching outfits, stands down right. Door, left, leads to rest of house.

AT RISE: MILLIE *is dusting "furniture," which occasionally sneezes, twitches, and coughs.* FREDDY *enters left.*

FREDDY (*Arms outstretched; dramatically*): Millie! Dearest Millie!

MILLIE (*Hands over her heart*): Freddy! Faithful Freddy!

FREDDY: I had to see you, for though I am a lowly footman, forced to wait hand and foot—well, foot, at least—on Madame Diamante Glitterata, my heart is yours, dear Millie.

MILLIE: And mine belongs to you, faithful Freddy.

QUARTET (*Singing to tune of "I'm a Little Teapot"*):
Millie is a housemaid, pure and sweet.
That is her Freddy; he's rather neat.
Though they'll work as servants all their days,
They'll be forever happy, because it pays.

MADAME DIAMANTE (*Calling from offstage*): Fred-er-ick! Where is that lazy footman?

FREDDY (*Sadly*): Duty calls. (FREDDY *exits.* MILLIE *resumes dusting.* MARIGOLD MAYFAIR *and* FLORIMOND FLOOTE *enter left.*)

MARIGOLD (*Gesturing*): Please come this way, Master Floote. (*To* MILLIE) It is time for my music lesson, Millie. You may go.

MILLIE (*With a little curtsy*): Yes, miss. (*Aside*) Music is not all these two are playing at! (*She exits.*)

FLORIMOND (*Ardently*): At last, my most precious Marigold, we are alone.

MARIGOLD: Oh, Florimond! How shall we go on? You are but an impoverished music intructor, and I, the orphaned heiress to millions. Aunt Diamante will never consent to our betrothal!

FLORIMOND: I fear you are right, my Marigold. (*They sigh deeply.*)

MADAME DIAMANTE (*Offstage*): Marigold, I hear no music playing! What is going on?

MARIGOLD: Oh dear! Aunt Diamante! (*Quickly sits at "piano"*)

FLORIMOND (*In stage whisper*): Quickly, Marigold! Play! (MARIGOLD *"plays piano" by patting heads of front row of* CHORUS *members, who sing out notes of the scale in turn.*)

MADAME DIAMANTE (*Poking head in door*): *Much* better! (*She exits.*)

MARIGOLD: I believe we are now in tune, Master Floote. (*Continues to play as piano sings softly*)

FLORIMOND (*Warmly*): Indeed we are, Miss Mayfair. (*She stops playing. He kisses her hand just as* MIMOSA *enters.*)

MIMOSA (*Innocently*): Oh, Marigold, I didn't mean to interrupt your music lesson.

MARIGOLD (*Rising*): That's quite all right Cousin Mimosa. I was just showing Master Floote out. (MASTER FLOOTE *bows to* MIMOSA, *then he and* MARIGOLD *exit left.* MIMOSA *walks to window, peers out wistfully, sighs, then walks about room idly. After a beat,* FLOYD BRIGHT *appears at window from outside, pulling aside curtains.*)

FLOYD (*In whisper*): Hist! Mimosa! Mimosa Meadows!

MIMOSA (*Turning to him, startled*): Floyd Bright, whatever are you doing here?

FLOYD: I followed you all the way from the country, Mimosa. I wanted to make sure you'd be happy here at Mayfair Meadows with your cousin Marigold and your Aunt Diamante Glitterata.

MIMOSA (*Delighted*): Oh, Floyd, you're so sweet.

FLOYD (*Shyly*): Shucks, Mimosa, I hope you know how I feel about you.

MIMOSA: I'll be coming home soon, Floyd. Frills and finery don't suit me. I miss my piglets and ducklings—and you.

FLOYD (*Bashfully*): Aw, shucks.

QUARTET (*To tune of "Home on the Range"*):
Oh, give her a home where the country folk roam,
And the cows and the chickens all play.
Where seldom is heard a discouraging word,
And she can see Floyd Bright all day.

FLOYD: I'm worried you'll get lonely here, Mimosa. These fancy folks aren't what you're used to.

MIMOSA: But I have my sweet cousin Marigold to keep me company.

MADAME DIAMANTE (*Offstage, calling*): Mimosa, where are you? I want you to pick some flowers for me.

MIMOSA: I must fly, dear Floyd, for Aunt Diamante Glitterata calls. (*She waves, exits. FLOYD sighs. DUNSTON DARK-STORM creeps up behind him, taps him on shoulder.*)

DUNSTON: Boo! (FLOYD *screams and runs off outside window.* DUNSTON *laughs evilly.*) I'm Dunston Darkstorm, and I'm bad, bad, bad!

QUARTET (*To tune of "Old MacDonald"*):
Dunston Darkstorm was a rat!

CHORUS *and* QUARTET (*Together*):
Eee! Eee! Eee! Eee! Oh! (*As song continues,* CHORUS *members change from furniture pieces to mime the following: Window members link arms as two elderly people, one using curtain rod as cane;* DUNSTON *kicks at cane and they trip and stumble back to their window position. Piano members play jump rope, which* DUNSTON *interrupts, scaring them back into their piano position. Another* CHORUS *member drops his glasses and* DUNSTON *steps on them.*)

QUARTET:
And what a rat he really was!

CHORUS *and* QUARTET (*Together*):
Eee! Eee! Eee! Eee! Oh!

QUARTET:
With a bad deed here and a bad deed there!
Here a deed, there a deed, everywhere a bad deed!
Dunston Darkstorm was a cad!

CHORUS *and* QUARTET (*Together*):
Eee! Eee! Eee! Eee! Oh! (DUNSTON *silences them with threatening gesture.* CHORUS *members resume furniture positions.* MILLIE *and* MARIGOLD *enter.* MILLIE *begins dusting;* MARIGOLD *sits at piano.* MIMOSA *pulls aside curtains and appears from outside at window, holding flowers.*)

MILLIE (*Sighing*): Freddy!

MARIGOLD (*Sighing*): Florimond!

MIMOSA (*Sighing*): Floyd! (*They sigh again in unison.*)

DUNSTON (*To audience*): How revolting. Nothing sickens me

more than true love. (*Rubbing hands together*) My dastardly work is cut out for me, I see. (*He creeps toward* MILLIE, *and follows her about the room, pestering her as she dusts.*)

QUARTET (*To the tune of "Pop Goes the Weasel"*):
All around the furniture
The villain chased sweet Millie.
He thought it was great fun, and then— (MILLIE *whacks him with feather duster.*)
Pop! She knocked him silly! (DUNSTON staggers to MARIGOLD. QUARTET *sings to tune of "Someone's in the Kitchen with Dinah."*)
Dunston's in the parlor with Mari,
Dunston's in the parlor, I know.
Dunston's in the parlor with Mari—(MARIGOLD *daintily stomps on* DUNSTON's *toe. He grabs his foot and grimaces in pain.*)
And Marigold stomped on his toe!
(DUNSTON *hops to* MIMOSA, *who steps in through window and hurries about, trying to avoid him.* QUARTET *sings to tune of "The Farmer in the Dell."*)
The villain's in the house,
The villain's in the house,
Look out, Mimosa dear,
The villain's in the house.

The scoundrel grabs her hand,
The scoundrel grabs her hand,
Look out, Mimosa dear,
The scoundrel's got your hand.
(MIMOSA *kicks* DUNSTON *in the leg and exits. He limps to center.*)

DUNSTON: Thrice foiled! Thrice scorned! (*Angrily*) Nobody, but *nobody*, crosses Dunston Darkstorm and gets away with it! (*Blackout; curtain*)

* * * * *

SCENE 2

TIME: *Later that day.*
SETTING: *Woods on the edge of Mayfair Meadows. Train track*

*is center; several chorus members stand upstage as trees, arms
outstretched.*

AT RISE: MILLIE, MARIGOLD, *and* MIMOSA, *hands tied behind their backs, are pushed on by* DUNSTON.

MILLIE (*Accusingly*): I should never have believed you when
you said you had a message for me from Freddy!

DUNSTON (*Laughing maniacally*): It was foolish of you.

MARIGOLD (*Indignantly*): I should never have listened when
you told me Florimond was calling for me!

DUNSTON (*With evil grin*): Sneaky of me.

MIMOSA (*In disbelief*): I never dreamed you were lying when
you said Floyd was waiting for me in the garden!

DUNSTON (*Matter-of-factly*): Clever, aren't I?

MILLIE: You're bad!

MARIGOLD: Despicable!

MIMOSA: Rotten to the core!

DUNSTON: But you three were the ones sneaking around behind Madame Glitterata's back! (MILLIE, MARIGOLD, *and*
MIMOSA *hang their heads.*) And now, my trio of oh-so-modest
maidens, you will learn just how foolish you have been. Heh,
heh, heh! (*Train whistle blows offstage.*)

MILLIE (*Aghast*): You can't mean—

MARIGOLD: Horrors! You wouldn't dream of—

MIMOSA: Not even you—

MILLIE, MARIGOLD, *and* MIMOSA: The railroad tracks?!

DUNSTON: But of course, my proud beauties. (*He ties them to
train tracks as* QUARTET *sings.*)

QUARTET (*To the tune of "Down by the Station"*):
Down by the train tracks
Near the Mayfair Meadows
See the lovely heroines
All in a row.

See the wicked villain
Tie them tight with scout knots.
Puff, puff, toot, toot
Away they'll go.

DUNSTON: And now for my most dastardly deed yet! The three

lovesick lotharios must stand by helplessly as their sweet-hearts—heh, heh, heh— catch the next train out of town! (*He runs offstage, then reenters, pulling* FREDDY, FLORIMOND, *and* FLOYD, *tied back-to-back.*)

FREDDY, FLORIMOND, *and* FLOYD (*Seeing heroines, ad lib*): Horrors! You cad! You villain! You varmint! (*Etc.*)

DUNSTON (*Gleefully*): I *am* a cad, aren't I?

FREDDY: Release my Millie right now, you wicked man!

DUNSTON: Never!

FLORIMOND: Untie my Marigold at once, you vile villain!

DUNSTON: Who is going to make me?

FLOYD: Let my Mimosa go, you nasty varmint!

DUNSTON: Not a chance. I'm having entirely too much fun seeing all six of you suffer! Unfortunately, I must now be off to plan more dastardly deeds. (*Prodding* FLOYD) For a *varmint's* work is never done. (*To audience*) There are so many misguided people out there trying to do good that I have to be alert every minute. (*He exits. Train whistle sounds louder offstage.*)

MILLIE: Oh, Freddy!

MARIGOLD: Florimond!

MIMOSA: Floyd!

MILLIE, MARIGOLD, *and* MIMOSA: Save us before it's too late! (FREDDY, FLORIMOND, *and* FLOYD *murmur frantically to one another, as though forming a plan. Train whistle blows louder. Then they lurch toward tracks, each trying to save his sweetheart.*)

QUARTET (*To the tune of "Chattanooga Choo-Choo"*):
Pardon them, boys,
But it's the 7 p.m. choo-choo!
It's heading this way,
They'll really hold you at bay.
(*Train enters, made up of* CHORUS *members: One rides on shoulders of another to make smoke stack; caboose is made of two* CHORUS *members carrying a third behind them across their backs, in a fireman's carry.*)

MILLIE: Quick! There's no time to save all three of us!

MARIGOLD: Working together you can rescue one of us!

MIMOSA: The other two of us must be sacrificed!

FREDDY, FLOYD, FLORIMOND: No! No! A thousand times no!

MILLIE, MARIGOLD, *and* MIMOSA: It's the only way!

FREDDY: But Millie—

FLORIMOND: But Marigold—

FLOYD: But Mimosa—

DIRECTOR (Entering; through megaphone): Cut! Look, fellows, we're running out of time! Just choose one of the heroines and save her.

FREDDY, FLORIMOND, *and* FLOYD: We cannot!

MILLIE, MARIGOLD, *and* MIMOSA: You must!

FREDDY, FLORIMOND, *and* FLOYD: But we won't!

DIRECTOR (*Interrupting*): All right. If you can't decide, then we'll leave it to the audience. (*To audience*) Folks, could you vote by applause, please? Should they save Millie the housemaid? (*Pauses until applause dies down*) Marigold, the young lady from a good family? (*Pauses*) Mimosa, the country maiden? (*Pauses*) O.K. The votes are in. (*To* FREDDY, FLORIMOND, *and* FLOYD) Get busy, fellows. We're on a tight schedule here. (*Exits. Train moves closer, humming "Chattanooga Choo-Choo," as three heroes work together to rescue the winning heroine.*)

MADAME DIAMANTE (*Entering, leading* DUNSTON *by the ear*): What do you mean, you've tied my girls to the track? You scoundrel! (*She holds hand in front of train; in commanding tone*) Stop! (*Train stops.*) Untie my girls at once, you villain! (DUNSTON *frees other two heroines. The heroes remain tied together.* MADAME DIAMANTE *waves train on imperiously.*)

DUNSTON (*Simpering*): But they scorned me. Thrice! (*Sneering*) I never would have caught them if they hadn't been sneaking out to meet their swains behind your back!

MILLIE: Alas! Discovered!

MARIGOLD: Alack! Found out!

MIMOSA: Ah, me! He's spilled the beans!

MADAME DIAMANTE (*Aghast*): My girls were sneaking out to meet these three? A lowly footman? An impoverished music instructor? A—good gracious—farm boy?

MILLIE, MARIGOLD, *and* MIMOSA (*Ad lib*): Yes. It's true. You've found us out. (*Etc.*)

MADAME DIAMANTE: Well! (*Long pause*) Why didn't you just tell me you loved them? Silly girls, all I want is for you to be happy! (MILLIE, MARIGOLD, *and* MIMOSA *hug* MADAME DIAMANTE, *then run to their heroes and embrace them.*)

DUNSTON: What? You want them to be—happy?

MADAME DIAMANTE: Of course I do, you villain.

DUNSTON: How could you want such a revolting thing?

MADAME DIAMANTE (*Threateningly*): Perhaps you would like to wait on the tracks for the next train while you're figuring it out, Dunston Darkstorm.

DUNSTON (*On his knees*): Have mercy, Madame Glitterata!

MADAME DIAMANTE: I don't know whether I should. (*To audience*) What do you think? Vote by applause, please. Should I show mercy? (*Pauses for applause to subside*) Should I be as nasty as he is? (*Pauses again*) Just as I thought. Thank you for your cooperation. We'll see that it's taken care of as soon as the curtain goes down. Meanwhile, there's dusting to be done, Millie. And Marigold, I haven't heard the piano in quite some time. Mimosa, pick up that rope, would you dear? (MIMOSA *gathers rope attached to heroes, and they follow her behind* MADAME DIAMANTE.) Come along, boys. Don't dawdle. (*They exit. Curtain*)

THE END

Production Notes

MELODRAMA AT MAYFAIR MEADOWS

Characters: 4 female; 4 male; male or female for Director, Quartet, and Chorus.

Playing Time: 25 minutes.

Costumes: Victorian dress. Millie wears black dress with white apron and cap; Freddie, knickers and jacket; Mimosa and Floyd, country clothing and straw hats; Marigold and Madame Diamante, elegant dresses (Madame Diamante also wears glittery jewelry); Florimond, slightly tattered suit; Dunston, black cape and top hat; Quartet, matching outfits; Chorus members, neutral clothing, except for piano members, who wear black and white.

Properties: Feather duster; bouquet of flowers; four ropes; megaphone.

Setting: Scene 1, the parlor of Mayfair Meadows, with door left. Scene 2, woods on the edge of Mayfair Meadows, with train tracks center.

Lighting: Blackout between Scene 1 and 2, as indicated.

Sound: Train whistle, as indicated.

~Bandit Ben Rides Again

by *Helen Louise Miller*

Could this be how the West was won? . . . .

Characters

WILD BILL
PEANUT BUTTER PETE
JESSE JONES ⎫ *cowboys*
SAD SAM ⎭
SHERIFF BUNCOMBE
MIRANDA, *his daughter*
RED CHIEF
RED SQUAW
WHITE CHIEF
WHITE SQUAW
BLUE CHIEF
BLUE SQUAW
YELLOW CHIEF
YELLOW SQUAW
GREEN CHIEF
GREEN SQUAW
TILLY ⎫
MILLY ⎬ *city slickers*
WILLY ⎭
BANDIT BEN

TIME: *Just after the days of the wild West.*
SETTING: *Sheriff's office near the Tumbleweed* Ranch. Crudely lettered sign left reads TUMBLEWEED RANCH; *sign right reads* SHERIFF'S OFFICE. *There is a rail fence left, and a desk with swivel chair stand right. There is a large hand bell on desk.*

AT RISE: WILD BILL, PEANUT BUTTER PETE, JESSE
JONES *and* SAD SAM *are perched on rail fence, idly twirling
their lassos.* SHERIFF BUNCOMBE *is slouched in swivel
chair, his hat pushed back on his head, feet on the desk. He is
polishing his badge with bandanna.*

COWBOYS (*Singing to the tune of "Git Along Little Doggie"*):
    We're four little cowboys
    From Tumbleweed Ranch,
    We're four little cowboys
    Just waiting our chance
    To do something useful,
    To do something bold,
    Like real western heroes
    In brave days of old.

WILD BILL:
    We've counted our cattle,
    We've herded our sheep.

PEANUT BUTTER PETE:
    There's nothing to do
    But to eat and to sleep.

JESSE JONES:
    We're quick on the trigger.
    We're fast on the draw.

SAD SAM:
    We'd risk any danger
    Upholding the law.

ALL: But we've run out of robbers
    And bad men, you see,
    'Cause all of them lately
    Have jobs on TV!

SHERIFF (*Singing to the tune of "Reuben, Reuben"*):
    I'm the Sheriff of Hokum County
    And I'm shining up my star,
    'Cause it's getting kind of rusty
    With affairs the way they are.
    Why, there hasn't been a hold-up
    Since I couldn't tell you when,
    And the rustlers do not rustle—

Now they're honest cattlemen.
So my star is getting rusty,
And my pistols are the same,
And my saddle's getting dusty,
Now the West is strictly tame!

BILL: Well, boys, what shall we do this afternoon?

PETE: I'm going to make some fresh peanut butter sandwiches.

JESSE: I'm going to write a letter.

SAM: I'm going to read a sad, sad story, so I can have a good cry.

BILL (*Yawning and stretching*): In that case, I might as well take a nap. (*As they exit, he sings to tune of "On Top of Old Smokey."*)

It's back to the bunkhouse
For me and for you,
Because there's just nothing,
Just nothing to do! (*Cowboys exit.*)

SHERIFF: I might as well go fishing. (*Calls off*) Miranda, will you please bring me my fishing rod and that can of worms in the shanty? (MIRANDA *enters with rod and can.*)

MIRANDA: Fishing again, Father?

SHERIFF: A man has to keep busy somehow. (*Picks up rod and can*)

MIRANDA: But we've had so much fish lately, I've started to sprout fins. I hope you don't catch any.

SHERIFF (*Sighing*): But I'm the Sheriff. If I can't catch outlaws, I might as well catch fish. (*Exits*)

MIRANDA (*Sitting in* SHERIFF's *chair*): Poor Father. He still misses the old days when there was a highwayman behind every bush. It certainly is quieter now. (*Five* CHIEFS *and five* SQUAWS *enter in single file. They wear Indian costumes in colors of their names.* SQUAWS *carry camping equipment.* GREEN CHIEF *carries bows and arrows.*)

INDIANS (*Singing*):

One little, two little, three little Indians.
Four little, five little, six little Indians,
Seven little, eight little, nine little Indians,
Ten little Indians all!

RED CHIEF: This is a good place for camp. (*All set equipment down.*)

YELLOW CHIEF: Put the bows and arrows in a dry place, Green Chief.

GREEN CHIEF: Why bother? We never use them any more.

YELLOW CHIEF: They'll come in handy some day.

MIRANDA: Howdy, strangers.

INDIANS: Howdy.

MIRANDA: Welcome to Hokum County. You aim to pitch camp here?

RED CHIEF: Yep.

MIRANDA: Good! It'll be nice to have some new neighbors. (*Sighing*) Though I have to warn you, nothing ever happens here. (TILLY, MILLY, *and* WILLY *enter, screaming.*)

TILLY: Help, help! Sheriff!

MILLY: We've been robbed!

WILLY: Help!

BLUE CHIEF: What's wrong?

TILLY: Help!

MILLY: Help! Help!

MIRANDA: Stop that screaming and tell us what's wrong.

WILLY (*Breathlessly*): We've been robbed! We've been robbed!

MIRANDA: In Hokum County? Impossible. Who are you, anyway?

TILLY, MILLY, *and* WILLY (*Singing to tune of "Old Smokey"*):
We're three City Slickers,
As green as can be.
We don't know a cactus
From a Joshua Tree!

TILLY: I'm Tilly!

MILLY: I'm Milly!

WILLY: I'm Willy!

MIRANDA: How did you get here? Where are your horses?

TILLY (*Singing*):
We never ride horses,
We're fresh from New York.
Our stagecoach was held up
At Red River Fork!

MIRANDA: How exciting!

MILLY (*Pointing at Indians; screaming in terror*): Indians! Help, help!

MIRANDA: Calm down. These Indians won't hurt you.

WILLY (*Trembling*): We'll never see home again.

MILLY (*Whimpering*): We'll be their captives for life.

TILLY (*Falling on her knees*): Spare, oh spare us, merciful Chief.

WHITE CHIEF (*Shaking head*): Too much sun can make you crazy.

YELLOW CHIEF (*Firmly*): This calls for a council. (*To* TILLY) Sit down. Tell us your story. (*Indians sit in semicircle, while* TILLY, MILLY, *and* WILLY *stand center.* MIRANDA *goes to desk.*)

MIRANDA: Now, tell us what really happened to you.

MILLY: Our stage was held up at Red River Fork . . .

WILLY: By a bandit wearing a black mask.

TILLY: He took all my bracelets.

MILLY: And all of my rings.

WILLY: And all of our money.

GREEN CHIEF: What happened to the stagecoach driver?

TILLY: The horses ran off with the coach and driver.

MIRANDA: I'll call my father. He'll know what to do. This is our alarm bell. (*Rings bell*) We always ring it when there is trouble. It will rouse the boys at the Tumbleweed Ranch, too. We haven't had so much excitement in years. (*Cowboys run in left.* PETE *is munching on a sandwich.*)

JESSE: What's up, Miranda?

MIRANDA: Plenty. A bandit just held up the stage at Red River Fork. These people were robbed.

BILL: Come on, men. We'd better see if the cattle are all right.

SAM: Let's go! Pete, finish up that sandwich, and we'll saddle the horses. (*Cowboys exit.*)

RED CHIEF (*To* RED SQUAW): Get the bows and arrows.

GREEN CHIEF (*To* GREEN SQUAW): Bring the war paint, too.

MIRANDA (*Objecting*): You don't need war paint to catch a bandit.

GREEN SQUAW: War paint is good medicine. It scares bandits.

SHERIFF (*Entering with rod and pail*): Miranda, what in tarnation is going on here? You scared me to death ringing that bell, and my biggest fish got away.

MIRANDA: Father, I'm glad you're here!

TILLY: Our stage was held up at Red River Fork.

MILLY: And the bandit took all our money and jewelry.

WILLY: You must catch him at once.

SHERIFF: That we'll do. (*Pompously*) Sheriff Buncombe always gets his man. I'll round up a posse right away.

WHITE CHIEF: Your Indian neighbors are ready to ride with you.

SHERIFF (*To* MIRANDA): Where did these Indians come from?

MIRANDA: They're our new neighbors. They're very friendly.

SHERIFF (*To Indians*): Then get your horses at once. (CHIEFS *exit.*) Did you see which way the bandit went?

TILLY, MILLY, *and* WILLY (*Each one pointing in a different direction*): He went that-a-way!

SHERIFF: Did you call the boys from Tumbleweed Ranch?

MIRANDA: They've gone to check on their cattle and saddle their horses.

SHERIFF: Good. I'll saddle Old Paint and be ready to ride. (*Exits. Cowboys enter on broomstick horses.*)

BILL: That miserable bandit stole some of our best cattle.

JESSE: The varmint! He'll never get away with it. (*Indians enter on broomstick horses.*)

MIRANDA: Our new Indian neighbors are joining the posse.

BILL: Good.

SHERIFF (*Entering on broomstick horse*): No doubt the villain is hiding in Cabbage Canyon. We'll cut him off at Snake Tooth Gap.

WILLY: Maybe I'd better go with you.

SHERIFF: No, you stay here with the ladies. (*To posse*) Come on, fellows, let's go. (*Cowboys and Indians circle stage once, shouting and yelling, then exit left.*)

YELLOW SQUAW: We'd better set up camp.

MIRANDA (*To* TILLY, MILLY, *and* WILLY): Make yourselves at home. (SQUAWS *busy themselves with camp equipment.*) I'll help the squaws. (*She joins* SQUAWS. MILLY, TILLY, *and* WILLY *sit on floor as* BANDIT BEN *enters, wearing black half-mask. He carries bag of loot in one hand and brandishes toy pistol in the other.*)

BANDIT: Stick 'em up. (SQUAWS *and* MIRANDA *turn, surprised.* MILLY, TILLY, WILLY *jump up.*)

ALL (*Ad lib*): The bandit! The bandit! He'll kill us! Help!

BANDIT (*Pointing pistol*): Reach for the sky! (*All raise their hands.*) Now . . . (*Looks around*) nobody here but the ladies, I see. Where are the men?

WILLY: I'm right here. And if you think I'm afraid of that gun, you . . . (*Stammering*) you're right.

MIRANDA (*To* BANDIT): What's your name? And what do you think you're doing here?

BANDIT (*Removing mask; swaggering as he recites*):
I'm a big, bad bandit, by the name of Ben.
I'm a rootin', tootin' rascal from El Gaucho Glen!
All the cowboys tremble, and their horses shy,
And the Injuns quake and quiver when I just ride by!
I'm a big, bold, bad man from the wild, wild West,
And of all the old-time outlaws, I'm the last and the best!
I'm a big bad bandit, as bad as I can be,
It'll do you no good to try to catch me!

MIRANDA (*Defiantly*): Well, my father will catch you. He's out looking for you right now.

BANDIT: He's wasting his time. I knew he'd go that-a-way (*Pointing*), so I came this-a-way.

MILLY *and* TILLY: Help! Help!

BANDIT: Stop that screeching. Be quiet, and you won't get hurt.

MIRANDA: What do you want?

BANDIT: First of all, I want something to eat. Have you any pie?

MIRANDA: I—I think so.

BANDIT: Bring me a nice, big piece. And while you're at it, fry some potatoes and cook a steak. I like it rare and juicy.

MIRANDA: I'm not the cook here.

BANDIT: Don't put on airs. (*Brandishing gun*) Just do as I say.

MIRANDA: But I'm really *not* the cook. Grub Smith is our cook, and he's a good one, too.

BANDIT: Then tell him to get moving and bring me some food.

MIRANDA: He—he's not here right now. He's out in the barn. (*Starting left*) I'll go get him.

BANDIT: No tricks, little lady. You stay right here where I can keep my eyes on you.

MIRANDA: Oh, I don't need to go to the barn. I can call him with this bell. He'll come running the minute he hears it.

BANDIT: O.K., then. Go ahead and ring it, and make it plenty loud. (*Hands to stomach*) I'm as hungry as a grizzly bear.

MIRANDA (*Ringing vigorously, then pausing*): I guess he's in the barn. Maybe he can't hear me. I'll ring again. (*Rings bell. SHERIFF, Cowboys, and Indians gallop on.*)

COWBOYS and INDIANS (*Ad lib*): The bandit! Nab him! (*Etc.*)

SHERIFF: Tie him up. (*Cowboys and Indians disarm BANDIT. BILL ties him up.*) I told you Sheriff Buncombe always gets his man. Now, what shall we do with him?

SAM: There's no punishment too severe for him!

PETE: He'll pay for his crimes now!

JESSE: Yeah! We've got him, and there's no escape!

MIRANDA: Easy, boys—easy. First we must give him a fair trial.

RED CHIEF: He doesn't deserve a trial.

MIRANDA (*To SHERIFF*): Father, as the sheriff you must stand for law and order.

SHERIFF: But this man is a dangerous outlaw, daughter.

WILLY: I have an idea, Sheriff.

SHERIFF: We don't need any of your big-city ideas. We have our own laws here in the West.

WILLY: But this is a great idea, sir.

SHERIFF: O.K., let's hear it.

WILLY: Just turn him over to me.

SHERIFF: What for? What would you do with him?

WILLY (*Producing card and handing it to SHERIFF*): Sir, my card.

SHERIFF (*Reading*): Willy Winkum, President of Reluctant TV Talent, Inc.

WILLY: If you turn him over to me, I'll put him on television and keep him there for the rest of his life. He'll be the last of the bad guys.

BANDIT (*Pleading*): Oh, please no, Sheriff. Anything but that. I don't want to be a bad guy on television. The bad guys always get caught.

SHERIFF: Well, you're caught now, and it's up to us to decide. All those in favor of putting this weasel on television, say "aye"!

ALL: Aye!

SHERIFF: So be it. Mr. Winkum, he's your prisoner. Take him away. (*Pushes* BANDIT *toward* WILLY, *who takes him by his arm*)

WILLY: I promise you he will never escape. He will be caught and punished on every TV show.

ALL: Hurray! Hurray!

BILL (*Singing to tune of "Git Along Little Doggie"*):
And now, my little friends
When you're watching TV,

JESSE:
Just think how unhappy
This bandit will be!

PETE:
No matter how quick,
The hero is quicker!

SAM:
No matter how slick,
The good guys are slicker!

SHERIFF:
And not once, but always,
Again and again,
They'll capture the bandit,
And that will be Ben!

MIRANDA:
'Twill be a lot safer
For you and for me,
To keep this bold bandit
For life on TV! (*Curtain*)

THE END

Production Notes

BANDIT BEN RIDES AGAIN

Characters: 12 male; 8 female.
Playing Time: 20 minutes.
Costumes: Sheriff, Miranda, Cowboys, Indians, traditional costumes. Bandit Ben, dark outfit and black half-mask. Tilly, Milly, Willy wear city clothes.
Properties: Sheriff's badge; lassos; fishing rod; bait can; camping equipment; bows and arrows; sandwich; broomstick horses; bag of loot; toy pistol; rope; business card.
Setting: Sheriff's office near the Tumbleweed Ranch. Crudely lettered sign at left reads TUMBLEWEED RANCH. Another sign at right reads SHERIFF'S OFFICE. Rail fence is left. Desk with swivel chair is right. Large hand bell is on desk.
Lighting: No special effects.

~The Clever Maakafi

by Virginia A. Artist

Girl outwits her elders in African village . . .

Characters

AMIRA, *the narrator*
OBASU, *a healer*
SESI, *his wife*
MAAKAFI, *their daughter*
JUDGE
BAUNDI, *goldsmith*
TOTHI, *an apprentice to Baundi*
OTHER APPRENTICES, *at least four extras*
TOWNSPEOPLE, *extras*

TIME: *Long, long ago.*
SETTING: *An open area near the city wall in the imaginary African city of Dzharka.*
AT RISE: *Sound of African music is heard.* TOWNSPEOPLE *sit or stand in small groups around stage.* AMIRA *enters carrying basket, which she sets down.*
AMIRA (*To audience*): Good day! My name is Amira. Amira means "Teller of Tales." Today I am going to tell you the story of the Clever Maakafi. (*Pause*) One day in the ancient city of Dzharka, Obasu, the healer, his wife, Sesi, and their daughter Maakafi appeared before a judge. Now, in ancient times judges did not hold court in just one place. They traveled from city to city hearing cases and upholding the King's laws. (AMIRA *picks up basket and exits.*)
JUDGE: I will now hear the case of Obasu versus Sesi and Maakafi.

OBASU: It is a very simple case, my lord Judge. My daughter wants to do something I am opposed to. She wants to go to school.

JUDGE (*Horrified*): To school! A girl! Whoever heard of such a thing?

OBASU: That is exactly what I said, my lord Judge. In the history of Dzharka, no girl has ever gone to school. Now my daughter wants to overturn three hundred years of tradition. And to make a bad matter worse, her mother supports her.

SESI (*Matter-of-factly*): Many fine families in other cities are now sending their daughters to school. Maakafi is so clever, she deserves to go.

JUDGE (*Sternly*): You may speak when your turn comes, woman! (*Kindly*) Now, Obasu—poor man—how did your daughter get such an outlandish idea in her head?

OBASU (*Shaking his head*): I only wish I knew, my lord Judge.

JUDGE: Is she willful and disobedient?

SESI: Maakafi is a good girl and, after me, she is the best cook and housekeeper in the city.

JUDGE (*Sharply*): Your turn has not come. Tell me, Obasu, has your daughter had any unusual privileges for a young girl?

OBASU (*Hesitantly*): Well . . .

JUDGE: The court is your friend, Obasu. You may speak frankly.

OBASU: Well, I did teach her to be a healer like me, but only because none of my sons has the wit or the will to learn. A man must pass his skills on to someone.

JUDGE: Aha! I begin to see where the trouble lies!

TOWNSPEOPLE (*Ad lib*): He sees the trouble. He's going to get to the bottom of it. What will he do? (*Etc.*)

SESI: My lord Judge, may I speak?

JUDGE: Not yet! Obasu, how often does a woman become a healer?

OBASU: Only once every hundred years or so does a woman become a healer.

JUDGE: Ah-ha! Maakafi *has* been unusually privileged for a girl. You have been too good to her! Now, Sesi, it is your turn to speak. Tell this court how your daughter has abused this poor man because he has been too kind a father to her!

SESI: Maakafi has not abused anyone. Every one of our sons has gone to school. I am sure Maakafi could do as well as they did. She is very clever.

JUDGE: Maakafi, have you anything to say?

MAAKAFI: My lord Judge, I am a good healer. I could be a better healer if I could read medicine books as my father does. If you let me go to school, I will study night and day to bring honor to my father's house.

OBASU (*Sighing*): You see how it is, my lord Judge. When ideas like these come into a young girl's head, peace flies out the window. Already other young girls are asking their families why they can't go to school. If I send my daughter to school, where will this business of educating women end?

JUDGE (*Gravely*): Obasu, you were right to bring this case to me. This is a matter without precedent in our time and one that could have serious repercussions.

TOWNSPEOPLE (*Ad lib*): Serious repercussions. Did you hear those big words. A wise judge! A clever judge! (*Etc.*)

JUDGE: It is written that three things are most dangerous to a man: a beast that walks upright, a friend who becomes an enemy, and a woman with a little learning.

MAAKAFI (*Skeptically*): Where is that written? I will not believe it until I read it myself.

SESI: Well said, my daughter!

JUDGE: If Maakafi is allowed to go to school, other girls will demand the same privilege. Soon the whole order of nature will be overturned. Do you think men will want to marry learned women?

MAAKAFI: They will if there is no other kind for them to marry.

SESI: Well said, my daughter!

JUDGE: It is a great and terrible mistake to be too indulgent to our daughters, for some women are quick to get too high an opinion of themselves.

OBASU: True, true.

JUDGE: So, Maakafi, stop healing. Stay home and help your mother until you are married—if a husband can be found for you which I seriously doubt, for no man wants a troublesome woman.

MAAKAFI (*Upset*): You mean I can't go to school?

JUDGE: No, you must stay home and tend your yam patch.

SESI *and* MAAKAFI (*In unison*): Oh, no!

JUDGE: Oh, yes.

OBASU (*Pleased*): They said you were a clever judge, and you surely are that! Come, wife. Come, daughter. Let us go home—and no more talk of school for our Maakafi. (OBASU, SESI, *and* MAAKAFI *begin to move slowly away. Suddenly, angry voices are heard off.*)

TOWNSPEOPLE (*Ad lib*): What's that noise? That howling! It's Baundi, the goldsmith! (*Etc.* TOTHI *and* FOUR OTHER APPRENTICES *run on pursued by* BAUNDI *who has stick raised above his head threateningly. He sees* JUDGE *and lowers stick.*)

BAUNDI: Thank goodness the court is still in sitting! Are you the Clever Judge?

JUDGE: I am. Who are you?

BAUNDI: I am Baundi, the goldsmith, as was my father before me and his father before him and—

JUDGE: Enough! What is your problem?

BAUNDI: My lord judge, three months ago the King himself—may his name be praised—

ALL: May his name be praised!

BAUNDI: The King himself sent me a large pearl, as large as the top of my thumb and like the very moon for beauty.

TOWNSPEOPLE (*Ad lib*): The King himself! What an honor! Such a beautiful jewel! (*Etc.*)

BAUNDI: The pearl was to be set in a gold bracelet, which was to be a gift from the Crown Prince to his bride-to-be. (TOWNSPEOPLE *gasp in admiration.*)

JUDGE: Go on, Baundi.

BAUNDI (*Proudly*): My lord Judge, I am the only goldsmith in the city, in the kingdom, who could have set that pearl without harming it. The bracelet I made was a masterpiece, if I do say so myself. (*Angrily*) Now, both pearl and bracelet are gone! Stolen! (TOWNSPEOPLE *gasp.*) And what makes it worse is that the thief had to be one of my own apprentices!

TOWNSPEOPLE (*Ad lib*): Who would do such a thing? What a disgrace! A hanging crime! (*Etc.*)

JUDGE (*Holding up hands to quiet* TOWNSPEOPLE): What do you want this court to do?

BAUNDI: I want you to find the thief.

JUDGE: Has anyone confessed?

BAUNDI: I have begged them on my knees to confess. I have given them my word that the thief will not be punished. I have beaten them until my arm is ready to fall off. All any of them will say is, "I am innocent."

TOTHI *and* APPRENTICES (*In unison*): I am innocent!

BAUNDI (*Shaking stick at them angrily*): Thieves! Ingrates! (*To* JUDGE, *pleadingly*) Unless the real thief is revealed, I will be hanged as a thief and a traitor. My workshop will be burned to the ground. My family will be disgraced forever!

JUDGE (*Unconcerned*): Since no one has confessed, I can do nothing.

BAUNDI (*Shocked*): But you are known as the Clever Judge.

JUDGE: So I am. I am clever enough to stay out of the King's affairs. (*With a sweeping gesture*) Remove yourself and your apprentices from my court at once.

BAUNDI (*Desperately*): Oh! My poor wife! My poor children! They will starve to death, and I will be hanged.

MAAKAFI: One moment, please. I think I can identify the thief.

OBASU (*Sternly*): Daughter, this is none of our business.

MAAKAFI: Father, yes it is. Think what will happen to all the businesses in Dzharka if the King says, "I sent a pearl to Dzharka, and I, the King, was robbed?"

TOWNSPEOPLE (*Ad lib*): She has a point! The whole city would fall under the King's displeasure. Maakafi speaks the truth! (*Etc.*)

OBASU: By heavens, you think like a man. That is something I had not considered. People will say this whole city is a den of thieves. We will all suffer if the King's pearl isn't found.

BAUNDI: Find the thief for me, Maakafi, and I will dress you in jewels fit for a queen.

JUDGE: But she is only a girl!

BAUNDI: I don't care if she's a girl or a goat. I am a dead man unless the King's pearl is found!

JUDGE (*With resignation*): What do you suggest we do, Maakafi?

MAAKAFI: Someone must run to my house and get my work basket.

SESI: I will go, daughter. I know just where it is. (*She runs off.*)

OBASU: Find the King's pearl, my daughter, and you shall go to school—even to the university.

MAAKAFI: My father, you know my only wish is to bring honor to your house. (SESI *returns carrying basket; plants hang out of it.*)

SESI: Here is your work basket, Maakafi.

MAAKAFI: Thank you, Mother. (*To the others*) Now you all know that I am a healer.

TOWNSPEOPLE (*Ad lib enthusiastically*): That is so. Maakafi is a great healer. (*Etc.*)

MAAKAFI: I know the secret virtues of plants and minerals and animal organs.

TOWNSPEOPLE (*Ad lib agreement*): She knows these things. She is very wise. (*Etc.*)

MAAKAFI: So I know that this plant will help us find the thief. (*Pulls plant from basket*)

SESI: Daughter, that plant is—

MAAKAFI (*Interrupting her quickly*): A plant that will let us know who the thief is. (TOWNSPEOPLE *gasp*.) Master Goldsmith, have your apprentices squeeze this plant.

BAUNDI: Squeeze this plant, ingrates!

JUDGE (*Sternly*): You heard Baundi! Squeeze the plant. (*One by one*, TOTHI *and* APPRENTICES *squeeze plant*.)

MAAKAFI: Now, Master Goldsmith, look at their hands. Do you see anything strange?

BAUNDI (*Surprised*): Why, their hands are stained dark red!

MAAKAFI: Are all their hands stained?

BAUNDI: No. Tothi's are nearly clean.

MAAKAFI (*Matter-of-factly*): Then Tothi is your thief.

TOTHI: What!

MAAKAFI (*To* TOTHI): You are the thief. Give Baundi the King's pearl at once, or we will turn you over to the King.

TOTHI (*Terrified*): No! No! I stole the pearl, it is true. (*Drops to his knees*) Have mercy. I will tell you where it is hidden.

BAUNDI (*Hotly*): Thief! Ingrate! Where is the King's pearl?

TOTHI: Under a yellow brick on the floor of my room.

JUDGE: Seize him and hold him until we have the pearl. (TWO APPRENTICES *seize* TOTHI *and hustle him off.*) What magic is this you practice, Maakafi?

MAAKAFI: No magic, my lord judge, only something my mother taught me. This plant is used for making soap—red soap. The others knew they hadn't stolen the King's pearl, so they squeezed the plant as hard as they could to prove their innocence. The oil from the bark stained their hands and fingers dark red, as you all saw. Tothi knew he was guilty so he only *pretended* to squeeze the plant. That is why his palms were clean.

JUDGE: Maakafi, you are indeed a clever young woman.

OBASU: I have always said that Maakafi is as good as a son to me—every bit. She gets her clever wits from me, you know.

SESI *and* MAAKAFI: *We* know.

BAUNDI (*Gratefully*): Maakafi, my word is my bond. I will give you the finest jewelry any woman ever wore.

MAAKAFI: Father is sending me to school. That is reward enough for me.

BAUNDI: If you won't take the jewels as a reward, then take them as a gift. (*To crowd*) Call the drummers! Call the pipers! Let there be music and song and dancing! I will give a feast for the whole city. The King's pearl is safe, and so is my life! (*Drums and pipes are heard. All dance.* AMIRA *enters.*)

AMIRA: So it came about that Maakafi was allowed to go to school. She was even allowed to go to the university, and there she was so very clever that she soon married a learned professor. When the people of Dzharka heard *that*, they all sent their daughters to school. Now that city of Dzharka is as famous for its learned women as it is for its beautiful jewelry and art-

work. Some say this state of affairs is all due to the Clever
Judge. But I ask you—who was the Clever Judge? (AMIRA
joins others in dance as curtains close.)
THE END

Production Notes

THE CLEVER MAAKAFI

Characters: 4 male; 3 female; 4 male or female for Apprentices; male and female extras as needed for Townspeople.

Playing Time: 15 minutes.

Costumes: African clothing. Since Dzharka is a major trade center, the clothing may represent diverse ethnic groups. Judge carries a cow tail switch or long gourd rattle to call court to order and as a symbol of his authority.

Properties: Two baskets, one with a plant in it; a large stick.

Setting: Simple set. Backdrop may be painted to represent a large stone wall with grass growing at its base and palm trees painted here and there. Potted palms or other tall foliage may be placed on stage.

Sound: Recordings of African music, as indicated.

Lighting: No special effects.

~The Zeem Dream

by Gart Westerhout

A nightmare rescue from the Horrible Hogglewart . . .

Characters

STEPHEN
JENNIE, *his sister*
MOTHER, *offstage voice*
FOUR ZEEMBIRDS
MEETER
GREETER
FREDDIE
KATHY, *his sister*
SEVEN BUBBLE BLOWERS
ZORT
OGGLE
HORRIBLE HOGGLEWART

SCENE 1

TIME: *Evening, the present.*
SETTING: *Bedroom with twin beds. May be played before curtain.*
BEFORE RISE: STEPHEN *and* JENNIE *enter left, wearing pajamas.*
MOTHER (*Offstage*): Now, you two, I want you to go straight to bed! No talking, no flashlights, no nothing!
STEPHEN *and* JENNIE (*Together*): Yes, Mother. (*They lie down.*)
STEPHEN (*After a pause, sitting up*): Hey, Jen, are you awake?
JENNIE (*Angrily*): I don't want to talk to you, Stephen! It's just

not fair! Kathy and I were having a nice time jumping rope, when all of a sudden you get in a fight with her horrible brother Freddie, and get me in trouble, too. It's way before my bedtime—I'll never get to sleep, and it's all your fault!

STEPHEN (*Petulantly*): No it's not, it's *Freddie's* fault. Some friend he is! (*He lies down. Lights dim, and short interlude of dreamy music is heard.*)

* * *

TIME: *Short time later.*

SETTING: *Planet Zeem. Landscape is stark, with strange trees, big rocks, and sign that reads,* WELCOME TO PLANET ZEEM.

AT RISE: *Music fades and lights flicker for a moment.* STEPHEN *and* JENNIE *enter, still in pajamas, looking dazed and confused.*

STEPHEN: Wow! Where are we, Jen?

JENNIE: How should I know? (*Notices sign*) Wait, look—there's a sign. (*Reads*) "Welcome to Planet Zeem."

STEPHEN: Planet Zeem? Weird. Well, if we're lucky, Freddie isn't on this planet, too.

JENNIE: I'm not sure I like the looks of this place—it could be dangerous. (FOUR ZEEMBIRDS *enter left, doing somersaults or rolling sideways, dressed in brightly colored leotards with feathers attached. They do not notice children.*) Hey, what funny-looking birds! (JENNIE *and* STEPHEN *hide behind large rock.* ZEEMBIRDS *roll to center and stand.* JENNIE *and* STEPHEN *peek out during following exchange.*)

1ST BIRD (*Breathlessly*): Am I worn out!

2ND BIRD (*Grumpily*): Stop your complaining!

3RD BIRD: I'm tired, too.

4TH BIRD: But this is what we do every day. We roll across the desert, and then we roll back.

1ST BIRD (*Sadly*): Maybe we're just bored. Nothing much happens here on Zeem. (*Suddenly,* STEPHEN *loses balance and rolls out from behind rock.* JENNIE *tumbles out after him.* ZEEMBIRDS, *curious, cross over to them.*)

4TH BIRD: Well, look here.

STEPHEN (*Terrified; on his knees, pleading*): Spare me! Spare me! I'll do anything you ask.

2ND BIRD: Spare you? Spare you from what?

JENNIE (*Desperately*): From your evil intentions. Please, don't kill us! (ZEEMBIRDS *look at each other, then burst out laughing.*)

3RD BIRD: Kill you! Why would we do that? This is a peaceful planet. Nobody is mean to anybody here. (JENNIE *and* STEPHEN *sigh in relief.*)

BIRDS (*Together*): Except for the Horrible Hogglewart!

STEPHEN *and* JENNIE (*Together*): The horrible *what*?

1ST BIRD (*Shuddering*): The Horrible Hogglewart. Surely you've heard of him.

JENNIE: Uh, no, but he does sound horrible. (*Pointing to sign*) We're not on Earth, are we? (MEETER *and* GREETER *rush on. They wear silver robes and turbans.*)

MEETER: Of course not. This is Planet Zeem.

GREETER: Welcome, friends, to Zeem, the 24th planet in the wonderful gappersnort solar system in the galaxy of Zod. I'm the Greeter . . .

MEETER: And I'm the Meeter, officially assigned to welcome all visitors to Planet Zeem.

STEPHEN (*Tentatively*): Nice to meet you. I'm Stephen, and this is my sister, Jennie. (JENNIE *waves uncertainly.*) We're from (*Names town of production*)—uh, in the U.S.A., Planet Earth.

MEETER: Ah, yes, Earth: the third planet in the solar system that revolves around the sun, in the far corner of the Milky Way. Isn't that where TV dinners were invented?

GREETER: Yes, as were portable CD players, high-priced sneakers, and toast.

4TH BIRD: We were just telling them about the Horrible Hogglewart.

GREETER (*Ominously*): Oh, yes, whatever you do, watch out for the Horrible Hogglewart. He eats little children!

JENNIE (*Sarcastically*): Hey, maybe we can take him home and introduce him to Freddie. (*She and* STEPHEN *snicker.*)

4TH BIRD: Well, we were just rolling home for supper—would you two care to join us? (ZEEMBIRDS *start to roll to exit.*)

STEPHEN *and* JENNIE (*Together*): Oh, yes, thanks! We're

starving! (ZEEMBIRDS *roll off.* JENNIE *and* STEPHEN *look at each other, shrug, then follow them off, doing somersaults.*)

* * * * *

SCENE 2

TIME: *A short while later.*
SETTING: *Same.*
AT RISE: FREDDIE *and* KATHY *enter right, dazed and confused.*
FREDDIE (*Looking about*): Where are we?
KATHY: I have no idea. The last I remember, you and Stephen were fighting, and his mom called him and Jennie inside. Then we climbed to the tree fort to spy over the fence at them with our flashlights, and suddenly I was very tired.
FREDDIE: Yeah, so was I. But I'm not tired anymore, and we're not in our tree fort, either. (*Points to sign*) We're on Planet Zeem, whatever that is! (MEETER *and* GREETER *enter.*)
MEETER: Welcome to Planet Zeem! I'm the Meeter . . .
GREETER: And I'm the Greeter of Zeem, the 24th planet in the wonderful gappersnort solar system in the galaxy of Zod.
KATHY: But how did we get here, and what are we doing here? (MEETER *and* GREETER *exchange glances, shrug.*) Tell me. (*Pause, then louder*) Tell me! (SEVEN BUBBLE BLOWERS *come laughing and prancing through the aisles onto stage. They wear white shirts with big, colorful spots, party hats, and are blowing soap bubbles.*)
BUBBLES (*Mockingly*): Tell me! Tell me! (*The following introductions should go in rapid succession, and though the number of Bubbles may vary, the last is always named Sam.*)
1ST BUBBLE: Hi! I'm Bubbles.
2ND BUBBLE: I'm Bubbles' brother, Bubby.
3RD BUBBLE: I'm Bubble Trouble.
4TH BUBBLE: And I'm Bubble Trouble's double!
5TH BUBBLE: I'm Chubble Rubble.
6TH BUBBLE: I'm Hubble Gubble.
7TH BUBBLE: And I'm Sam.

ALL OTHER BUBBLES (*Together*): Sam?!

7TH BUBBLE: All right, all right, I'm not Sam, but my name is so complicated!

FREDDIE: What is it?

7TH BUBBLE: Well, if you must know, it's Bubbleheimer Iddlesquatter Funneltrooper Flooper.

FREDDIE *and* KATHY: *What?*

BUBBLES (*Singing to tune of "Supercalifragilisticexpialidocious" from "Mary Poppins"*):
He's Bubbleheimer Iddlesquatter Funneltrooper Flooper
Bubbleheimer Iddlesquatter Funneltrooper Flooper
Bubbleheimer Iddlesquatter Funneltrooper Flooper
Bubbleheimer Iddlesquatter Funneltrooper Flooper!

7TH BUBBLE: See what a pain that is?

KATHY: I have an idea. Why don't you just use your initials instead of your whole name?

7TH BUBBLE: What do you mean?

KATHY: Well, "B" stands for Bubbleheimer, "I" stands for Iddlesquatter, "F" stands for Funneltrooper, and "F" stands for Flooper.

FREDDIE: Right! and B-I-F-F spells Biff. Just call yourself Biff!

6TH BUBBLE: What a super idea!

1ST BUBBLE: I'd call it super duper.

2ND BUBBLE: A super duper Funneltrooper!

3RD BUBBLE: Now you'll never make a blooper, Biff!

5TH BUBBLE: Oh, super super poodle grouper!

4TH BUBBLE: Well, in my opinion, that's just super, Biff!

7TH BUBBLE: Incredible! Fantastic! I shall be happy to call myself Biff!

1ST BUBBLE: Wonderful!

2ND BUBBLE: Just super.

3RD BUBBLE: Let's not start that again!

5TH BUBBLE: We're so thankful for your idea.

7TH BUBBLE (*Elatedly*): Yes, thank you, thank you, thank you!

1ST BUBBLE: What are your names?

FREDDIE: I'm Freddie.

KATHY: And I'm Kathy.

1ST BUBBLE (*Frowning*): Your names are strange. (*Smiling*) But you seem nice.

2ND BUBBLE: Perhaps you can help defend us against our biggest bubble—I mean, trouble.

BUBBLES (Together): Yes, maybe you can help capture the Horrible Hogglewart!

FREDDIE *and* KATHY (*Together*): The horrible what?

2ND BUBBLE (*Looking off*): Look out! Here come his henchmen! (ZORT *and* OGGLE *rush onstage; they are dressed in black, wear white gloves, and carry a rope.* FREDDIE, KATHY, *and* BUBBLE BLOWERS *run off, screaming.*)

ZORT: Blast! They got away, Oggle!

OGGLE: Foiled again! The Horrible Hogglewart will be very angry with us for not capturing those earthlings.

ZORT (*Fearfully*): He'll probably twist our ears and stretch our noses.

OGGLE: Or even worse, make us eat chocolate-covered worms for a week.

ZORT *and* OGGLE (*Grimacing; together*): Yuck!

OGGLE: I hear someone coming! Quick, Zort, *hide!* (*They crouch behind large rock as* JENNIE *and* STEPHEN *enter.*)

JENNIE: Boy, that was the best supper I've ever had!

STEPHEN: You said it! Those Zeembirds may have trouble flying, but they sure can cook! (STEPHEN *and* JENNIE *start to sit on large rock.* ZORT *and* OGGLE *swoop up and capture them, then tie them together with rope.*)

ZORT: Aha! Gotcha!

STEPHEN *and* JENNIE (*Ad lib*): Hey! Let us go! (*Etc.*)

OGGLE: Hey, these aren't the ones we were chasing earlier.

ZORT: So what? The Horrible Hogglewart will eat any youngster—even a funny-looking one.

JENNIE: Talk about funny-looking!

OGGLE: Wait until you see the Horrible Hogglewart! (*They exit;* JENNIE *and* STEPHEN *protest loudly as* ZORT *and* OGGLE, *laughing wickedly, push them ahead. Curtain*)

* * * * *

SCENE 3

TIME: *Later that day.*
SETTING: *Same.*

AT RISE: SEVEN BUBBLE BLOWERS *rush onstage, all appear upset.*

6TH BUBBLE: Have you heard the news? Two earthlings have been captured by the Horrible Hogglewart's assistants!

5TH BUBBLE: Oh, the poor earthlings.

BUBBLES (*Together*): Poor, poor earthlings. (FREDDIE *and* KATHY *enter.*)

FREDDIE *and* KATHY: Poor earthlings? What are you talking about? We're fine.

2ND BUBBLE: Two other children are now prisoners of the Horrible Hogglewart, and he will surely eat them alive.

FREDDIE *and* KATHY (*Ad lib*): Oh, no! That's terrible! (*Etc.*)

KATHY: There must be something we can do to help. (MEETER *and* GREETER *enter, followed by* ZEEMBIRDS.)

GREETER: Greetings!

MEETER: Meetings! (*To* KATHY) There is something you might be able to do.

FREDDIE: Tell us!

MEETER: Well, legend says that if an earthling is brave enough to throw a cup of water in the face of the Horrible Hogglewart, he will fall asleep for exactly one minute—just long enough for us to capture him.

GREETER: But he eats children up so fast, no one has ever had the chance to throw water on him.

FREDDIE: We have to try and help, Kathy. Come on, lead us to the cave of the Horrible Hogglewart! (*All exit. Curtain*)

* * * * *

SCENE 4

TIME: *Shortly thereafter.*

SETTING: *Cave of the Hogglewart. Previous setting may simply be rearranged, and sign removed.*

AT RISE: ZORT *and* OGGLE *enter, pulling* STEPHEN *and* JENNIE *on by rope. Ominous music is heard and lights flicker a moment as* HORRIBLE HOGGLEWART *enters from back of theater, growling and hissing as he lumbers down aisle and onto stage.*

HOGGLEWART (*Bellowing*): Make way for the Horrible Hog-
glewart! (*Chanting*)
Oh, yes, I am the Hoggle,
And as a little sport,
I'll chop you up, then eat you up
I am the Hogglewart.
ZORT *and* OGGLE (*Chanting*):
He loves to eat umbrellas
And squirmy wormies, too.
But most of all he likes to eat
Children just like you.
Oh, watch out for the Hoggle
He's horrible and gross.
He'll put you in the blender
And spread you on his toast.
ZORT, OGGLE, *and* HOGGLEWART:
So, scrawny little earthlings,
We'll get you very soon.
Oh, yes we're going to eat you for
A snack this afternoon! (*They laugh hysterically.*)
HOGGLEWART (*Looking closely at* STEPHEN *and* JENNIE):
Hm-m-m. Rather scrawny, aren't they? Our magical meal
chant will turn them into tastier morsels. (*They kneel and
mumble jibberish.* FREDDIE *enters, carrying cup of water,
followed by* KATHY, FOUR ZEEMBIRDS, SEVEN BUB-
BLES, MEETER, *and* GREETER. *They surround* HOG-
GLEWART, ZORT, *and* OGGLE. *All at once, some of them
jump* OGGLE *and* ZORT, *pinning them down, while* FRED-
DIE *throws water in* HOGGLEWART'*s face.*)
OGGLE *and* ZORT (*Ad lib*): Hey, let go of us! We'll get you for
this! (*Etc.*)
HOGGLEWART (*Angrily*): Who dares to—(*Suddenly falls into
trance*)
STEPHEN *and* JENNIE (*Ad lib; gratefully*): We're saved!
Thank you! (*Etc.* BUBBLES *remove rope from* STEPHEN *and*
JENNIE *and tie* HOGGLEWART, OGGLE, *and* ZORT *to-
gether. Others cheer.*)

STEPHEN (*Suddenly noticing* KATHY *and* FREDDIE): Freddie! Kathy! What are you doing here?

FREDDIE: I was about to ask you the same thing, Stephen.

JENNIE: That was very brave of you, Freddie, sneaking up and splashing the Horrible Hogglewart.

STEPHEN: Yes, you saved our lives. (*Pause*) Maybe you're not so bad after all. (*Extends hand*) Friends?

FREDDIE (*After a moment; smiling*): Friends! (*They shake, and all cheer.* HOGGLEWART *wakes up with a roar. All laugh as they drag him,* OGGLE, *and* ZORT *offstage. Curtain*)

* * * * *

SCENE 5

TIME: *Next morning.*

SETTING: *Same as Scene 1, bedroom. May be played before curtain.*

BEFORE RISE: STEPHEN *and* JENNIE *wake up, stretch, and yawn.*

JENNIE: I had the strangest dream last night. I feel as if I haven't slept at all. (*Stands and rubs eyes*)

STEPHEN: Same here. And you know what I've been thinking? Maybe Freddie isn't such a creep after all! (*They nod in agreement, then start to giggle as lights dim to blackout.*)

THE END

Production Notes

THE ZEEM DREAM

Characters: 2 male; 2 female; 16 or more male and female for inhabitants of Planet Zeem; offstage female voice.

Playing Time: 20 minutes.

Costumes: Stephen and Jennie, pajamas; Freddie and Kathy, play clothes; Zeembirds, leotards, solid, brightly colored shirts, feathers attached to costume; Meeter and Greeter, silver robes and turbans; Bubble Blowers, leotards, large white shirts with big, colorful spots, bright party hats or hair ribbons with helium balloons attached; Zort and Oggle, all-black clothing and white gloves; Horrible Hogglewart, black cape and wild hair.

Properties: Soap bubble bottles; rope; cup of water (or confetti).

Setting: Before rise, Scenes 1 and 5: bedroom, with two twin beds or cots, played before curtain. At rise, Scenes 1, 2, and 3: Planet Zeem, a stark landscape with strange trees, big rocks, and sign reading WELCOME TO PLANET ZEEM. Scene 4: Hogglewart's cave, a rearrangement of Planet Zeem landscape, minus sign.

Lighting: Flickering lights and blackout, as noted in text.

Sound: Dreamy music for transition to Planet Zeem; ominous music for Hogglewart's entrance.

❧The Mother Goose Olympics

by Robert A. Mauro

Calling all candlestick-jumpers and nursery-rhyme gymnasts . . .

Characters

JIM McCLOUD } *sportscasters*
CATHY LEE SUNSHINE
JUNE WARNER, *director*
PHOTO FOSTER, *camera operator*
TWO MAKE-UP ARTISTS, *extras*
OLD KING COLE
THREE FIDDLERS
TWO ASSISTANTS
SIX JUDGES
WEE WILLIE WINKIE
JACK BE NIMBLE
COW, *two actors*
MARGERY DAW
TWO DUCKS
MOTHER GOOSE

TIME: *Once upon a time.*
SETTING: *Stadium, where Mother Goose Olympics will take place. Upstage center, there is a throne for Old King Cole, down left a booth with two chairs, for TV sportscasters, and nearby, a director's chair. Banner, reading* THE MOTHER GOOSE OLYMPICS, *hangs overhead. Crowd is shown on backdrop. Pennants, flags, and balloons fly from upstage walls.*
AT RISE: JIM McCLOUD *and* CATHY LEE SUNSHINE *sit in*

267

TV booth. TWO MAKE-UP ARTISTS *work on them, adjust clothing, etc.* CATHY LEE *holds microphone;* JIM *has stopwatch and binoculars, microphone.* JUNE WARNER, *wearing earphones, enters right and crosses to booth, followed by* PHOTO FOSTER, *who carries portable TV camera.*

JUNE: O.K. Places everyone! (MAKE-UP ARTISTS *exit right.* FOSTER *focuses on sportscasters.* JIM *and* CATHY LEE *smile into camera.* JUNE *counts down.*) Seven . . . six . . . five . . . four . . . three . . . two . . . one. (*Points to* JIM *and* CATHY LEE) You're on the air! (JUNE *sits in director's chair.*)

JIM (*Speaking into mike*): Hello, sports fans! This is your TV Action Sports Reporter, Jim McCloud—

CATHY LEE (*Into her mike; brightly*): And Cathy Lee Sunshine—

JIM: Coming to you live from Mother Goose Land!

CATHY LEE: We're here today to bring you action coverage of the Mother Goose Olympics, via the Mother Goose Satellite! (*Sound of cheering is heard offstage.*)

JIM: Just listen to that crowd roar! Yes, it's going to be an exciting day here! In just a few moments, the games will begin. Tell us what we'll be seeing, Cathy Lee.

CATHY LEE: All our favorite Mother Goose characters will be competing for those coveted Mother Goose Gold Medals!

JIM (*Looking offstage*): And here comes our royal dignitary, Old King Cole, for the opening ceremonies. (OLD KING COLE *enters, followed by* THREE FIDDLERS *who carry violins, and* TWO ASSISTANTS, *one carrying a pipe, the other, a bowl of soap solution for blowing bubbles.*)

CATHY LEE: Old King Cole! What a merry old soul he is.

JIM: A merry old soul is he. (KING *sits on throne.* JIM *recites.*) He called for his pipe . . .
(KING *beckons to* 1ST ASSISTANT, *who bows and gives him his pipe.*)
He called for his bowl . . .
(2ND ASSISTANT *bows and hands bowl to* KING. *During following dialogue,* KING *blows soap bubbles with pipe.*)

CATHY LEE (*Reciting*):
And he called for his Fiddlers Three!

(KING *beckons to* FIDDLERS, *who cross to throne, bow, and pantomime playing. Music is heard.* ASSISTANTS *stand at attention.* KING *blows bubbles.*)

JIM: The fiddlers are playing the Mother Goose National Anthem.

CATHY LEE: What an exciting moment!

JIM (*As music ends*): The Mother Goose Olympics are about to begin! (FIDDLERS *and* ASSISTANTS *exit.* KING *remains on throne. During following dialogue, he watches action and blows bubbles intermittently.* WEE WILLIE WINKIE *enters, wearing nightshirt, nightcap, and running shoes. He begins to do warm-up exercises and to jog in place.*) The first event is the 5,000 meter dash. Here's our first contestant!

CATHY LEE: It's that famous Mother Goose Land long-distance runner, Wee Willie Winkie.

WILLIE (*Waving to audience*): Hi there, everyone!

JIM: Two years ago Willie set an Olympic record when he ran through the town, upstairs and down, in his nightgown.

CATHY LEE: But in our last Olympics, Jim, Willie's record was beaten by Tom, the piper's son.

JIM (*Reciting*):
Tom, Tom, the piper's son
Stole a pig and away he run.

CATHY LEE: Yes, Tom was quick, but Willie's been training all year for this event, and he has a good chance of beating Tom's record. I see he's wearing his lucky nightshirt.

JIM: Yes, and for your information, folks, that is a regulation nightshirt, approved by the Mother Goose Olympics board.

CATHY LEE: His sneakers meet Mother Goose requirements, too, Jim.

JIM: They certainly do. Those sneakers were made especially for Willie by the little old woman who lived in a shoe. At one time, she had so many children, she didn't know what to do.

CATHY LEE: She finally got a job as a shoemaker. She now owns her own company and brings out an entire line of athletic footwear! (1ST JUDGE *enters, holding starting gun.*)

JIM: Cathy Lee, here comes the judge. (WILLIE *gets on his mark.*)

CATHY LEE: Willie's on the mark! (JUDGE *fires starting gun.*)

JIM: And there he goes! (WILLIE *runs offstage and up aisle, as* JIM *starts his stopwatch and looks through binoculars at* WILLIE. *Running,* WILLIE *exits at rear of auditorium.* 1ST JUDGE *exits.*)

CATHY LEE: He'll be gone for a while, Jim, so let's move on to our next event: the high jump. (JACK BE NIMBLE *enters, wearing shorts and tank top. He holds three candles.*)

JIM: Here comes Jack Be Nimble! (JACK *crosses to* JIM *and* CATHY LEE.) Good to see you, Jack. Tell our audience about your event. (*Holds microphone up to* JACK, *who speaks into it.*)

JACK: I'd be happy to, Jim. (*To audience*) I'm a candle-jumper, and today I'll be trying to top all candle-jumping records.

CATHY LEE (*To audience*): According to our computer, the record is 17.999 inches.

JACK: That's right, Cathy Lee. That record is currently held by my little dog. (*Recites*)
Leg over leg,
As the dog went to Dover;
When he came to a stile,
Hop! He went over.

JIM: Let's hope you hop right over today, Jack! I see you have a few candles with you.

JACK: Right, Jim. (*Displays candles*) This one is 18 inches. Here we have a 24-incher. And this third is a full three feet long! (2ND JUDGE *enters, takes candles.*)

JIM (*To audience*): O.K., sports fans, you've heard it straight from the champ, Jack Be Nimble. Now it's time for the event you've all been waiting for!

CATHY LEE: All I can say is (*Recites*)
Jack be nimble,
Jack be quick,
Jack jump over the candlestick!

JACK: Thanks, Cathy Lee. I'll try the biggest one first. (JUDGE *sets candle down, center.*)

JIM: Good luck, Jack! (JACK *crosses to right.*)

CATHY LEE: There he goes! (JACK *runs toward candle.*) He's

running, running, running! (JACK *attempts to jump candle, but knocks it down.*)

JIM: Too bad. He didn't make it at three feet.

JACK (*Breathlessly*): I'll try the 24-incher. (JUDGE *sets up second candle.*)

CATHY LEE: Jack is going to try the 24-inch candle now. And it's a veritable giant! (JACK *crosses right, starts running center again.*)

JIM: And there he goes! (JACK *jumps over candle.*) He's up—and over!

CATHY LEE *and* JIM (*Together*): He made it! (*Roar of crowd is heard. KING applauds.*)

JIM: It's a new candle-jumping world's record! (JACK *waves hands in air, then exits, followed by* 2ND JUDGE.)

CATHY LEE: Next, Jim, we're going to meet our first animal contestant. (COW *enters.*) Another entry in the high-jump event.

JIM: It's the famous Cow who jumped over the moon!

CATHY LEE: What's the Cow going to try today, Jim?

JIM: Let's ask. (*They walk over to* COW.) Cow, can you tell our audience what you plan to jump over today?

COW (*Proudly*): Moo moo moo-oo! Moo moo moo-oo!

CATHY LEE (*Astonished*): You don't say!

COW (*Firmly*): Moo moo moo!

JIM: I don't believe it, Cathy Lee. (*To audience*) Sports fans, Cow is going to attempt to jump over the planet Jupiter!

CATHY LEE: Jumping Jupiter! That's never been done before.

COW (*Proudly*): Moo-oo! (3RD JUDGE *enters, carrying ball, labeled,* JUPITER. COW *directs* JUDGE *to place ball at center.*)

JIM: There we have Jupiter being carefully set up. As we mentioned before, Cow cleared the moon last year. Do you think she'll be able to jump over Jupiter?

CATHY LEE: We'll soon see. (COW *warms up at right, shuffling hooves, jumping, etc.* JIM *and* CATHY LEE *return to booth.*)

JIM: The Cow is warming up now, with the usual Moo Cow calisthenics. (COW *begins to run toward center.* JIM *speaks excitedly.*) There she goes! (COW *jumps over globe.* JUDGE *signals.*)

CATHY LEE *and* JIM: She's up and over! She's jumped Jupiter!

JIM: That was amazing! Another record, folks! (*Roar is heard.* KING *applauds.* COW *bows, then exits, right.* 3RD JUDGE *removes globe, and exits.* MARGERY DAW *enters.*)

CATHY LEE: Look, Jim. Here comes Margery Daw, better known to all you balance beam fans as See-Saw Margery Daw. (MARGERY *warms up.* 4TH *and* 5TH JUDGES *enter, carrying board. They set it down on floor, then adjust until it is parallel to front of stage.*)

JIM: The judges have set up the balance beam and checked it carefully, to make sure that it's not dangerous.

CATHY LEE: Right, Jim. (*Seriously*) The Mother Goose Olympics Commission has tightened its safety codes, after what happened to Humpty Dumpty.

JIM: In case you don't remember, sports fans (*Recites*)—
Humpty Dumpty sat on a wall,
Humpty Dumpty had a great fall;
All the King's horses and all the King's men
Couldn't put Humpty together again.

CATHY LEE (*Shaking head*): That was terrible, Jim. Humpty was such a good egg! (MARGERY DAW *steps up on end of board, poised.*)

JIM: I think Margery Daw is ready to perform. (*Music is heard from offstage.* MARGERY DAW *begins to dance on board.*) There she goes! Look at her keep in step with that music!

CATHY LEE: That's what I call style! She should get all sevens for her score!

JIM: I agree, Cathy Lee. (*Pause*) I believe she's just about finished. (MARGERY DAW *jumps from board and strikes a triumphant pose. Music stops. Roar of crowd is heard as she bows.*)

CATHY LEE: That was perfect! A perfect performance!

JIM: Our audience certainly was impressed. (JUDGES *take out cards and pretend to mark them.*)

CATHY LEE: Any second now we'll know Margery Daw's score. Remember, the current world's record was set by Humpty Dumpty!

JIM: Although Humpty's balance wasn't as good as Margery's, he ended up with a shattering 6.9!

CATHY LEE: The suspense here is unbelievable! (JUDGES *face audience and hold up cards. Each one reads* 7.0)

JIM (*Enthusiastically*): And it's a perfect score!

CATHY LEE: A perfect seven for Margery Daw! (MARGERY *jumps excitedly. She may do a few cartwheels, then runs off.* JUDGES *remove board and exit.*)

JIM: This certainly is an exciting day! Don't you agree, Cathy Lee?

CATHY LEE: I certainly do, Jim. (*To audience*) I'm sure our viewers at home are just as thrilled.

JIM: The swimming event is next. (TWO DUCKS *waddle on and stand poised, center.* 6TH JUDGE *enters, with starting gun.*) And here are the ducks. Remember them, Cathy Lee?

CATHY LEE: I sure do, Jim. (*Recites*)
The cock's on the housetop
Blowing his horn;
The bull's in the barn
A-threshing of corn;
The maids in the meadow
Are making of hay . . .

JIM (*Reciting*):
And the Ducks in the river
Are swimming away!
(JUDGE *fires starting gun.* DUCKS *cross from right to left, flapping their wings and waddling frantically.*)

CATHY LEE: They're really moving!

JIM: Last year, Goosey Goosey Gander received the gold medal in this event.

CATHY LEE: Look, Jim! That little ugly duckling from Long Island is in the lead!

JIM: But here comes the Peking duck! Look at him cut through the water! (DUCKS *continue "swimming," making turns at left and heading back right.*)

CATHY LEE: The Long Island duckling is catching up!

JIM: They're beak to beak!

CATHY LEE: They're coming to the finish! (JUDGE *raises arm.*)

JIM: It's going to be close. (1ST DUCK *reaches* JUDGE, *who drops arm.*) The Long Island duckling wins! (*Crowd is heard cheering.* KING *applauds.* DUCKS *exit, followed by* 6TH JUDGE.)

CATHY LEE (*Pointing into audience*): Here comes Willie, our long-distance runner! (WILLIE *enters at back of auditorium, runs down aisle.*)

JIM (*Raising binoculars*): I see him! (*Roar of crowd is heard.* JIM *checks stopwatch.*) He has ten seconds left to beat the record of 13 minutes, 20.8 seconds! (1ST JUDGE *reenters with* 2ND JUDGE. *They hold red tape, down center.*)

CATHY LEE (*Dramatically*): That's going to be close!

JIM (*Counting*): Seven . . . six . . . (WILLIE *rushes up onto stage.*) five . . . four . . . (WILLIE *breaks tape, hands in the air.*)

CATHY LEE (*Jumping excitedly*): He did it! He's broken the record! (*Roar is heard from crowd.* WILLIE *waves arms triumphantly.*)

JUNE (*To* CATHY LEE *and* JIM, *as she crosses to booth*): That's all the time we have. Let's cut to the award ceremonies.

JIM (*Into mike*): Looks as if our time is about up, folks. And here comes Mother Goose to present the medals! (*Roar is heard.* MOTHER GOOSE *enters, carrying a long pole over her shoulders, with a sack hanging from each end of it.*)

MOTHER GOOSE (*Puffing and struggling to balance pole*): One of these giant sacks is full of solid-silver medals and the other is full of solid-gold ones! (*Sets pole down on stage*) They're for our new Mother Goose Olympics champions. (*Entire cast reenters;* JACK BE NIMBLE, COW, MARGERY DAW, 1ST DUCK *join* WILLIE *at center.*) There's one medal especially for our grand champion.

JIM: Who's that, Mother Goose?

MOTHER GOOSE (*Lifting pole and heavy sacks over her head, with difficulty*): Who?

CATHY LEE: Yes, Mother Goose, who is this year's grand champion?

MOTHER GOOSE (*Triumphantly raising pole*): Me!

JIM *and* CATHY LEE: You? For what?

MOTHER GOOSE (*Fighting to balance heavy weight; straining*

to speak): For weight-lifting! These sacks of medals weigh a ton! (*Roar of crowd is heard. All cheer for* MOTHER GOOSE, *as curtains close quickly.*)

THE END

Production Notes

THE MOTHER GOOSE OLYMPICS

Characters: 4 male, 4 female; 18 male and/or female, for Photo Foster, Make-Up Artists, Fiddlers, Assistants, Judges, Cow (two actors), and Ducks.

Playing Time: 20 minutes.

Costumes: Appropriate athletic attire for all Olympic contestants. Two actors wear Cow costume, one in front, one in rear. Ducks wear yellow with construction paper "feather" wings, orange beaks, swimming goggles. Willie has on nightshirt, nightcap, running shoes. Mother Goose wears frilly white dress, blue sash, flowery bonnet, and spectacles. King wears royal attire, crown. Fiddlers wear jester costumes. Judges wear black slacks, white shirts with judge on shirt. June, Photo Foster, Cathy Lee, and Jim wear modern, everyday dress.

Properties: Stopwatch; binoculars; earphones; make-up powder puff; portable TV camera; three fiddles; starting "guns" (cap pistols may be used); bowl of soap bubble solution; bubble pipe; cards for 4th and 5th Judges, with large number 7.0 on each; three candles of graduated sizes; board; red ribbon; ball, reading JUPITER; pole with two sacks suspended from it, one reading SILVER, the other GOLD.

Setting: Stadium. Throne, up center. Booth with two chairs, down left. Nearby, director's chair. Banner, reading THE MOTHER GOOSE OLYMPICS, plus pennants, balloons, and flags, decorate stage. Backdrop shows outline of crowd. Exits are right and at rear of auditorium.

Lighting: No special effects.

Sound: Roar of crowd; recorded fiddle music and dance music, as indicated in text.

~Madame Zena's Séance

by Mary E. Hanson
and David P. Sheldon

A summons to the spirit world brings unexpected guests . . . .

Characters

PRINCESS
ROXY
JOE } *mobsters*
MOE
GRANDMOTHER
MRS. ALICE PORTER
AUNT PHYLLIS } *her daughters*
BOBBY PORTER, *Alice's son*
ABDUL
OMAR
MADAME ZENA, *a psychic*
CINDY PORTER, *Alice's daughter*
TWO POLICE OFFICERS

TIME: *Early afternoon, the present.*
SETTING: *Living room of the Porter house. Front door is down right; kitchen door is up right; bedroom door, up left, and basement door, down left. Sofa and coffee table are center. To the right of sofa is table with four chairs; a candle and matches rest on table. Folding screen stands down right. Windows with blinds are on rear wall. Candle sits on table.*
AT RISE: *Sounds of gunshots and shouting are heard from offstage. Front door bursts open, and through it enters PRINCESS, who is wearing a gag, pushed on by JOE. ROXY, carrying a rope, and MOE follow close behind. PRINCESS*

wears turban with jewel set in front, and a sari. Mobsters wear cheap-looking suits.

ROXY (*Urgently*): Close that door, Moe, before someone sees the princess.

MOE: Right, Roxy. (*He closes door.*)

ROXY (*To* PRINCESS): Don't try to escape, or you'll end up in the morgue!

JOE (*With bravado*): She won't get away. Not as long as *I'm* around. (*Lets go of* PRINCESS *and beats his chest proudly.* PRINCESS *dashes to door, but is pulled back by* ROXY.)

ROXY (*Holding out rope; sarcastically*): That's why we use lots of rope in this business, Joe. (MOE *takes rope and begins to tie* PRINCESS*'s hands together in front of her.*) Check out this house, Joe. See if there's a good place to hide.

JOE (*Eagerly*): You got it, Roxanne.

ROXY (*Threateningly*): What did you call me?

JOE (*Frightened; backing away toward basement door*): Whoops! *Roxy!* You got it, *Roxy!* (*He exits.* ROXY *points to* PRINCESS*'s turban.*)

ROXY (*Smoothly*): Well, well, what do we have here, Princess? I think this little trinket would go very nicely with my entire wardrobe. (*Roughly removes stone from* PRINCESS*'s turban and drops it into her pocket, as* PRINCESS *stomps on* MOE*'s foot. He howls in pain, letting go of her hands.* PRINCESS *removes her gag.*)

PRINCESS (*Incensed; to* ROXY): Fool! An ancient curse protects that sacred jewel! It can be worn only by members of my royal family. Many have died trying to steal it! (MOE *quickly reties her gag, then finishes tying her hands.*)

ROXY (*Mockingly*): Hear that, Moe? The princess is concerned about us. I am deeply touched. (*Checking gag*) I'll be even happier when her father pays the ransom and we're *all* living on Easy Street.

JOE (*Reentering; eagerly*): Roxa—(ROXY *growls*) Er—Roxy, this house has a huge basement. We can hide down there.

ROXY: Good. After it gets dark, we'll make a break for our hideout. (ROXY, JOE, *and* MOE *exit with* PRINCESS.

GRANDMOTHER *enters up right, holding a feather duster, humming.*)

GRANDMOTHER: Bobby, is that you? (*Pauses*) Hm-m-m. That's odd. I thought I heard voices. Maybe the spirits are arriving early for the séance. (GRANDMOTHER *dusts furniture, then arranges chairs around table, humming while she works.* AUNT PHYLLIS *and* MRS. ALICE PORTER *enter, carrying shopping bags.*)

MRS. PORTER: Hello, Mother.

GRANDMOTHER: Alice, you're just in time for the séance. Madame Zena is coming this afternoon to summon Harold from the other world.

MRS. PORTER (*Depositing bags on table; distractedly*): That's fine, Mother, so long as it doesn't interfere with dinner.

AUNT PHYLLIS (*Sharply, to* GRANDMOTHER): This foolish séance is nothing but rubbish! (*To* MRS. PORTER) Alice, I don't know why you encourage Mother. It's a waste of time and money! (BOBBY *enters down right, holding a squirt gun.*)

BOBBY (*Excitedly*): Mom! Mom!

MRS. PORTER: Bobby, how many times have I told you not to bring that water pistol in here! Go outside and play with it.

BOBBY (*Breathlessly*): But, Mom, I just saw two strange guys wearing turbans sneaking around in the bushes outside!

MRS. PORTER (*Exasperated*): Now, Bobby, not another of your wild stories! Last week it was flying saucers, and the week before that it was giant spiders! (*Dryly*) I suppose these two fellows were carrying sabers, too?

BOBBY (*Incredulously*): They were! How did you know? And they had big bushy beards and were talking funny.

AUNT PHYLLIS (*Sighing*): There he goes again telling another of his tall tales! That's what comes of watching too much television.

GRANDMOTHER (*Excitedly*): I wonder if what he saw were ghosts. Only a few minutes ago I heard voices in this very room!

AUNT PHYLLIS: Please, Mother, don't start on that again! You've all given me a splitting headache. I'm going to my room and lie down. (*Exits*)

GRANDMOTHER: Poor Phyllis. I think I'll go into the kitchen and make her some seaweed tea. (*Exits*)

MRS. PORTER (*Shaking her head*): Seaweed tea? (*Calls*) Mother, Mother, wait a minute! I think I'd better help you! (MRS. PORTER *exits*.)

BOBBY (*Going to window and peering out*): Here come those guys with the turbans! I'd better find a place to hide! (*Looks around room and runs behind sofa. Front door opens, and ABDUL and OMAR cautiously enter room. Each wears turban, flowing trousers, and a saber tucked into his belt.*)

ABDUL: Omar, I swear on the head of my father that this is the house those running dogs entered with the princess.

OMAR: If it is not the right house, you son of a beetle, the sultan will be most angry!

ABDUL (*Shuddering*): The sultan's wrath is fearsome indeed! (*Puts hand to neck*) I do not wish to lose this head of which I am most fond.

OMAR: Your head will not be a great loss, but, mine—ah, that is a different story! (*Looks around room*) Abdul, I see no sign of the princess!

ABDUL: They must be hiding her. Come, let's look.

BOBBY (*Jumping up from behind sofa*): Stick 'em up! (OMAR *and* ABDUL *scream in terror and clutch each other.* BOBBY *points his water pistol at them, and they fall to their knees, imploring.*)

OMAR *and* ABDUL (*Ad lib*): Mercy! Spare us! (*Etc.*)

BOBBY: What are you two doing sneaking around my house? Don't move, or I'll blast you!

ABDUL: Sorry, Master, but we are looking for our stolen princess.

OMAR: Have mercy on us! Have mercy, please! If we don't find her, our sultan, Alacazar the Magnificent, will chop off our heads! (*Knock on front door is heard.* BOBBY *goes to door, still pointing his water pistol at* OMAR *and* ABDUL.)

BOBBY: Stay where you are while I open this door. (BOBBY *opens door and* MADAME ZENA *enters. She wears a flowing caftan with a shawl about her shoulders.*)

MADAME ZENA (*Mysteriously*): Good afternoon. I am Madame

Zena, and I have an appointment to conduct a séance. (*Peers at* BOBBY *intently*) You must be Edith's grandson.

BOBBY (*Impressed*): Wow! How did you know?

MADAME ZENA (*Knowingly*): I am a psychic. It's my job. (*Sees* OMAR *and* ABDUL) Who are you? No, don't tell me—it's coming to me—I know! You are from a foreign country—but, which one? Maybe the spirits will help me. (*Ominously*) They speak to me in many ways.

ABDUL: We've come from a faraway land searching for the lowly dogs who kidnapped our princess.

OMAR (*Hopefully*): Can your spirits help us find her?

MADAME ZENA (*Slyly*): Perhaps they can. (*Holds hand to fore-head and speaks as though in a trance*) The spirits are talking to me; the spirits have a plan. (*Drops hand from forehead and pulls* ABDUL *and* OMAR *aside; suddenly matter-of-fact*) If you will hide during my séance, I'll say that I see two men wearing turbans. Then you two will jump up as if you had suddenly materialized! If you do that little job for me, I'll do what I can to help you find your princess. Is it a deal?

ABDUL (*Seriously; to* OMAR): Omar, if the spirits can find our princess . . .

OMAR (*Nodding*): Then we can keep our heads, Abdul.

MADAME ZENA (*Pushing them toward sofa*): Trust me! Now, stay out of sight until I give the signal. (ABDUL *and* OMAR *crouch behind sofa.*)

BOBBY: But, Madame Zena, I thought you were here to help Grandmother. (*Skeptically*) You can't really talk to ghosts, can you? (ABDUL *and* OMAR *peer over sofa.*)

MADAME ZENA (*Coolly*): The ways of the spirit world are clothed in mystery, known to only a few mere mortals. (ABDUL *and* OMAR *exchange frightened looks.*)

BOBBY (*Insistently*): Grandma's really looking forward to talk-ing to the ghost of my Grandpa. (*Looking at* OMAR *and* ABDUL *dubiously*) Grandpa didn't look like either of them.

CINDY (*From off left*): Slinky! Here, boy! (*Exasperated*) Oh, where is he now? (ABDUL *and* OMAR *stand, looking about in confusion.*)

MADAME ZENA (*Alarmed*): Quick, everybody hide! (*Pushes*

ABDUL *and* OMAR *behind screen, down right; to* BOBBY *as she opens front door and pushes him out.*) Go take a walk, kid. You're interfering with the spirit world. (*As she shuts door,* CINDY *enters from left.*)

CINDY: Oh, hello! You must be Grandma's psychic. I was looking for Slinky. Have you seen a snake? (*Holding her hands two feet apart*) He's about this long.

MADAME ZENA (*Looking about floor, shuddering*): I haven't seen anyone except a few stray spirits.

CINDY: I wonder where he can be? (MRS. PORTER *reenters.*)

MRS. PORTER (*Seeing* MADAME ZENA): Why, you must be Madame Zena. My mother is expecting you. Won't you have a seat? (*Points to sofa*)

MADAME ZENA: Thank you. (*Seats herself gingerly, checking cushions for snake*)

CINDY: Mom, have you seen Slinky? He's not in my room, and I can't find him anywhere.

MRS. PORTER: Cindy! Have you lost that snake again? If he gets out of the house, he'll scare the neighbors to death!

CINDY: Oh, he wouldn't hurt anyone

MRS. PORTER: A nine-foot snake would scare any reasonable human being.

CINDY (*Rolling her eyes*): Oh, Mom! He's not nine feet long. I'm going to check the garage. (*She exits.* GRANDMOTHER *reenters.*)

GRANDMOTHER: There! The tea is brewing. (*Notices* MADAME ZENA; *delighted*) Madame Zena, I'm so glad you're here. (*They shake hands.*) I'm ready to start whenever you are.

MADAME ZENA (*Pointing to windows; mysteriously*): It is too bright in here for the spirits. (MRS. PORTER *goes to windows and draws blinds.* AUNT PHYLLIS *enters.*)

AUNT PHYLLIS (*Testily*): I couldn't sleep a wink, so I thought I might as well join you and see what's going on.

GRANDMOTHER: I'm so glad you've changed your mind, Phyllis. This is Madame Zena. (MADAME ZENA *nods imperiously.*)

AUNT PHYLLIS (*Boldly*): I must warn you, Madame Zena. I do not believe in ghosts one bit.

MADAME ZENA: Perhaps what you see today will change your mind. (*Picks up matchbook from table and lights candle. GRANDMOTHER turns switch on wall and lights dim. They seat themselves around table.*)

GRANDMOTHER (*Excitedly*): I cannot wait to speak to Harold!

MADAME ZENA (*Holding up a hand for silence*): Hush! We must be silent. Our hands must touch. (*They join hands. MADAME ZENA bows head, all is silent for a moment. Suddenly, BOBBY bursts in through front door, startling others.*)

BOBBY (*Excitedly*): Mom! Mom! The neighborhood is being invaded!

MRS. PORTER (*Stands, wagging her finger at BOBBY*): Young man, can't you see we are in the middle of something?

BOBBY: But, Mom, it's true! I saw guys with walkie-talkies next door and—

MRS. PORTER (*Interrupting*): Bobby, I do not want to hear another one of your stories. Now go fix yourself a snack and leave us in peace. (*Grumbling, BOBBY exits. MRS. PORTER sits at table.*)

MADAME ZENA (*Coldly*): The spirits do not look kindly on disrespectful behavior. (*They join hands again and bow heads. After a moment, MADAME ZENA begins to sway and moan as if in a trance. Suddenly, she looks up and screams.*)

AUNT PHYLLIS (*Nervously*): Gracious! What is it?

MADAME ZENA (*Dramatically*): I see two men. They are from foreign parts. They have large, bushy beards and moustaches! They are coming nearer, nearer, nearer. They are in this very room!

GRANDMOTHER (*Fascinated*): Goodness!

MADAME ZENA: They are materializing! I can see them! Come out, foreign spirits! Come out. (*ABDUL and OMAR step out from behind screen. AUNT PHYLLIS, MRS. PORTER, and GRANDMOTHER scream.*)

AUNT PHYLLIS (*Hysterically*): Ghosts! Ghosts! Standing right over there! Real, live ghosts! I see them myself!

MRS. PORTER: I don't know what they are!

GRANDMOTHER: They don't look like my Harold, I know that much!

MADAME ZENA: You must not be frightened. These spirits are your friends. They want to help you find your husband. (*Mysteriously*) Foreign spirits, you have come to us from the other world. You are telling me that all is well—

ABDUL *and* OMAR (*In ghostly voice; together*): All is well—

MADAME ZENA (*Interrupting; nervously*): Do not try to speak, foreign spirits. I will read your thoughts. You are telling me that though we may feel our loved ones are lost forever—

ABDUL *and* OMAR (*Eerily*): Lost forever—

MADAME ZENA (*Quickly*): Yes, though they may seem lost forever, they are actually very near to us—

ABDUL (*In his own voice*): The princess is near?

OMAR (*Fiercely*): Tell us where she is!

MADAME ZENA (*Quickly*): Foreign spirits, listen to me! It is time for you to return to the other world. Do you hear? Your questions will be answered in due course. Now go! (*Grumbling,* ABDUL *and* OMAR *retreat behind screen.* MADAME ZENA *closes her eyes and begins to sway.*) And now I will communicate with your departed husband. (*Calls*) Harold! Speak to me, Harold. (*Knock is heard on front door; taken aback*) Oh, you are knocking. How surprising. (*Knocking continues; aside*) Dear me, this really works. (*Calls*) If you are well, knock twice. (*Knocking continues.*)

MRS. PORTER (*Wryly*): I believe that's the front door.

TWO POLICE OFFICERS (*Calling from offstage*): Police! Open the door! We have a warrant to search the premises.

MRS. PORTER, AUNT PHYLLIS, *and* GRANDMOTHER (*Together*): The police?

MADAME ZENA (*Aside; guiltily*): The police? I didn't think it was that serious! Well, they can't prove anything! (*She drapes her shawl over her head to hide her face.* MRS. PORTER *rises, turns on light, and opens front door.* TWO POLICE OFFICERS *enter.*)

MRS. PORTER (*Alarmed*): Good afternoon, Officers. What can I do for you?

1ST OFFICER (*Sternly; to* MRS. PORTER): We're investigating a kidnapping, and have heard reports of gunfire in the neighborhood. (MRS. PORTER *gasps and* AUNT PHYLLIS *rushes to her side.*)

2ND OFFICER: Has anyone seen any suspicious characters or noticed anything unusual?

GRANDMOTHER (*Rising*): We did see two bearded men wearing turbans—they were here only moments ago.

2ND OFFICER (*Crossing to her*): Which way did they go?

GRANDMOTHER (*Innocently*): Oh, I wouldn't worry about them. They returned to the spirit world. (ABDUL *and* OMAR *peek out from behind screen, unnoticed by others, and then retreat.*)

2ND OFFICER (*Narrowing his eyes; suspiciously*): So, you're not willing to cooperate, is that it?

GRANDMOTHER (*Patting his shoulder comfortingly*): I can tell you're a bit tense, Officer. (*Leads* 2ND OFFICER *toward kitchen*) Why don't I get you some nice, soothing, seaweed tea. (*They exit.*)

AUNT PHYLLIS (*Heading to kitchen; nervously*): I never thought I'd say this, but I think I could use some seaweed myself. (*Exits*)

1ST OFFICER (*To* MRS. PORTER): We're looking for a gangster who goes by the name of Roxy. I should tell you that harboring criminals is a serious offense.

MRS. PORTER: Honestly, Officer, we have nothing to hide. Feel free to look around the house. (*Heading toward kitchen*) In the meantime, I'd better go check on my mother. (*She exits, leaving door open behind her.* 1ST OFFICER *looks about room, then notices* MADAME ZENA, *still hiding under her shawl and sitting at table. He crosses to her.*)

1ST OFFICER (*Trying to get a look at her*): Excuse me, ma'am, but do you know anything about a kidnapping? (MADAME ZENA *removes shawl and assumes an innocent expression.*)

MADAME ZENA: I know nothing about a kidnapping, sir. (*Mysteriously*) All my dealings are with the spirit world.

1ST OFFICER (*Peering at her intently*): You look awfully familiar. What is your name?

MADAME ZENA (*Rising and going to sofa*): I am Madame

Zena, and I am sure we have never met—at least not in this lifetime.

1ST OFFICER (*Following her to sofa*): I never forget a face. (*Both their backs are turned to screen. ABDUL and OMAR crawl out from behind screen and hide behind kitchen door.*) Though I'm sure I'd remember a name like Madame Zena.

MADAME ZENA (*Pointing to screen; excitedly*): Something moved behind that screen!

1ST OFFICER (*Crossing to screen and looking behind it*): There's nobody there.

MADAME ZENA (*Surprised*): There isn't?

1ST OFFICER (*Suddenly; wagging his finger at her*): I know why you look so familiar. Your name isn't Madame Zena. It's Wendy Wong of Wendy's All-Night Laundry Service. (*Accusingly*) You ruined all my shirts. I told you to starch them, but you scorched them instead!

MADAME ZENA (*Laughing nervously*): How ridiculous! (*At that, GRANDMOTHER enters carrying teacup, then closes kitchen door behind her, exposing OMAR and ABDUL.*)

GRANDMOTHER (*Dropping her cup*): Eek! Ghosts!

OMAR and ABDUL (*Looking at each other; horrified*): Eek! Ghosts!

1ST OFFICER (*Pointing pistol at OMAR and ABDUL*): Police! Hold it! (2ND POLICE OFFICER *runs on right, blowing whistle. ABDUL and OMAR run around sofa, with OFFICERS chasing them. MRS. PORTER, BOBBY, and AUNT PHYLLIS reenter, as ABDUL and OMAR exit to bedroom with OFFICERS in pursuit.*)

BOBBY (*Pointing off left; excitedly*): Those are the guys I told you about earlier!

MRS. PORTER (*Aghast*): All right, young man. You have some explaining to do!

AUNT PHYLLIS (*Sputtering*): I should say so! Did you allow those strangers into our living room? You almost had me believing in ghosts!

BOBBY (*Insistently*): I *tried* to tell you, but you wouldn't listen! (CINDY *enters.*)

CINDY (*To* BOBBY): Bobby! I have been looking all over for you. What have you done with Slinky?

BOBBY: I didn't touch your dumb snake!

CINDY: Slinky is *not* dumb, and I'll bet you let him out of his cage. If anything happens to him, you'll be in for it!

MADAME ZENA (*Shouting*): Quiet! All this noise is disturbing my vibrations. (*Scream is heard off.*)

BOBBY: Someone's in the basement!

MRS. PORTER: Oh, dear!

GRANDMOTHER (*Hopefully*): Maybe it's more spirits.

BOBBY (*Moving toward basement door*): I'll go check it out.

MRS. PORTER (*Pulling him back*): No, Bobby. You might get hurt!

AUNT PHYLLIS: If I see another strange person in this house, I'm leaving. (JOE *and* MOE *lead* PRINCESS *on left, followed by* ROXY, *who is waving a gun. All gasp.*)

ROXY: Nobody move! Put up your hands. (*All except mobsters raise hands.* ROXY *glares at them, furious.*) All right, who's the wise guy who planted a snake in the basement? What kind of monsters are you folks? (CINDY *drops her hands and rushes to basement door in excitement.*)

CINDY (*Calling*): Slinky! Slinky! (*Happily*) There you are, Slinky! (*She picks up "snake" from just offstage and strokes it.*) There, there, you're safe now. (JOE, MOE, *and* ROXY *scream.*)

ROXY, MOE, *and* JOE (*Ad lib; hysterically*): Yipes! Get that thing away from me! Get it out of here! Snake! (*Etc. Panicked,* ROXY *drops gun, and* GRANDMOTHER *picks it up.*)

GRANDMOTHER (*Pointing gun at mobsters*): All right, hands up! Don't move. (JOE *and* MOE *release* PRINCESS *and raise hands in the air.* ROXY *raises hands, keeping an eye on the snake all the while.* AUNT PHYLLIS, MRS. PORTER, MADAME ZENA, *and* BOBBY *lower their hands in relief.*)

BOBBY (*Delightedly*): Nice work, Grandma!

MADAME ZENA (*Attempting nonchalance*): I can see you're all very busy. (*Moving to front door*) We will have our séance another time. (GRANDMOTHER *turns, inadvertently aiming gun at* MADAME ZENA.)

GRANDMOTHER: Don't go! I still want to speak to my Harold. (MADAME ZENA *turns, sees gun pointed at her, and stops abruptly.*)

MADAME ZENA (*As though suddenly remembering*): Harold! Of course. I forgot. (*Laughs nervously*) I can stay as long as you like. (*Just then,* OMAR *and* ABDUL *run in, followed by* OFFICERS. OMAR *and* ABDUL *see* PRINCESS, *stop suddenly, and fall to their knees before her.* OFFICERS *stare in bewilderment.*)

ABDUL: Hail, O beloved Princess.

OMAR: Our prayers have been answered.

1ST OFFICER (*To* PRINCESS): You must be the sultan's daughter. We've been looking for you, Your Highness. Are you all right? (PRINCESS *nods.* OFFICERS *handcuff mobsters.*) So, Roxy, you'll be brought to justice at last. You and your men are wanted in ten counties.

2ND OFFICER (*To* ROXY): We're going to put you away for a long time.

ROXY (*Nervously*): That's fine with me. So long as I'm far away from that snake.

PRINCESS (*Holding out hand to* ROXY): I believe you have something that belongs to me. (ROXY *reaches into her pocket and hands jewel to* PRINCESS.) You should have listened to me. I told you no good would come of taking the sacred jewel. (2ND OFFICER *goes to* GRANDMOTHER, *who is still pointing gun at* MADAME ZENA, *and takes gun from her.*)

2ND OFFICER (*To* GRANDMOTHER): You've done a fine job, ma'am. (*Looking closely at* MADAME ZENA) Say, don't I know you from somewhere?

MADAME ZENA (*Sighing, in resignation*): Probably.

2ND OFFICER: Sure, I do. You're Maria Treble. (*Accusingly*) Last year I hired you to teach my daughter how to play the piano, and you taught her how to play poker instead.

MADAME ZENA (*Aside*): This will teach me to do business with the police. (*To* GRANDMOTHER) Forgive me, Edith, but I won't be holding any more séances. (*Looking apprehensively at* OFFICERS) I see a lot of laundry and music lessons in my future. (*She starts toward front door, followed by* OFFI-CERS, *with* ROXY, JOE, *and* MOE *in tow. They exit.*)

PRINCESS (*To* GRANDMOTHER, CINDY, *and* BOBBY): Thank you for your help. I wish to give you a token of my appreciation. (*Removes turban and gives it to* BOBBY; *gives bracelet to* CINDY. *To* GRANDMOTHER) And you were the most brave. What can I give you?

GRANDMOTHER (*Rather sadly*): I don't suppose you can bring back my Harold. (*She sniffs.* PRINCESS *unwinds scarf from around her neck and uses it to daub* GRANDMOTHER's *tears, then drapes scarf about* GRANDMOTHER, *who then brightens.*) Thank you, Princess. (PRINCESS *nods, then exits, followed by* OMAR *and* ABDUL. *All gather around* GRAND-MOTHER.)

AUNT PHYLLIS (*Affectionately*): Well, Mother, it seems you're stuck with us. (GRANDMOTHER *smiles and shrugs.*)

MRS. PORTER (*Cheerily*): Well, now that we have our house to ourselves again, we ought to celebrate! (*Others ad lib enthusiastic agreement.*)

GRANDMOTHER: And I know just how we'll celebrate . . . I'll make us a big pot of seaweed tea! (*She starts toward kitchen. All groan, then laugh. Quick curtain*)

THE END

Production Notes

MADAME ZENA'S SÉANCE

Characters: 7 female; 5 male; 2 male or female for Police Officers.

Playing Time: 30 minutes.

Costumes: Everyday modern dress. Princess wears turban with jewel set in front, bracelet, scarf, and sari or long robe; Roxy, Joe, and Moe wear cheap-looking suits; Abdul and Omar each wear turban, flowing trousers, and saber tucked into belt; Madame Zena wears billowy caftan and shawl; Police Officers are in uniform, with pistols and night sticks.

Properties: Pistols; rubber snake; handkerchief; feather duster; shopping bags; squirt gun; tea cup.

Setting: The Porter living room. Front door is down right, kitchen door is up right, bedroom door is up left, and basement door is down left. A table, on which rests candle and matches, is right center, surrounded by four chairs; sofa and coffee table are center; folding screen is down right. A light switch is on wall near table. Windows with blinds are on rear wall.

Lighting: Lights dim for séance, as indicated in text.

Curtain Raisers

❦ Boarder Skirmish

by *Christina Hamlett*

Just another manic day at Magic Manor . . .

Characters

RHONDA MARQUART, *boarding house owner*
WANDA, *her sister*
PRINCE CHARMING
GOLDILOCKS
OLD WOMAN
JACK
FROG PRINCE
BRUNHILDA
HANSEL
GRETEL
KIDS, *extras*

TIME: *Long ago.*
SETTING: *Office of Magic Manor Boarding House, a cozy room with business counter right. There is phone on counter, and chair in front of it. Exit down left leads to rest of house. Door up left leads outside. Window overlooking street is a few feet from door. Portraits of Red Riding Hood, Cinderella, etc., on walls add to "homey" effect. Pots of colorful flowers are down left.*
AT RISE: WANDA *is watering flowers.* RHONDA *is on phone.* PRINCE CHARMING *sits on chair in front of counter, looking anxiously at* RHONDA.
RHONDA (*Hanging up with a sigh*): I'm sorry, Your Highness, but there's still no answer. Would you like to leave her a message?

291

PRINCE: Are you sure we're talking about the same person? She has blond hair, blue eyes—

RHONDA: And wears a crown? Yes, that's the one. And I must say, she's one of the quietest tenants my sister and I have ever had here at Magic Manor.

WANDA (*Looking up*): Are you talking about Sleeping Beauty? Yes, that's true. We haven't heard a peep out of her.

PRINCE: And she hasn't gone out?

RHONDA: No, not since the delivery three days ago.

PRINCE (*Puzzled*): What delivery?

WANDA: Quite a large box, as I recall. Do you remember where it came from, Rhonda?

RHONDA: The Acme Spinning Wheel Company.

WANDA (*Beaming*): Isn't it nice to see a young woman take up spinning? It's so practical.

PRINCE (*To* RHONDA): Would you mind ringing her room again?

RHONDA (*As she picks up phone*): O.K., but she's probably sleeping. (*As* RHONDA *and* PRINCE *are busy at counter, door up left bursts open and* GOLDILOCKS *runs in.*)

WANDA (*Startled, then concerned*): Oh, good heavens, child! You flew through that door as if you had a pack of wild animals after you!

GOLDILOCKS: Isn't *that* the truth! Listen, Wanda, if anyone comes around asking for me, you haven't seen me, O.K.?

WANDA: Like whom, dear?

GOLDILOCKS: Oh, it's some stupid mixup with the police. This crazy family of bears told them I broke into their house.

WANDA (*Astonished*): Did you?

GOLDILOCKS (*Sheepishly*): Yeah, well, sort of. And they also said I messed up their furniture.

WANDA: Did you?

GOLDILOCKS (*Embarrassed*): Kind of. But look, they don't build stuff the way they used to. The capper, though, is that they said I ate all their oatmeal while they were out for a walk.

WANDA: Oh, dear! What would possess them to say *that?*

GOLDILOCKS (*Defiantly*): Circumstantial evidence. Just because a person has a spoon in her hand and an empty dish in front of her, everyone jumps to all the wrong conclusions. (*Crosses to door down left*) Anyway, I'm going to keep a low profile for the next couple of days, O.K.? You haven't seen me. You haven't talked to me. You don't even know who I am. (*Exits quickly*)

RHONDA (*To* PRINCE *as she puts down phone*): I'm sorry, but there's still no answer.

PRINCE: Well, thanks for trying. Let me go ask around the other kingdoms and I'll stop back later. (*Exits*)

RHONDA (*To* WANDA): Was that Goldilocks who just ran in?

WANDA (*Shrugging*): I don't know. I've never seen her before in my life. (OLD WOMAN *tentatively opens door, then enters. She wears long dress and apron, under which she has large whistle around her neck, and she carries a piece of paper in one hand.*)

OLD WOMAN (*Checking piece of paper*): Excuse me, but is this the Magic Manor Boarding House?

RHONDA: Yes, it is. (*Shaking* WOMAN's *hand*) I'm Rhonda Marquart and this is my sister, Wanda. We're the owners.

WOMAN: Oh, thank goodness I found you. You people come highly recommended by my neighborhood cobbler.

WANDA (*Puzzled*): Your cobbler?

WOMAN: Yes, that's right. I left my shoe for him to repair this morning, and he gave me your address.

RHONDA: Shoe? Just one shoe?

WOMAN: Yes—just one. It gets so much wear and tear, you know, that I have to have it restitched twice a year.

WANDA: I'm confused. What does that have to do with us?

WOMAN: Well, I'm going to need a place to live. A week at the most. Do you have a large room available?

RHONDA: Certainly. Now, is this just for yourself?

WOMAN: Well, I do have a few children. Is that a problem?

WANDA: My sister and I love children. How many?

WOMAN: At last count (*Thinking, counting on fingers*) . . . about thirty.

RHONDA (*Gasping*): Thirty?

WOMAN: Give or take a few. (*In reassuring tone*) But don't

worry. I run a very disciplined household. You'll never even know they're around.

WANDA (*To* RHONDA): What do you think, Rhonda?

RHONDA: Well, they can't be any worse than those musicians who moved in last week.

WOMAN: Musicians? (*On cue, cacophony of music is heard.*)

WANDA: *Those* musicians. I know they have to practice, but—

RHONDA: Now, Wanda, you have to admit they're well behaved, even if they *are* an odd mix .

WOMAN: How odd?

RHONDA: A donkey, a dog, a cat, and a rooster. They call themselves the Bremen Town Four.

WANDA: They expect to hit the big time any day now.

RHONDA: They were even on *Oprah* last week.

WOMAN: Really?

WANDA: Yes, it was the episode on Musical Animal Quartets.

WOMAN: How exciting to live in a house with musicians! The children will love it. May I see the room now, please?

WANDA: Would you mind showing her, Rhonda? I want to finish watering the plants.

WOMAN (*Noticing flower pots*): What beautiful flowers!

WANDA: Oh, I can't take all the credit. They belong to one of our tenants, Mary Contrary. She has the greenest thumb I've ever seen!

RHONDA (*Leading way down left*): This way, ma'am. (RHONDA *and* WOMAN *exit, as* JACK *enters.*)

JACK: Morning, Miss Marquart!

WANDA: Why, hello, Jack! Back already from marketing for your mother?

JACK: Yep. And boy, is she going to be pleased!

WANDA: You got a good price for the family cow, then?

JACK (*Reaching into pocket*): You bet. A guy in a plaid jacket gave me these nifty beans!

WANDA: Beans?

JACK: He said if I throw 'em in a patch of dirt and water it really well, I'll get a surprise.

WANDA (*Shaking her head*): Oh, Jack, I'm afraid the only surprise you're going to get is a patch of soggy dirt. Those beans look totally worthless.

JACK: But the man said—

WANDA: Now, Jack, haven't we always told you never to listen to strangers? (*Accompanying him to door*) We're going right back to that marketplace and retrieve Bessie the cow before your mother comes home. (*As they exit,* RHONDA *and* WOMAN *reenter.*)

WOMAN: The room is perfect. And a view besides!

RHONDA: Don't you have a view where you are now?

WOMAN: Only if you like looking at leather and laces all day.

RHONDA: Let me get you an application. (*As they cross to counter, sawing, hammering, and pounding are heard offstage.*)

WOMAN: What are your musicians doing up there now?

RHONDA: That's not the band. It's that silly trio of pigs on the top floor.

WOMAN: What are they doing?

RHONDA: They carry on like that all the time. They're very security conscious, you see. They're always hauling straw and wood and bricks up there, as if they're building a fort or something. (*Hands paper and pen to* WOMAN) Just fill out the middle section and the back, please, and we'll be in business. (FROG PRINCE *enters up left, wearing green suit and crown, and carrying frog in palm of his hand.*)

FROG (*Talking to frog in hand*): You'll love this place, Gwendolyn. The people are friendly, there's a pond just outside, and plenty of flies to dine on night and day!

RHONDA: Hello, Your Highness.

FROG (*Bowing deeply*): M'lady.

RHONDA (*Indicating frog in his hand*): A new acquaintance, I see?

FROG: Lady Gwendolyn. She hopped on my knee while I was visiting the old lily pad, and it was love at first sight! Mind if I show her around?

RHONDA: Your friends are our friends, Your Highness. (FROG PRINCE *exits down left.*)

WOMAN: What was that all about?

RHONDA: Oh, the poor man's been heartsick ever since he got turned back into a human. (WOMAN *hands application and pen to* RHONDA.)

WOMAN: Done!

RHONDA: Thank you. (*Reaches into pocket and pulls out key*) And here's your key. (*Hands to* WOMAN) Nice to have you with us.

WOMAN: Thank you. (*Goes to door up left, opens it, pulls whistle out from under apron, blows it. After a moment,* KIDS *run in, making the most noise possible. They follow* WOMAN *down left.* WANDA *enters, perplexed.*)

WANDA: Goodness, there were a lot of them, weren't there?

RHONDA: Where have you been?

WANDA: Well, I went to the market with Jack to track down a shifty salesman.

RHONDA: Were you successful?

WANDA: Yes and no. We didn't find the salesman, but look at this great bargain I picked up! (*Takes brass lamp from apron pocket*)

RHONDA: Good grief, Wanda! What are you going to do with *that* ugly thing?

WANDA: It's not ugly at all! Why, with a little bit of polish, it would look beautiful on the mantle.

RHONDA: We don't *have* a mantle, Wanda.

WANDA: I can always wish for one, can't I?

RHONDA: Wishing doesn't make it true, dear. Now, put that silly thing away. We've got work to do. (*Door up left opens to reveal* BRUNHILDA, *a wizened crone in a black cloak carrying basket of red apples.*)

WANDA: Hello! May we help you?

BRUNHILDA: Yes, dearie, I'm looking for my ... uh ... my niece. Perhaps she lives here?

RHONDA: What's her name?

BRUNHILDA: White.

WANDA (*Frowning*): Hm-m-m. Common name. Is there anything special about her?

BRUNHILDA (*With a malevolent snarl*): Only that she's cheery all the time and lives with seven strange little men who work in the silver mines.

RHONDA: Oh, you mean Snow?

BRUNHILDA (*Excitedly*): Yes, yes, that's the one.

WANDA (*Pointing down left*): Second floor, last door on the left.

BRUNHILDA (*Quickly*): No, no, I don't actually want to *see* her.

RHONDA (*Puzzled*): You don't?

BRUNHILDA (*Setting basket on counter*): It's her . . . uh . . . birthday, and she loves fresh apples.

WANDA (*Admiringly*): Oh, they're beautiful! So shiny and red.

RHONDA: Those are definitely apples to kill for.

BRUNHILDA (*Laughing wickedly*): Yes, aren't they? I just made them—(*Quickly correcting herself*) I mean, just *picked* them. You *will* see that she and the little men get them as soon as possible?

WANDA: We'd be happy to.

RHONDA: By all means.

BRUNHILDA: Thank you, my dears. (*Exits with a maniacal laugh*)

WANDA (*Walking around to join RHONDA behind counter*): Wasn't that nice of her to drop them off?

RHONDA: Hm-m-m . . . do you think Snow would mind if—

WANDA: Now, Rhonda, those apples are not for us.

RHONDA: Yes, but there are more than enough to go around. What harm would it do?

WANDA: I suppose you're right. (*Takes apple, hands it to* RHONDA) One for you. (*Takes another apple*) And one for me. (*They toast with apples.*) Cheers! (*They simultaneously bite into apples and fall down behind counter, just as HANSEL and GRETEL enter.*)

HANSEL: Hello!

GRETEL: Anybody here?

HANSEL (*With hands on hips*): What did I tell you, Gretel?

GRETEL: You're absolutely right, Hansel. You can *never* find a landlord when you need one! (*Quick curtain*)

THE END

Production Notes

BOARDER SKIRMISH

Characters: 6 female; 4 male; male and female extras for Kids.

Playing Time: 20 minutes.

Costumes: Rhonda and Wanda, peasant dresses and long aprons with large pockets. Prince Charming, tights, satin jacket, crown. Goldilocks, blue dress, white knee socks, black patent shoes. Old Woman, peasant dress, apron, whistle on cord around neck. Jack, short pants, jacket, feathered cap. Frog Prince, green suit and crown. Brunhilda, witch costume. Hansel and Gretel, lederhosen and shirts. Extras, shirts and short pants for boys, dresses and knee socks for girls.

Properties: Watering can; note; beans; toy frog; key; paper and pen; brass lamp; basket of shiny red apples.

Setting: Office of Magic Manor Boarding House. Business counter with phone on it is right. Chair is in front of counter. Exit down left leads to rest of house. Door up left leads outside. Window overlooking street is a few feet from door. Portraits of various famous tenants (Red Riding Hood, Cinderella, etc.) grace walls and add "homey" effect. Pots filled with colorful flowers are down left.

Lighting: No special effects.

Sound: Cacophonous music; sawing, hammering, pounding.

～Name That Book!

by Helen Louise Miller

A TV quiz show for Book Week . . .

Characters

MASTER OF CEREMONIES
SEVEN PANELISTS, *male or female*
CAMERA OPERATOR
ASSISTANT
1ST GIRL, *Anne of Green Gables*
MARILLA
1ST BOY, *Pip*
CONVICT
2ND GIRL, *Jo March*
2ND BOY, *Jim Hawkins*
BEN GUNN
3RD GIRL, *Becky Thatcher*
4TH GIRL, *Amy Lawrence*
3RD BOY, *Oliver Twist*
ARTFUL DODGER
5TH GIRL, *Alice in Wonderland*

SETTING: *A television studio. There is a large sign on back wall that reads,* NAME THAT BOOK! *Table and chairs for Panelists are up left. Down left is a TV camera on a tripod. Podium for M.C. is at center. Chair, large gong, and buzzer are up right.*
AT RISE: PANELISTS *are sitting at table left.* ASSISTANT *is stationed at gong.* CAMERA OPERATOR *down left follows action with camera as* MASTER OF CEREMONIES *enters and goes to podium.* PANELISTS *applaud.* NOTE: *A stagehand may encourage audience to applaud by walking across apron while holding up sign reading* APPLAUSE.

MASTER OF CEREMONIES: Good afternoon, and welcome to our television special, a quiz show for Book Week. With us today is a panel of literary experts, and we're going to test their knowledge of famous books. Let me introduce the panel to you. (*Introduces* PANELISTS, *each of whom may ad lib on their "expertise."*) And now, on with today's show! For our quiz, we will be presenting scenes from some of the world's best-known and favorite books. Our contestants must identify the book and its author, in exchange for some fabulous prizes! My helpful assistant (*Points to* ASSISTANT) will tell you if you are right (ASSISTANT *bangs gong.*)—or wrong! (ASSISTANT *sounds buzzer.*) Members of the panel, are you ready?

PANELISTS (*Ad lib*): You bet! Let's go! (*Etc.*)

M.C.: All right! Our first scene takes place on Prince Edward Island and represents a real tragedy in a young girl's life. (1ST GIRL *enters, her head wrapped in a towel. She is sobbing, hiding her face in her hands.* ASSISTANT *brings chair center, helps* 1ST GIRL *to sit, and returns to gong. After a moment* MARILLA *enters. She is an older woman, severely dressed, wearing a grim expression.*)

MARILLA (*To* 1ST GIRL): Mercy on us! Have you been asleep, child?

1ST GIRL (*Still sobbing*): No.

MARILLA: Are you sick, then?

1ST GIRL: No. Please, Marilla, go away. (*Dramatically*) I'm in the depths of despair. My career is ended. Please go away.

MARILLA: Did anyone ever hear the like? (*Firmly*) Now you get up this minute, and tell me what you've done. Take that towel off your head, I say. What is this all about?

1ST GIRL: I can't let you see. I simply can't. (*Miserably*) Oh, Marilla, it's my hair!

MARILLA: Your hair! Let me see! (*Removes towel to reveal green wig; stunned*) Heavens above! What have you done? Your hair! It's green!

1ST GIRL (*Bitterly*): I thought nothing in the world could be as bad as red hair; but now I know it's ten times worse to have green hair. (*Imploringly*) Oh, Marilla, what can I do?

MARILLA (*Shaking her head*): How did you ever get into this fix? You've got to tell me. What did you do to your hair?

1ST GIRL: I dyed it.

MARILLA (*Outraged*): You *dyed* your hair? Didn't you know that was a wicked thing to do?

1ST GIRL (*Sobbing*): I knew it was a *little* wicked, but I meant to be extra good in other ways to make up for it.

MARILLA: Well, if I decided it was worthwhile to dye my hair, I'd at least have dyed it a decent color—not green!

1ST GIRL: But I didn't mean to dye it green. He said it would turn my hair a beautiful raven black. How could I doubt his word?

MARILLA: *Who* said? What are you talking about?

1ST GIRL: The peddler that was here this morning. I bought the dye from him.

MARILLA (*Sternly*): How often have I told you never to let one of those peddlers in?

1ST GIRL: I didn't let him in. I remembered what you said, and I went outside and looked at his things on the step. That's when I saw the bottle of hair dye. The peddler said it would dye any hair a beautiful raven black that wouldn't wash out. It cost seventy-five cents, but I had only fifty cents from my chicken money. The peddler had such a kind heart he let me have it for fifty cents. I put the dye on just as the directions said . . . and now look at me! Oh, Marilla, what shall I do?

MARILLA: Goodness knows what is to be done, but we'll start by giving your head a good washing. Come along. (*They exit.* ASSISTANT *removes chair.*)

M.C. (*To* PANEL): What a tragedy! We'll give our panel and our television audience a few moments to identify the heroine, book and author. At the sound of the buzzer, your time will be up. (*Musical interlude is heard, during which time* PANEL-ISTS *write answers on cards. After a pause,* ASSISTANT *sounds buzzer and music stops.*) Time's up! We'll collect all the cards with your answers at the end of our show. Now let's have our next scene. This story involves a boy in a desperate situation. We'll give you one very important clue: The scene takes place in an English graveyard. (1ST BOY *is shoved on by* CONVICT, *who follows wearing a ball and chain attached to his ankle.* CONVICT *grabs* BOY *by the collar.*)

1ST BOY: Oh, don't hurt me, sir! Please! Please!

CONVICT (*Shaking him roughly*): Show me where you live! Point out the place!

1ST BOY (*Pointing toward audience; timidly*): Right down there, sir, in the village.

CONVICT: Where's your mother and father?

1ST BOY (*Pointing; sadly*): There, sir. There among the tombstones.

CONVICT: Who do ye live with, then—supposin' I let ye live at all?

1ST BOY: With my sister, sir—Mrs. Joe Gargery, wife of Joe Gargery, the blacksmith, sir.

CONVICT (*Craftily*): Blacksmith, eh? That gives me an idea. You know what a file is, boy?

1ST BOY (*Gulps*): Yes—yes, sir. A file is used to saw through iron.

CONVICT: And you know what victuals is?

1ST BOY: Yes, sir.

CONVICT: You get me a file, and you get me victuals. You bring 'em both to me tonight, and if you never say a word or dare to make a sign, I'll let ye live. (*Threateningly*) You fail me, and your heart and your liver shall be torn out . . . roasted . . . and ate!

1ST BOY (*Terrified*): I'll do it, sir, I'll do it! Only let me go! Please, let me go!

CONVICT: On your way then, and mind ye! . . . I'll be keepin' my eye on ye! Understand? (*Shoves* BOY *ahead of him offstage and follows slowly, dragging his chain with effort.*)

M.C.: Now, panel, identify that character, the book, and its author. (*Music is heard, and* PANEL *members jot down answers on cards. After a pause,* ASSISTANT *sounds buzzer and music stops.*) Pencils down! Our next character is a New England girl of Civil War days. Strangely enough, her problem, too, has to do with her hair. Only in this case, the young lady *sold* her hair to help raise money for her father, who was lying in a Civil War hospital. This is what she tells her mother when she comes home from the barber. (2ND GIRL *enters*.)

2ND GIRL (*To audience*): I hadn't the least idea of selling my hair at first, but I kept wondering what I could do, when in a barber's window, I saw swatches of hair with the prices marked, and one black swatch, not nearly as thick as mine, was forty dollars . . . . So I walked right in and asked if they'd buy mine. The barber stared at me at first and said he didn't care much for mine because it wasn't a fashionable color. But I begged him to take it . . . finally, I got so excited I told him the whole story, all about Father being in the hospital, and how much we needed the money to buy things for him. His wife heard me and she said, "Oh, take it, Thomas, and oblige the young lady." It turned out their son was in the army, too. So the barber agreed. I took a last look at my hair while he got his scissors. But I must admit I felt a bit queer when I saw my own hair laid out on the table and I could feel only the short, rough ends on my head. The barber's wife took pity on me and she gave me a lock to keep. (*Pulling lock of hair from pocket and holding it out*) Here it is, Marmee, I'll give it to you to remember past glories. (*Exits*)

M.C.: And her past glories *are* remembered today by everybody who reads the book in which she is one of four central characters. (*Music is heard, and* PANELISTS *write on cards*.) Write down her name, panelists, as well as the book and its author. (ASSISTANT *sounds buzzer and music stops*.) Time is up. O.K., we're going to move on to our next scene, from a book of English literature. Our story takes us to an island where our young hero encounters a strange character. (2ND BOY *enters cautiously, as if exploring strange territory. He wears a smock open at throat, knee breeches, and is barefoot. As he peers around stage,* BEN *enters in an odd costume of rags and goat skins. Each is startled at the sight of the other.*)

2ND BOY: Who are you?

BEN: I'm Ben Gunn, I am, and I haven't spoken with a living soul these three years.

2ND BOY (*Amazed*): Three years! Were you shipwrecked?

BEN: Nay, mate, marooned! Marooned three years ago, and

lived on goats since then, and berries and oysters. But, mate, my heart is sore for some real food. (*Hungrily*) You mightn't happen to have a piece of cheese about you now? (2ND BOY *shakes head. Dejected*) No? Well, many's the long night I've dreamed of cheese . . . and woke up again, and here I were.

2ND BOY: If ever I can get aboard ship again, you shall have cheese by the stone, I promise.

BEN (*Taken aback*): If ever you can get aboard again, says you? Who's to hinder you?

2ND BOY (*Amiably*): Not you, I know.

BEN (*Grins*): What do you call yourself, mate?

M.C. (*Breaking in*): That's far enough, fellows. You'll have to cut the scene right there and make your exit. I'm sure you've given our experts enough clues. (2ND BOY *and* BEN *exit. Music is heard as* PANELISTS *write on cards.*) Our panelists are now trying to come up with the name of that boy, the book, and its author. (*After a pause,* ASSISTANT *sounds buzzer and music stops.*) It's time to move on to our next story, and this time it's from an American author. (ASSISTANT *brings in bench from offstage and sets it down center.*) And here come the girls now, on their way home from school. (3RD *and* 4TH GIRLS *enter, carrying books, lunch pails, and slates, and sit on bench.*)

3RD GIRL: Do you like rats?

4TH GIRL (*In disgust*): Of course not. I hate rats! Whatever made you ask such a question?

3RD GIRL (*Distractedly*): Oh, I don't know. I was just thinking. (*Pauses*) Do most boys like rats?

4TH GIRL (*Shrugging*): I guess so. But I'm not sure. I've seen some boys who collect dead ones, just to swing them around on a string and chase the girls.

3RD GIRL (*Nodding*): Uh-huh. Boys are funny, aren't they? What else do they like besides dead rats and candy and getting into fights?

4TH GIRL: Circuses, I guess. Most boys I know like circuses more than anything.

3RD GIRL (*Dubiously*): Even more than they like girls?

4TH GIRL (*Emphatically*): Oh, sure. They only like to chase girls and make them cry.

3RD GIRL: I don't believe all boys are like that!

4TH GIRL: You don't? Do you know any that are any different?

3RD GIRL (*Hesitantly*): I—I think so. (*Abruptly*) Say, were you ever engaged?

4TH GIRL: Oh, yes. A long time ago.

3RD GIRL: What was it like?

4TH GIRL: Well, it wasn't like anything. You only tell a boy you won't have anybody but him, ever, and then you kiss, and that's all. Anybody can do it.

3RD GIRL (*Shocked*): Did *you* kiss the boy you were engaged to?

4TH GIRL: Sure. That's part of it. Then after that you can't love anybody but him. And you can't ever marry anybody but him, ever, ever, ever.

3RD GIRL: And he never marries anybody but you, ever, ever, ever.

4TH GIRL: That's right. And when you're coming to school or going home, you walk together. And you choose him and he chooses you at parties, because that's what you do when you're engaged.

3RD GIRL (*Dreamily*): It's so nice. I never heard of it before today.

4TH GIRL: Oh, it's ever so nice . . . why, me and Tom Sawyer . . .

3RD GIRL (*In distress*): Then I'm not the first girl he's been engaged to! Oh, dear! (*Starts to cry*) I hate him! And I hate you, too! Go away, you wicked girl, I'll never speak to you again as long as I live, or to him either! So there! (*Runs off-stage, followed by* 4TH GIRL)

4TH GIRL (*Calling*): Please, please . . . wait for me! It was a long time ago. Let me explain! (4TH GIRL *exits.* ASSISTANT *removes bench.*)

M.C. (*To* PANELISTS): But all *you* have to come up with, in addition to the full name of the book and its author, is the identity of these two girls, both engaged at different times to the same boy. (*Music is heard as* PANELISTS *write on cards.*) Their names are famous the world over, wherever books are read and loved. (*After a pause,* ASSISTANT *sounds buzzer and music stops.* 3RD BOY *enters, walking wearily, with small bundle of clothing tied on the end of a stick.*) Here comes another young hero who seems a bit down on his luck. Let's listen to his story. (3RD BOY *goes to center and sits on floor. Presently* ARTFUL DODGER *enters, wearing an ill-fitting suit and a battered hat. He walks around* 3RD BOY, *examining him from all angles.*)

DODGER: Hello, my covey. What's the row?

3RD BOY (*Wearily*): I'm very hungry and tired. I have been walking these seven days.

DODGER: Walkin' these seven days? Oh, I see . . . Beak's orders, eh? I suppose you know what a beak is . . .

3RD BOY: I always supposed a beak was the mouth of a bird.

DODGER (*Laughing*): My, how green you are! Why, a beak's a magistrate. And when you walk by a beak's order, it's not straight forward, but always a goin' up and niver a-comin' down again. But come. You want grub and shall have it. I'll fork out. Up with you, on your pins. (3RD BOY *rises.*) There! Now, then. Hurry. (*They start to walk offstage together.*) Going to London?

3RD BOY: Yes.

DODGER: Got any lodging?

3RD BOY: No.

DODGER: Money?

3RD BOY: No. (DODGER *whistles in surprise.*) Do you live in London?

DODGER: I do when I'm at home. I suppose you want some place to sleep in tonight, don't you?

3RD BOY: I sure do. I have not slept under a roof since I left the country.

DODGER: Don't fret your eyelids on that score. I've got to be in London tonight, and I know a respectable old gen'leman as lives there, what'll give you lodgins for nothin' and never ask for the change . . . that is, if any gen'leman he knows interduces you! And don't he know *me*? I'll say he does! (*They exit,* DODGER *laughing heartily.*)

M.C.: Now there are two characters you should recognize right away. (*Music is heard, and* PANELISTS *write their answers.*)

Write down the answer, if you know it. (*After a pause,* AS-SISTANT *sounds buzzer; music stops.*) On to the next scene, panelists. I hope you're not too confused by this next charac-ter, who seems to be in quite a muddle herself. (5TH GIRL *enters.*)

5TH GIRL: Dear! Dear! How queer everything is today. I wonder if I've been changed into something else during the night. I'll see if I know all the things I used to know. Four times five is twelve. And four times six is thirteen! And four times seven is . . . . Oh, dear! I'd better try geography. London is the capital of Paris, and Paris is the capital of Rome, and Rome is . . . no! That's all wrong! I'll try reciting "How Doth the Little Busy Bee."
How doth the little crocodile improve his shining tail,
And pour the waters of the Nile on every golden scale.
How cheerfully he seems to grin, how neatly spread his claws,
And welcomes little fishes in with gently smiling jaws.
(*She exits.*)

M.C.: It's plain to see that this heroine is mixed up. She doesn't know her own name, but no doubt our experts can supply the missing identification. We'll ask our first panelist to come out here as we call our performers back for proper identification. (1ST PANELIST *crosses center, bringing her answer card with her.*) First, the young lady with the green hair. (1ST GIRL *reenters, wearing green wig.*) Panelist, name that book!

1ST PANELIST (*Checking card*): That character's name is Anne, from *Anne of Green Gables* by L.M. Montgomery. (AS-SISTANT *bangs gong.*)

M.C.: That is correct! The rest of our panelists can check their own cards to see how they fared. (PANELISTS *check cards, ad libbing elation or dismay.*) Let's ask Anne to explain how she happened to live at Green Gables—Anne?

ANNE: I had been in an orphanage, but then went to live with Marilla and Matthew. They had asked the orphanage for a boy to help them on the farm. When they got me, instead, they were disappointed. But after a while we grew very fond of each other, despite the fact that I was always getting into mischief. (*She exits.* 1ST PANELIST *returns to seat.*)

M.C.: And that green-hair episode was only one of dozens. Since its publication in 1908, *Anne of Green Gables* has been popular with readers of all ages all over the world. Will our next panelist please come forward to identify our next character. (2ND PANELIST *comes forward carrying card and stands beside* M.C. *Throughout play, panelists step forward when called.*) We call our English hero who was almost frightened to death by an escaped convict. (1ST BOY *enters.*) Now, who is this famous boy of fiction?

2ND PANELIST (*Looking at card; uncertainly*): His name is— Tip? (ASSISTANT *sounds buzzer.*)

M.C.: Oh, no, that's wrong. But you're close. The boy's name is Pip! Luckily, you have another chance: Can you name that book?

2ND PANELIST (*Still uncertain*): Is it *Great Expectations* by Charles Dickens? (ASSISTANT *bangs gong.*)

M.C.: That's right! (*To* 1ST BOY) Tell us, Pip, how did you ever get such a strange name?

PIP: My father's family name was Pirrip, P-I-R-R-I-P, and my given name was Philip. The combination was more than I could say when I was small, so I called myself Pip.

M.C.: And did you help that convict escape?

PIP: Yes, I brought him some food and the file for his chain, and it was the beginning of a great adventure for me. *Great Expectations* is a wonderful story. I think you'll enjoy it. (*Exits*)

M.C.: We've certainly enjoyed meeting Pip! And now for our next mystery character—the girl who sold her hair. (*To* 3RD PANELIST) Do you know her name? Can you name that book? (2ND GIRL *enters.*)

3RD PANELIST (*Waving card excitedly*): She's Jo March, the feisty, independent sister in *Little Women* by Louisa May Alcott. (ASSISTANT *bangs gong.*)

M.C.: You're right! All the world loves this classic. Jo, can you tell us about your family?

JO: While my father was in the hospital, we—that is, my sisters, Meg, Beth, Amy, and my mother, Marmee, and I, lived in the

Orchard House near Concord, Massachusetts. We are a closely knit family, and we tried our best to look after one another while Father was away. If you ever go traveling that way, you're welcome to stop by and see our house. (*Exits*)

M.C.: In our next scene . . . a boy promised to bring some cheese to poor Ben Gunn, marooned on the island for three years. (2ND BOY *and* BEN GUNN *enter. To* 4TH PANELIST) Can you name that book?

4TH PANELIST (*Checking card*): I'm pretty sure the book is *Treasure Island*. (ASSISTANT *bangs gong*.) The boy's name is . . . Jim Hawkins. (*Gong*) And the author's name is—(*After a pause, buzzer sounds*.) I can't remember.

M.C.: Robert Louis Stevenson is the author of *Treasure Island*. (*To* JIM) Would you like to tell us the rest of your story, Jim?

JIM: I managed to get back on board my ship, but so much happened in between.

BEN: You'll have to read *Treasure Island* to find out the rest. (*They exit.*)

M.C.: And now, let's have the two girls who got engaged when they were very, very young. (3RD *and* 4TH GIRLS *enter. To* 5TH PANELIST) Panelist, the boy they were engaged to was mentioned in their scene, and his name is part of the title of this book. Name that book!

5TH PANELIST (*Checking card*): *The Adventures of Tom Sawyer* by Mark Twain. (ASSISTANT *bangs gong*.) And the girls are named Becky Thatcher and Amy Lawrence. (*Another gong*.)

M.C.: That's right! (*To* GIRLS) Welcome, Becky and Amy. Did you two ever make up?

BECKY: Of course, we did.

AMY: We're really pretty good friends.

M.C.: And did you ever forgive Tom Sawyer for his first engagement, Becky?

BECKY: Yes, I did. You could never stay mad at Tom. Read about us and our great adventure when we were lost in a cave. It's really exciting. (*They exit.*)

M.C.: Now, back to merry England for our next book. (3RD BOY *and* ARTFUL DODGER *enter. To* 6TH PANELIST) Do you know these fellows?

6TH PANELIST (*Confidently*): Do I ever! Their names are Oliver Twist and Jack Dawkins, otherwise known as the Artful Dodger, from *Oliver Twist* by Charles Dickens. (ASSISTANT *bangs gong.*)

M.C.: Good job! And what a pair these two fellows are. Tell us, Oliver, were you boys good friends?

OLIVER: No, sir! And if I had ever guessed where the Artful Dodger was taking me on my first night in London, I would never have gone with him. That merry old gentleman he talked about ran a school for pickpockets, and before I knew it I was up to my ears in trouble.

DODGER: He never had no interest in his work, he didn't, and never learned to dodge the traps like I did. (*Craftily*) That's why my name suits me so well. (*They exit.*)

M.C.: And I'm sure *Oliver Twist* by Charles Dickens will suit us all for excitement and adventure. (5TH GIRL *enters.*) And here's another child who holds an honored place in the world of books. (*To* 7TH PANELIST) Do you know this famous heroine?

7TH PANELIST (*In frustration*): Her name is right on the tip of my tongue, but I just can't recall it. (ASSISTANT *sounds buzzer.*) Oh, wait, I remember now. She's Alice! (*Gong*)

M.C.: Nice work! I'll help you out with the title, which is *Alice's Adventures in Wonderland* by Lewis Carroll. (*To* ALICE) Alice, are you still as confused as ever?

ALICE: Not right this minute. But I am going back to my bookshelf before I get mixed up again. Goodbye, everyone. (*She exits.*)

M.C.: Goodbye, Alice. (*To* PANELISTS) You've done an excellent job on "Name That Book!" and now it's time to find out about our fabulous prizes! (ASSISTANT *rolls out bookcase full of books from offstage.*) Just look what we have here—all the books we just learned about on our show. They are yours to take home and enjoy—congratulations! (*He starts up a round of applause as* PANELISTS *go to bookcase and browse. To audience*) And thank you all for joining us today on "Name That Book!" Remember, any of the books you've heard about on our show—and many more—can be found at your library! (*Music is heard, and all wave to audience as curtain closes.*)

THE END

Production Notes

NAME THAT BOOK!

Characters: 6 male; 6 female; 3 male or female for M.C., Camera Operator, and Assistant; 7 male and female for Panelists.

Playing Time: 25 minutes.

Costumes: Modern, everyday dress for M.C., Cameraman, Assistant, and Panelists. 1st Girl, gingham dress, towel wrapped around green wig. Marilla, old-fashioned dress, very plain. 1st Boy, knee breeches, loose smock. Convict, striped shirt and pants, chain connected from ankle to "iron" ball. 2nd Girl, Civil-War period dress, with floor-length skirt and bonnet. 2nd Boy, knee breeches, open-necked smock; bare feet. Ben, a costume of tattered rags and "goat skins" tied together. 3rd and 4th Girls, gingham dresses, bonnets. 3rd Boy, simple shirt and pants. Dodger, ragged, ill-fitting suit; tall, black, battered hat. 5th Girl, long blond hair or wig, sailor-style Victorian dress. For further costume suggestions, consult illustrated editions of the books mentioned.

Properties: Cards and pencils; bench; bundle of clothing tied to the end of a stick; lock of hair; two lunch pails; two slates; bookcase on wheels, filled with books.

Setting: Television studio, with a large sign on back wall reading, NAME THAT BOOK! Table and seven chairs are at left. Podium is at center. Down left is a TV camera on a tripod. Chair, large gong, and buzzer are up right.

Lighting: No special effects.

Sound: Music, live or recorded; gong; buzzer, as indicated in text.

❧Yankees *vs.* Redcoats

by Claire Boiko

A baseball fantasy about the American Revolution . . .

Characters

PATRICK HENRY, *commentator*
JUDGE WOOLLY MATHER, *umpire*
CIDER VENDOR
TEA VENDOR
GENERAL THOMAS GAGE
GENERAL WILLIAM HOWE
GENERAL RICHARD HOWE } *Redcoats*
GENERAL JOHN BURGOYNE
GENERAL CHARLES CORNWALLIS
LORD NORTH
PAUL REVERE
GENERAL GEORGE WASHINGTON
GENERAL NATHANAEL GREENE } *Yankees*
NATHAN HALE
BENEDICT ARNOLD
MARQUIS DE LAFAYETTE
KING GEORGE III, *British cheerleader*
YANKEE FANS, *extras*

SETTING: *Continental Ball Park. Stadium is represented on backdrop by large scoreboard showing bottom of the ninth,* REDCOATS 2, YANKEES 0. *Up right are bleachers; up left is throne. A baseball diamond is laid out on stage, with home plate up center.*
AT RISE: YANKEE FANS *are seated in bleachers right. One* FAN *has slide whistle to play for sound of pitches; another*

313

FAN *has woodblock for hits.* KING GEORGE III *is sitting up left on throne, holding British flag. He wears crown, robes, and belt with sheathed sword underneath robes.* PAUL REVERE, GEN. GEORGE WASHINGTON, GEN. NATHANAEL GREENE, NATHAN HALE, BENEDICT ARNOLD, *and* MARQUIS DE LAFAYETTE *sit on bench up right.* GEN. THOMAS GAGE *is on pitcher's mound;* GEN. WILLIAM HOWE *is at first base;* GEN. RICHARD HOWE *is at second;* GEN. JOHN BURGOYNE *is at third.* GEN. CHARLES CORNWALLIS *is warming up in bullpen down left on apron.* LORD NORTH *squats behind home plate as catcher.* JUDGE WOOLLY MATHER *stands behind him wearing powdered wig, black robes, and beneath robes, a belt with sheathed sword attached.* PATRICK HENRY, *holding microphone, is down right.*

HENRY: Ladies and gentlemen, welcome to Continental Ball Park, here in the heart of downtown North America. (YANKEE FANS *cheer.*) I am your baseball commentator, Patrick "Give-Me-Liberty" Henry. It's the bottom of the ninth, folks, with the Redcoats leading the Yankees two to zero, and the entire world is looking on, as two teams battle it out for the pennant and victory in the Colonial series. On the field are the mighty Redcoats, recent victors in the French and Indian series.

KING (*Waving flag*): Hip-hip-hurrah. Pip-pip, and all that sort of thing.

HENRY: At bat are the Yankees, the underdog minor league team.

YANKEE FANS (*Waving pennants and cheering wildly*): Y-e-a, Yankees!

HENRY: In the field for the Redcoats are some fancy generals. At first base is General William Howe—a general nuisance. (*As their names are called,* GENERALS *salute and bow to each other and to* KING.) Second base is held down by General Richard Howe, a general bore. At third is General John Burgoyne, generally busy with the ladies. And on the mound we have General Thomas Gage, a general disaster. Catching for the Redcoats is Lord North—you might say that without him, we might not be having today's game. Warming up in the bullpen is General Cornwallis, generally late for everything but his meals.

KING (*Applauding*): I say, boys, let's have a go at it, shall we?

WOOLLY MATHER (*Shaking fist at* KING): *You* don't tell 'em to play ball. *I* tell 'em to play ball. (*Loudly*) Play ball!

HENRY: That was the umpire for today's game, Judge Woolly Mather, great-great nephew of Cotton Mather, and one of the meanest Mathers.

YANKEE FANS (*Together*): Boo! (MATHER *shakes fist at* FANS. CIDER VENDOR *and* TEA VENDOR *enter left and right, hawking their wares.*)

CIDER VENDOR: Cider! Get your good old American cider right here.

TEA VENDOR: Cider? You don't want cider. It'll curl your tongue and rot your stomach. What you want is nice British tea. Tea, hot tea right here.

CIDER VENDOR (*Squaring off with* TEA VENDOR): Tea? Did you say tea? (*He grabs* TEA VENDOR *by collar and shakes him. To* FANS) He's selling tea, folks. What shall I do with him?

YANKEE FANS (*Ad lib*): Throw the bum out! Throw him overboard! Dump him! (*Etc.* CIDER VENDOR *rushes* TEA VENDOR *offstage. There is a splash.* YANKEE FANS *applaud.*)

HENRY: Egad! What a rhubarb over the tea. Oh-oh. The umpire's mad.

MATHER: Are you going to play ball or not? You Yankees had better shake a bat, or you'll forfeit the game.

YANKEE FANS (*Together*): Boo! (PAUL REVERE *comes forward on a stick horse.*)

HENRY: Here we go, folks. Paul Revere steps up to bat. Good old Paul—always horsing around. (REVERE *dismounts, picks up plastic bat and bangs it on plate.*) And now Gage winds up for the pitch. (GAGE *winds up and throws. Slide whistle sounds.* NOTE: *All pitches are pantomimed.*) It's a fast ball. (REVERE *swings. Woodblock "tock."* REVERE *jumps onto stick horse and runs to second.*)

REVERE (*As he gallops*): The British are coming! The British are coming!

HENRY: Revere sockoed a cannonball that whistled through the British lines. A two-bagger! Maybe the Yankees will get the three runs they need this inning. (WASHINGTON *steps up to plate.*) Here comes George Washington. And listen to those fans!

YANKEE FANS (*Ad lib*): Yea, Washington! Chop 'em down George! (*Etc.*)

HENRY: Washington came out of the bush leagues of Virginia just a few seasons ago, and he is already first in hitting, first in pitching, and first in the hearts of the Yankee fans. (GAGE *begins his pitch.*) Gage is winding up. (*He throws.*) There it goes. A curve to Washington. (*Slide whistle is heard.* WASHINGTON *swings hard. Loud woodblock tock is heard.* WASHINGTON *runs to first.*) And it's a long, low hit across the Delaware. He's got to slide, folks. Hit the dirt, George! (RE-VERE *runs to third as* WASHINGTON *slides into first.* MATHER *runs down to first, waving his arms.* WILLIAM HOWE *catches ball.*)

MATHER: Safe! Safe at first!

YANKEE FANS: Hooray! Let's go, Yanks! Let's go, Yanks! (GREENE *steps up to bat, arrogantly blows kisses right and left, swings his bat fiercely and swaggers.*)

HENRY: Two men on, and Greene is at bat—a newcomer with a lot of self-confidence. But can he deliver those all-important runs? We'll soon see, folks. Gage is winding up like a wind-mill. (GAGE *swings his arm around and around. He throws.*) There goes the pitch. (GREENE *swings wildly and misses. Quick whistle.*)

MATHER: Strike *one!*

YANKEE FANS: Boo! (GAGE *winds up again and throws quickly. Quick whistle.* GREENE *swings wildly.*)

MATHER: Strike *two!*

YANKEE FANS (*Louder*): Boo! (GAGE *gives a short windup and pitches fast.* GREENE *swings so wildly that he whirls around and falls down.*)

MATHER: Strike *three!*

YANKEE FANS (*Together*): Kill the ump! Kill the ump! (MATHER *takes sword from sheath on belt and waves it threateningly at* FANS. GAGE *goes to* KING, *kneels in front of him.* KING *unsheathes sword from his belt and knights him.*)

KING: I dub the—Sir Shut-out. (GAGE *returns triumphantly to mound.*)

HENRY: One out for the Yankees. Now is the time for all good men to come to the aid of their team. Speaking of good men, here comes Nathan Hale, well known for his sacrifice tactics. Let's see what he does, folks. (GAGE *winds up, and throws. Short whistle.* HALE *bunts. Woodblock is heard.* WASHINGTON *runs to second.* GAGE *catches bunt, throws to* WILLIAM HOWE *who tags* HALE.)

HALE (*With hand on heart; dramatically*): I regret that I have but one out to give for my team! (*He returns to dugout.* YANKEE FANS *stand.*)

YANKEE FANS (*Putting hats on hearts*) A-men! (*All sit.*)

HENRY: Two away for the Yankees. They need a miracle! (BENEDICT ARNOLD *comes up to bat.*) Coming up to bat is Benedict Arnold. You all remember the fine batting he did at Saratoga. Can he pull the Yankees through today?

YANKEE FANS (*Together*): Hit 'em hard, Arnold! Hit 'em hard, Arnold! (ARNOLD *salutes* YANKEE FANS, *then shades his eyes and looks at* KING, *who holds up a sack labeled* GOLD, *and sign reading* WOULDN'T YOU RATHER SWITCH THAN FIGHT? ARNOLD *nods, drops bat, and joins* KING *sitting beside him as* KING *drapes red coat around his shoulders.*)

YANKEE FANS (*Together*): Boo! Boo!

HENRY: Did you see that? Arnold has just traded himself to the British.

MATHER: Error! Error! Shame on Benedict Arnold.

HENRY: Well, I guess this game is just about over, folks. Two outs, and the British two up on the Yanks. (LAFAYETTE *comes to plate.*) Wait a minute, folks, here's a pinch hitter. It's a Frenchman named Lafayette. Traded from Paris.

LAFAYETTE (*Striking a pose*): Mes amis—do not fear. Lafayette is here.

YANKEE FANS (*Chanting*):

Lafayette! Lafayette!

He'll get a hit! Wanna bet?

HENRY: The new player is a big favorite with the fans. But can he drive home that all important run? (KING *waves* GAGE *out.* GAGE, *crestfallen, leaves mound.* CORNWALLIS *leaves bullpen and trots to mound.*) What's this? Action on the British side. Gage has fallen out of favor, and Cornwallis is taking his place as relief pitcher.

KING: Hip-hip-hurrah. Pip-pip and all that rot. (CORNWALLIS *and other* GENERALS *go through a round of bowing and saluting.* CORNWALLIS *then goes up to* LAFAYETTE *and scrutinizes him from head to toe through his monocle, as* HENRY *speaks.*)

HENRY: And now, Cornwallis studies Lafayette. (CORNWALLIS *returns to mound.* LAFAYETTE *follows him, and looks him up and down.*) And Lafayette studies Cornwallis. (LAFAYETTE *returns to plate.*) Cornwallis winds up. And he winds up. (CORNWALLIS *keeps winding up.*) Ah—at last, the wind-up of the wind-up. (CORNWALLIS *throws. Slide whistle*) It's Cornwallis's triple-nervy-spit-ball-curvy-bounce-ball! Nobody in the world has ever hit one before. Lafayette is swinging, folks! (LAFAYETTE *swings. Loud woodblock tock*)

YANKEE FANS (*Standing and waving pennants and cheering*): He hit it!

HENRY: There goes the ball—sailing over Virginia, over the entire Atlantic ocean and right into the lap of His Royal Highness, King George the Third! (*Dull thump.* KING *falls over backward with his throne and scrambles up, furious.* RE-VERE, WASHINGTON, *and* LAFAYETTE *run around bases, coming across home plate, and are congratulated by some of the* YANKEE FANS. YANKEE FAN *changes score to* RED-COATS 2, YANKEES 3.)

MATHER: Safe at home!

HENRY: They did it! Those hometown boys scored three runs on Lafayette's homer, winning the series and gaining that coveted Colonial pennant. I can't believe it, but you saw it with your own eyes, folks. It happened right here in Continental Ball Park in the heart of downtown North America!

YANKEE FANS: Redcoats, go home! Redcoats, go home! (RED-COAT *team exits. An angry* KING *walks across field, to center. He wags his finger at audience.*)

KING: Foul! Foul! 'Tis a foul trick you've played on us. You haven't heard the last of us, you know. We'll get our innings. Just wait until the next series. Just wait until the series of 1812! (*Quick curtain*)

THE END

Production Notes

YANKEES *vs.* REDCOATS

Characters: 17 male (or female); male and female extras for Fans.

Playing Time: 15 minutes.

Costumes: Patrick Henry wears coat, stock, tricorn, breeches, stockings, buckled shoes. Redcoats wear red breeches, stockings, ruffled shirts, stockings, short red cloaks with epaulettes, red tricorns. Yankees wear the same, but in blue (no epaulettes for Revere or Hale). King wears purple robe, crown, under robe, a belt with sheathed sword attached. Boy Fans wear breeches, shirts with stocks, tricorns; girl Fans wear long dresses, mob caps. Cider Vendor wears blue and white, Tea Vendor wears red and white, similar to Fans' outfits. Judge wears long black robe, judge's wig, and under robe, a belt with sheathed sword attached. Cornwallis wears monocle.

Properties: Pennants, British flag, red cloak, plastic bat, baseball mitts, stick horse, sign reading WOULDN'T YOU RATHER SWITCH THAN FIGHT?, sack labeled GOLD, microphone, teapot, jug of cider.

Setting: Continental Ball Park. Backdrop shows large scoreboard at bottom of ninth, REDCOATS 2, YANKEES 0. At end, it reads REDCOATS 2, YANKEES 3. Up right are bleachers, up left a throne. Baseball diamond is laid out on stage, with home plate up center.

Lighting: No special effects.

Sound: Slide whistle indicates pitches, woodblock is hit to indicate hits; offstage splash, thud.

～The Western Civ Rap

by *Nancy Porta Libert*

A creative romp through history . . .

Characters

JACK, *lead rapper*
GROUP I ⎫
GROUP II ⎭ *mixed voices*
BOYS, *with low voices*
GIRLS I, *with low voices*
GIRLS II, *with high voices*

TIME: *The present.*
SETTING: *A classroom. Blackboard or painted backdrop on back wall reads* WESTERN CIVILIZATION FINAL EXAM. *Student desks line back and sides of stage.*
AT RISE: *Rappers, carrying books, notebooks, and talking amongst themselves, enter right and left. They place books on desks, then gradually form semicircle, arranged by group. When* JACK *makes his way to the middle of semicircle, murmuring dies down.* NOTE: *Each group steps downstage or away from semicircle in turn, and steps back when finished. Rappers may mime certain portions of story as the opportunity presents itself.*
GROUP I (*Leaping downstage, center*):
Now this story of ours,
If you want to know,
Goes a way, way back
To where the rivers flow.

In the Middle East,
North Africa, too,

321

India, China,
and even Peru.
BOYS:
  Well, a way back then,
  So the story goes,
  They had no language
  and they had no clothes.

  Even their food
  Was the simple kind—
  Seeds and berries,
  Whatever they could find.
JACK:
  Then they learned about hunting,
  And they learned about fire.
  And the prospects of man
  Rose higher and higher.
CHORUS (*All except* JACK *leaping forward and singing to the Ray Charles tune, "Hit the Road, Jack"*):
  Tell me more, Jack,
  And won't you go back some more, some more, some more,
    some more,
  Tell me more, Jack,
  And won't you go back some more.
JACK (*In gravelly voice*):
  What you say?!
CHORUS (*Repeating refrain*):
  Tell me more, Jack ... (*Etc. Meantime,* JACK *paces, deep in thought.*)
JACK:
  Well, ten thousand years,
  Maybe longer ago,
  There was ice all over—
  Just glaciers and snow.

  But the earth warmed up
  And the ice departed. (*To* CHORUS)
  What's the next big step?

CHORUS (*Shouting*):
  Farming started!
GROUP II:
  Now the earliest people,
  You'll know them by name,
  Came from different places
  Of equal fame.

  Sumer and Egypt,
  They left their traces—
  Strong early folks
  Of different races.
GIRLS I (*Confronting* JACK):
  Now, hold on, Jack!
  We happen to know
  That the ancient Greeks
  Were a part of this show.

  They came from the north
  Had a war to fight
  With Macedonia,
  They showed 'em their might.
GIRLS II:
  It was mountainous country
  In need of reparation,
  Took a long, long time
  To make one nation.

  Every city state
  Had its own pursuits,
  But Athens and Sparta
  Had the strongest roots.
JACK:
  They defeated the Persians,
  Had a Golden Age,
  Made democracy the rule,
  And sports the rage.

  They had poets like Homer
  Who wrote epics with ease,

And some dudes named Plato
And Socrates.

Alexander the Great
Spread the Greek ways.
The Hellenistic Age—
Those were civilized days.
1ST GIRL (*Stepping forward*):
Whoa! there, Jack,
It wasn't all Greek—
There were lots of other groups
Of which we should speak!
JACK (*Holding up hands defensively*):
O.K., O.K . . . now,
Give me some time.
I can give you the facts,
But they've got to rhyme!
(*He paces as though pondering, then spins around to audience.*)

On seven low hills
Some tough Latin tribes
Made plans to take over
Or, so say the scribes.

They fought their neighbors,
Hardly ever stayed home,
But they founded the great, great
City of Rome.
GROUP I:
Ah, the noble Romans
As an early nation,
Formed a strong republic
With representation.

There were consuls, a senate,
And a twelve-law credo—
And would you believe,
They invented the veto!

BOYS:

Soon the Romans fought others
And before they knew it,
They took on Carthage
And almost blew it.

But Hannibal was beaten
And in a short time,
They had Spain, and Greece,
And Palestine.

GIRLS I:

But the seeds of greed
Were in the grain,
And the Roman sense of duty
Was on the wane.

Some army generals
Had such great power
That the senators and consuls
Began to cower.

GROUP II:

So when Caesar declared
He would rule for life,
The chosen solution
Was to use the knife.

(*In stage whisper*)
Plots to kill him
Grew unabated.

CHORUS:

In a group attack,
He was assassinated!

GIRLS II:

Then the Roman Empire,
Rotten within,
Collapsed from folly,
Greed, and sin.

When German tribes
Took over their land,

Those ancient Romans
Made their last stand.
BOYS:
In the years that followed
Things were pretty dark.
There was great disorder
And it left its mark.

The Vikings and the Goths
And the Franks caused scandals.
They robbed, they pillaged
They were nothing but vandals!
GROUP I:
For the people of Europe
A new way of life
Was needed to save them
From war and strife.

So the king decided
To stand and deliver
His plan was to make him
A big land giver.

In return for land,
Men pledged to fight,
And with the tap of his sword
He dubbed each his knight.
JACK:
People lived in cities
Surrounded by walls
Where the king and his army
Protected them all.

A system of mutual aid
Had arisen
That got the name
Of Feudalism.

(CHORUS *sings "Tell Me More Jack" refrain;* JACK *chimes
in with "What you say?" and* CHORUS *sings refrain again.*
JACK *continues rapping.*)

By the year 1,000
They had it down pat,
Life on the manor—
That's where it was at.

Anything they needed
They made right there,
So trips into town
Were really quite rare.

GIRLS II:
This was the time
Of knighthood in flower,
When men were brave
And the gallant had power.

BOYS:
They marched to the east,
Fought eight crusades;
Showed skills in jousting,
Protected fair maids.

GROUP II:
But sooner or later
All things must cease,
And manor life declined
As travel increased.

With travel came trade
Which flourished and grew.
Smart people with skills
Could make money, too.

JACK:
So an age of business
Developed in stages,
As people with crafts
Were paid real wages.

They spent their time
Making products to sell,
The population grew
And merchants did well.

GIRLS I:
    There you go again, Jack!
    It wasn't so sunny!
    Don't paint this picture
    Of milk and honey.

    There were lots of things
    That weren't so hot.
    If you're gonna make soup—
    Put it all in the pot!
JACK (*Aside, to audience*):
    I see these girls
    Aren't easily led.
    They're sharp, they're quick,
    They're very well read.

    I've got to get down
    To the serious facts,
    Or my scholarly image
    Is bound to show cracks.

(*He pauses to consider his next move.*)
1215 in England
With clouds overhead,
King John taxed his nobles
Right into the red.

    He was forced to sign a charter
    That cut down his power
    At Runnymede the people
    Had their finest hour.
GROUPS I AND II:
    Soon a grand new age
    Got a really good start,
    With a lot of new thinking
    In science and art.
2ND GIRL:
    It was the Renaissance,
    An age that glistened.

JACK:
  When the poets spoke—
  The people listened.
GIRLS I:
  Now, the Renaissance
  Had some really fine fellows:
  Botticellis and da Vincis
  And Donatellos.

  Their sculpting and painting
  Sent the people reeling.
  Check out Michelangelo—
  He painted a ceiling.
JACK:
  Great men of letters
  Also arose,
  They began to write verse
  And classical prose.

  Their works got read much more,
  I guess—
CHORUS:
  When Gutenberg invented
  The printing press!
GIRLS II:
  Near 1500
  Some religious views
  Were tossed around
  'Til they made big news.

  Martin Luther, the German,
  Said the church must change—
BOYS:
  It's the hierarchy
  We ought to rearrange!
GROUPS I AND II:
  No immediate action
  Came about,

So Luther, being
Quite devout,

Led the people
In a new congregation,
And founded
The Protestant Reformation.
GIRLS I:
It was during this time
That ideas were big,
But there was one guy from Italy
That no one could dig.
ALL GIRLS:
It was clear that he marched
To a different drummer,
Said the world was round—
3RD GIRL:
Now, what could be dumber?
CHORUS (*Gathering downstage*):
He said, "To reach the East,
You gotta sail West!"
He got three Spanish ships
To make the test.

He found a new world
When he crossed that ocean—
JACK:
He reached America,
And set it in motion!
CHORUS:
Then came an age
Of exploration
That changed the lives
Of future generations.

The modern age came
In all its glory,
JACK:
But the truth is, friends,

That's a whole other story!
(*All strike rapper pose, followed by blackout. Curtain*)
                    THE END

Production Notes

THE WESTERN CIV RAP

Characters: 1 male for Jack; as many male and female as desired for other rappers: 2 mixed groups with medium-range voices; 1 group of males with deep voices; 1 group of females with deep voices, and 1 group of females with high voices.

Playing Time: 20 minutes.

Costumes: Modern. Members of each group may dress similarly to distinguish themselves from other groups.

Properties: None.

Setting: Classroom. Large blackboard or backdrop with WESTERN CIVILIZATION FINAL EXAM written in white is against back wall, center. Desks line back and sides of stage.

Lighting: Lights dim at end, as indicated.

Sound: No special effects.

ᴥBreakfast at the Bookworm Café

by Jane Tesh

Books come to the rescue when termite gang strikes . . . .

Characters

EMERSON BOOKWORM
HAWTHORNE BOOKWORM, *his son*
MR. CRAWLER
MRS. CRAWLER
CHEF VER DE TERRE
LADY WORM
BUGSY TERMITE
CHEWY TERMITE
WOODY TERMITE
MAYOR WORMER
LOUISA MAY, *his daughter*
OTHER GUESTS, *extras*
OTHER TERMITES, *extras*

TIME: *The present.*
SETTING: *Bookworm Café in Bugville. A counter divides the stage. On one side are tables and chairs. On the other side are cooking utensils, dishes, kitchen appliances, cardboard boxes, and stack of books.*
AT RISE: MR. CRAWLER *and* MRS. CRAWLER *are seated at one table,* LADY WORM *at another; they are studying menus.* CHEF VER DE TERRE *is cooking, and* EMERSON *and* HAWTHORNE BOOKWORM *are hurrying about, getting dishes.*
EMERSON (*Exasperated*): Hawthorne, for goodness' sake! Get

organized! The mayor and his daughter will be here any minute for their special breakfast.

HAWTHORNE: I'm hurrying, Dad. You know I want the café to look its best for Louisa May.

EMERSON: Son, I don't want to discourage you, but I don't think you have much of a chance with the mayor's daughter. She's a very rich young bookworm. Brought up on the classics.

HAWTHORNE: I know I'm just a lowly waiterworm, but I'm a bookworm, too. (*Fervently*) Some day I'll prove myself worthy of her.

EMERSON: Well, right now, you need to check on our customers. (HAWTHORNE *goes around counter and stops at* MR. *and* MRS. CRAWLER'*s table.*)

HAWTHORNE: Good morning, Mr. and Mrs. Crawler. Welcome to the Bookworm Café. I am Hawthorne, your waiterworm. Today's special is a slice of *Life* Magazine with *Huckleberry Finn* for dessert.

MR. CRAWLER: That sounds delicious. I'll have that.

MRS. CRAWLER: I'll have *Green Eggs and Ham*. (HAWTHORNE *writes down their orders and takes their menus.*)

HAWTHORNE: Thank you. Coming right up. (*He hurries to counter and calls over to* CHEF.) One special, one Seuss! (*Puts menus on counter*)

CHEF: One special, one Seuss. Right away. (LADY WORM *signals to* HAWTHORNE. *He goes to her table.*)

LADY WORM: Young worm, what is the book *du jour?*

HAWTHORNE: *Wonderful Flight to the Mushroom Planet* soup, ma'am.

LADY WORM: I'll have that and a cup of coffee, please. (*Hands him menu*)

HAWTHORNE: Right away! (*He runs to counter and calls to* CHEF.) One soup! (*Puts menu down*)

CHEF: One soup.

EMERSON: Hawthorne, come back here. (HAWTHORNE *goes around to other side of counter.* EMERSON *points to large pile of old thick books.*) What are all these old books doing here? I told you to get rid of them. They're useless. Too old, dry, and tasteless.

HAWTHORNE: Gosh, Dad, I can't believe any book is useless. We may need them some day.

EMERSON: I want them out.

HAWTHORNE: But—

EMERSON: I won't have that pile of junk in my café. Out they go!

HAWTHORNE (*Sighing*): O.K. (*He pushes books aside.*) Oof, talk about a heavy diet! (*He pauses to read some titles.*) *Farming Techniques. The Rise and Fall of Ancient Civilizations. Politics in the Fifties. The History of the Safety Pin.* Well, you never know. Not to everyone's taste, but it's vintage stuff. I can't throw out perfectly good food. I'll just hide them. (*He shoves books behind some boxes.*)

EMERSON: All right, let's go over the menu for the mayor's special breakfast. (HAWTHORNE *and* CHEF *join him at counter.*) *Scrambled Eggs Super,* followed by *Grapes of Wrath* and *Strawberry Girl,* and, for dessert, *Charlie and the Chocolate Factory* with *Ten Apples on Top.*

HAWTHORNE: Yum!

CHEF: I'll get started right away. (*He goes to cabinet, opens door, and stares.*) Horrible news, Monsieur Emerson! We are all out!

EMERSON: Out? Well, choose something from the storeroom. *Bread and Jam for Frances* is always good. Or *The Enormous Egg.* Very filling. (CHEF *dashes out and returns immediately, gasping.*)

CHEF: We're out of everything!

EMERSON: Everything? That's impossible!

HAWTHORNE: No books? No magazines? Not even a comic?

CHEF: Nothing! All the books are gone!

EMERSON: What could have happened? (BUGSY TERMITE, CHEWY TERMITE, WOODY TERMITE, *and* OTHER TERMITES *enter café.* WORMS *freeze in horror.*)

BUGSY (*Menacingly*): *We* happened, that's what!

ALL: Termites!

EMERSON: It's Bugsy Termite!

HAWTHORNE: And his Hole in the Wall Gang!

BUGSY: Yeah, that's right, and we're taking over, see?

EMERSON: Taking over my café? Never!

BUGSY: Me and the boys have been chewing our way across Bugville, Bookworm, and we're gonna eat your place to the ground.

EMERSON: No, no!

BUGSY: But before we do, we're gonna pull off a little caper. We heard the mayor is coming for breakfast. We're gonna kidnap him and his daughter, and then I'll be mayor of Bugville!

CHEWY: Great idea, boss!

WOODY: Yeah!

HAWTHORNE (*Upset*): You'll never get away with it.

BUGSY: Oh, yeah? For your information, pal, we termites should have been running this place long ago. We're the ones with all the smarts.

TERMITES (*Ad lib*): Yeah, you tell him. That's right. (*Etc.*)

BUGSY: We've been around for centuries, long before you puny worms crawled out of the dirt. So listen up! Everybody act natural. Chewy, you and Woody sit down over there and act like customers. The rest of you, do the same. When the mayor comes in, we'll grab him and the girl.

HAWTHORNE: Don't you dare harm Louisa May!

BUGSY: Don't *you* try to be a hero, or we'll beat you to a pulp— har, har, a little termite humor there. Serve these folks their books!

CHEWY: And bring us a little snack, too.

BUGSY: Good idea! We might as well eat while we wait.

EMERSON: Better do as they say, Hawthorne. (TERMITES *take seats.* WORMS *eye them nervously.* HAWTHORNE *and* EMERSON *confer behind counter*) What can we do? Those termites are so tough, and there's nothing left for them to eat!

HAWTHORNE: Oh, yes, there is! (*He pulls old books out from behind boxes.*)

EMERSON: Hawthorne, I told you to throw those away.

HAWTHORNE: Well, now aren't you glad I didn't? I have a plan. (*He whispers to* EMERSON *and* CHEF. *They nod and help him pull out books.* HAWTHORNE *chooses one.*) This is the very thing! Chef, can you make this look really tasty?

CHEF: Leave it to me!

BUGSY (*Loudly*): Hey, hurry up with that grub!

CHEF (*As he cooks and stirs*): You won't be able to judge this book by its cover! (*He puts food on plate and hands it to* HAWTHORNE, *who takes it to* TERMITES.)

BUGSY: What's this?

HAWTHORNE: Our very best seller. It's what we were planning to serve the mayor.

BUGSY: Hah! Too bad. We got here first. (*He grabs dish, and he and other* TERMITES *eat greedily, slurping and smacking their lips.*) More, more! (HAWTHORNE *serves them more.* MAYOR WORMER *and* LOUISA MAY *enter. They stop short when they see* TERMITES.)

MAYOR: What's this? Termites! (TERMITES *jump to their feet, and begin to sway.*)

BUGSY: Yeah, and we're taking over, see? (*Suddenly, he and his gang clutch their stomachs and double over, groaning.*) Gosh, what's happening? The pain is killing me! (*They fall writhing on floor.*) What was that book?

HAWTHORNE (*Grinning*): *The Rise and Fall of Ancient Civilizations.*

EMERSON: Good thinking, Hawthorne!

MAYOR: Yes, indeed. Take these creatures away! (WORMS *drag* TERMITES *off.*)

MAYOR (*To* HAWTHORNE): Young worm, you've saved the day. How can I ever thank you?

HAWTHORNE: Well, sir, I'd like to have breakfast with you and— (*Smiling at* LOUISA MAY) your lovely daughter.

MAYOR: Of course!

LOUISA MAY (*Admiringly*): Oh, Hawthorne, you were so clever.

HAWTHORNE (*Modestly*): I read a lot.

EMERSON: Breakfast for everyone!

CHEF: But Monsieur Emerson, we are out of books, remember?

HAWTHORNE: No problem! We'll just go back to the library. There's always something good there! (*All exit.*)

THE END

Production Notes

BREAKFAST AT THE BOOKWORM CAFÉ

Characters: 5 male; 3 female; male or female for Chewy, Woody, Chef Ver de
    Terre; male and female extras as needed for Guests and Termites.
Playing Time: 10 minutes.
Costumes: Worms wear brown or gray leotards and tights; Emerson and Haw-
    thorne wear large glasses; Chef wears chef's hat and apron; Termites wear
    brown clothes, trenchcoats or gangster costumes, antennae; Mayor wears
    top hat.
Properties: Plates of "food," notepad, pen.
Setting: Bookworm Café. A counter divides stage: on one side are tables and
    chairs; tables are set with dishes, silverware, menus, and centerpieces. On
    the other side are pots and pans, utensils, appliances made of cardboard
    boxes, if desired, a large pile of overly large, thick books, and boxes.
Lighting and Sound: No special effects.

Special Christmas Program

~The Birds' Christmas Carol

by Kate Douglas Wiggin
Adapted by Helen Louise Miller

Young girl brings comfort and joy to all . . .

Characters

CAROLERS
LEADER
NARRATOR
GRANDMA BIRD
DONALD ⎫
HUGH ⎪
PAUL ⎬ *the Bird children*
CAROL ⎭
NURSE PARKER
UNCLE JACK
MRS. RUGGLES
MRS. BIRD
SARAH MAUD ⎫
PETER ⎪
KITTY ⎪
LARRY ⎪
PEORIA ⎬ *Ruggles children*
SUSAN ⎪
CLEMENT ⎪
EILY ⎪
CORNELIUS ⎭

SCENE 1

TIME: *Late nineteenth century.*

SETTING: *A street in a big city. Scene is played before the curtain.*

BEFORE RISE: CAROLERS *and* LEADER *enter. Girls wear long skirts, cloaks, bonnets, muffs; boys wear knickers, heavy jackets, caps, and scarves. Narrator stands downstage, right.*

1ST CAROLER: Is this our last stop? My feet are nearly frozen!

LEADER: Yes, this is the last one. Then to my house for hot chocolate.

2ND CAROLER (*Looking out over audience*): Someone must be up late in that big house across the street. All the windows on the second floor are lighted up.

3RD CAROLER (*Stamping feet*): Maybe they'll invite us in to get warm.

LEADER: Think about the music instead of your feet, and you won't be so cold! Now, for our last performance, let's do our very best. Ready? (*He raises his hand and directs* CAROLERS *in singing "Deck the Halls."*) That was terrific! Anyone who heard that is bound to feel the Christmas spirit.

2ND CAROLER: I wonder if they were listening in that big house. The lights are still on, but no one is opening the door.

3RD CAROLER: I wonder how many people have heard our carols tonight, and what they thought of them.

LEADER: That's something we'll never know. But I have an idea that our Christmas caroling affects people more than we imagine. (CAROLERS *exit.*)

NARRATOR (*Moving center*): And even the leader would have been surprised at the result of their carol-singing in the big brownstone house. The family's name was Bird, and the house was called "Bird's Nest." It was all lighted up in the small hours of Christmas morning because a very precious baby Bird had come into the world shortly after midnight. As the other children gather in the living room after breakfast, their Christmas gifts are almost forgotten in the excitement. (*Exits*)

* * * * *

SETTING: *The Bird's living room, decorated for Christmas. Rocking chair is center.*

AT RISE: DONALD, HUGH, *and* PAUL, *in period costumes, crowd around* GRANDMA BIRD, *who sits in rocking chair.*

HUGH: What's the baby's name, Grandma?

GRANDMA: I can't say for sure, dear, but I think your mother's going to call her Susan. Would you like that?

HUGH: Oh, yes. It will do—for a girl! If it had been a boy, I think Texas would be a good name.

DONALD (*In disgust*): Texas isn't a real boy's name. It's the name of a state.

HUGH: Lots of boys are named Texas!

PAUL: I think Luella's a pretty name.

DONALD: Dorothy's a good name.

HUGH: Especially when it belongs to Dorothy Hagen, the girl who sits next to you in school.

DONALD (*Angrily*): Listen, you . . .

GRANDMA: Children! Children! Quiet down! We don't want to disturb your mother or wake the baby! Anyhow, we can't be absolutely sure what the baby's name is until we hear from your mother.

PAUL: Maybe Dad will have a good idea for a name.

HUGH: Dad named all three of us boys. He says it's mother's turn this time.

DONALD: Uncle Jack says a first girl baby should always be named for its mother.

GRANDMA: Well, one thing you can be sure of—the baby won't go without a name.

PAUL: When are we going to get to see the baby?

GRANDMA: As soon as the nurse says you may go up.

DONALD: I don't want to see it. I'd rather ride my new bicycle.

GRANDMA: Donald Bird! What a dreadful thing to say! Of course you want to see your little sister! (NURSE PARKER *enters.*)

NURSE (*To* GRANDMA): Excuse me ma'am, but Mrs. Bird would like you to bring the boys upstairs now to see the baby.

GRANDMA: Wonderful, Nurse. We'll be right up.

PAUL: What's the baby's name, Miss Parker? Has Mother decided yet?

NURSE: Indeed, she has, the perfect name for a Christmas baby. *Carol.*

BOYS: Carol?

GRANDMA: Is it short for Caroline?

NURSE: Heavens, no. It means just what it says, *Carol*—a song of joy for Christmas.

GRANDMA (*Puzzled*): Strange, she never mentioned that name before.

NURSE: The idea came to her early this morning. Right after the baby was born, Mrs. Bird heard the carolers singing outside her window, and she said it sounded as if the angels were bidding the baby welcome. "Carol," she said. "She's Mother's little Christmas Carol," and that's how she decided on the name.

PAUL: I guess if she had been born on the Fourth of July, Mother would have named her *Independence*!

DONALD: Carol! I think Carol's a pretty name. Let's go and see her. (*Starts for door*)

GRANDMA (*Amused*): I thought you didn't want to see the new baby at all.

DONALD: I've changed my mind since I know her name is *Carol.* I think it will be fun to have a little Christmas Carol around the house 365 days of the year. (*Curtain*)

* * * * *

SCENE 2

BEFORE RISE: NARRATOR *enters before curtain.*

NARRATOR: And it *was* fun to have Carol around the house 365 days of the year. She was a happy baby, and her tiny hands were forever outstretched in giving.

But by the time ten Christmases had come and gone, a sad change had come over the Bird's Nest; for the little child who once brought such an added blessing to the day, was terribly ill, and for month after month, she lay in bed, weak and help-

less. The doctor had warned the family that someday soon
Carol would slip quietly away from those who loved her so
dearly. In spite of their sorrow, the Birds determined to make
Carol's tenth birthday the very best Christmas ever. Carol
herself had planned the day down to the last detail, and she
could hardly wait to describe her plans to her beloved Uncle
Jack, just home from England for the holidays. (*Exits*)

* * * * *

SETTING: *Carol's bedroom. Bed is center, with straight-backed
chair beside it.*

AT RISE: CAROL *is in bed, propped up on pillows.* UNCLE
JACK *sits in chair.*

CAROL: I want to tell you about my plans for Christmas, Uncle
Jack, because I know it will be the loveliest one I've ever had.
You know, ever since I discovered how wonderful it is to be
born on Christmas Day, I've tried to make someone extra
happy on my birthday. This year it's to be the Ruggles family.

UNCLE JACK: The Ruggles family? That's the large brood of
children in the little house at the end of the back garden,
isn't it?

CAROL: Yes. (*Musing*) Uncle Jack, why do *big* families always
live in small houses, and the small families live in big houses?

UNCLE JACK: That's pretty hard to explain, Carol.

CAROL: Well, I'm sure the Ruggles children have a good time
in their little house. Ever since they moved in, I've watched
them play in their backyard. One day when they were extra
noisy, and I had a headache, Donald asked them not to scream
quite so loud, and what do you think they did?

UNCLE JACK: I hope they listened to Donald.

CAROL: They did. They played in pantomime all afternoon so
they wouldn't disturb me.

UNCLE JACK (*Laughing*): Quite an obliging family, I must say.

CAROL: Now, Sarah Maud—she's the oldest—stops everyday
to see how I am before they start their games. Then she and
Peter tell the others what to play.

UNCLE JACK: What is the pretty, little red-haired girl called?

CAROL: That's Kitty.

UNCLE JACK: And the chubby one?

CAROL: Little Larry. He's the youngest.

UNCLE JACK: And the most freckled one?

CAROL: Don't laugh! That's Peoria.

UNCLE JACK: Carol, you're joking.

CAROL: No, really, Uncle Jack, she was born in Peoria, Illinois.

UNCLE JACK (*Laughing*): And is there a Chicago and a Cincinnati?

CAROL: No. The others are Susan and Clement and Eily and Cornelius.

UNCLE JACK: How did you ever learn their names?

CAROL: When the weather is warm, I sit on the balcony, and the Ruggles children climb up and walk along our garden fence. They sit on the roof of our carriage house, and I tell them stories.

UNCLE JACK: And how do these children fit into your Christmas plans?

CAROL: I want to give the nine Ruggles children a grand Christmas dinner, and a tree, with lots of presents under it. Here, I've written the invitation. (*Hands him paper*) Please read it and tell me if it's all right.

UNCLE JACK (*Reading*): "Bird's Nest, December 17th, 1887: Dear Mrs. Ruggles: I am going to have a dinner party on Christmas Day, and I would like to have all your children come, every one of them, from Sarah Maud to little Larry. Mamma says dinner will be at half-past five, and lighting the Christmas tree at seven; so you may expect them home at nine o'clock. Wishing you a Merry Christmas and a Happy New Year, I am yours truly, Carol Bird." (*Curtain*)

* * * * *

SCENE 3

SETTING: *The kitchen of Ruggles home. Seven chairs, a coal hod, and a wood box are lined up across stage. A clock is on the wall.*

AT RISE: *The nine Ruggles children,* SARAH MAUD, PETER, KITTY, LARRY, PEORIA, SUSAN, CLEMENT, EILY, *and* CORNELIUS, *sit on chairs and wood box.* MRS. RUGGLES *inspects them.*

MRS. RUGGLES (*Walking from one child to another, examining their hands, ears, etc.*): Well, if I do say so, I've never seen a cleaner, more stylish mess of children in my life! I do wish your father could see you, even for a minute. (*Crossly, as* LARRY *tugs at sash.*) Larry Ruggles, how many times have I told you not to keep pulling at your sash! (LARRY *folds his hands.*) Haven't I told you if it comes untied, your shirtwaist and trousers will part company in the middle—and then where'll you be? (*Severely*) I've often told you what kind of people my family the McGrills were. We've reason to be proud. When my children go out, they've got to wear clean clothes and act proper. Now, I want to see how you're going to behave when you get to the Birds' house tonight! It isn't as easy as you think. Let's start at the beginning and act out the whole business. (*Pointing offstage*) Pile into the bedroom there and show me how you're going to come into the parlor. We'll pretend this is the parlor, and I'll be Mrs. Bird. (*Children go offstage.* MRS. RUGGLES *draws herself up with her nose in the air and speaks in "cultured" tones.*) Good afternoon, children. Come in. (SARAH MAUD *enters, and the other children straggle in after her, with* LARRY *last. They stand about awkwardly.*)

SARAH MAUD (*To* MRS. RUGGLES): How do you do, Mrs. Bird? (*As* LARRY *enters, he starts to run, then slips and falls. Children gasp and giggle.* MRS. RUGGLES *turns to him, her hands on her hips.*)

MRS. RUGGLES: There! I knew you'd do something foolish.

LARRY (*Ashamed*): I'm sorry, Ma.

MRS. RUGGLES: Well, go out and try it again, and Larry, if you can't come in on your two legs, you can stay at home, do you hear? (*Children exit again and reenter, marching in step, in single file.* MRS. RUGGLES *clasps her hands impatiently. Children stop in surprise.*) No! No! No!

PETER: What's wrong, Ma?

MRS. RUGGLES: You look like a line of soldiers. There isn't any style to that. Spread out more, and act kind of careless-like. This is a dinner party. (*Children exit again, then reenter, walking more carefully. They cross to chairs and sit down.*)

KITTY: Did we do all right, ma'am?

MRS. RUGGLES: Yes, that was better. (*To* CORNELIUS) Now, Cornelius, what are *you* going to say to make yourself good company?

CORNELIUS (*Startled*): Who? Me? I dunno!

MRS. RUGGLES: Well, you aren't going to sit there like a bump on a log, without saying a word, are you? Ask Mrs. Bird how she feels this evening, or if Mr. Bird's having a busy season, or how the weather agrees with him, or something like that. Now, we'll make believe we're having dinner. That won't be hard, because you'll have something to do. (*Pointing to each child as she says name*) If they have napkins, Sarah Maud, Peter, Kitty, Susan, and Peory may put them in their laps, and the rest of you, tuck them in your necks. (*Pacing up and down, shaking finger*) Don't eat with your fingers! Don't grab anything off one another's plates! Don't reach out for anything! Wait till you're asked! And if you never get asked, don't get up and grab it! Don't spill anything on the tablecloth, or like as not, Mrs. Bird'll send you away from the table. Susan, keep your handkerchief in your lap where Peory can borrow it if she needs it! Now, we'll try a few things to see how they go. (*In "cultured" tones; to* CLEMENT) Mr. Clement, do you eat cranberry sauce?

CLEMENT: You bet your life!

MRS. RUGGLES (*Shocked*): Clement McGrill Ruggles! Do you mean to tell me you'd say that at a dinner party? I'll give you one more chance. Mr. Clement, will you take some of the cranberry?

CLEMENT (*Meekly*): Yes, ma'am, thank you kindly, if you happen to have any handy.

MRS. RUGGLES: Very good indeed! But they won't give you two tries tonight. Miss Peoria, do you care for white or dark meat?

PEORIA: I'm not particular as to color. Anything nobody else wants will suit me!

MRS. RUGGLES: First-rate! Nobody could speak more genteel than that! Miss Kitty, will you have hard or soft sauce on your pudding?

KITTY: Hard or soft? Oh, a little of both, please, and I'm much obliged.

PETER: What a pig!

CHILDREN: Piggy! Piggy! (*They make grunting noises.*)

MRS. RUGGLES: None of that, Peter. Kitty wasn't being greedy. That was all right! It's not so much *what* you say, as the way you say it. Now, Eily and Larry, you are too little to train, so you two just watch the others and do as they do. Lord have mercy on you and help you to act proper. Is there anything more you'd like to practice?

PETER: I'm so cram full of manners now, I'm ready to bust without any dinner at all!

CORNELIUS: Me, too!

MRS. RUGGLES (*With sarcasm*): Well, I'm sorry for you both! Sarah Maud, after dinner, when you're in the living room, every once in a while, you must get up and say: "I guess we'd better be going." Then, if they say: "Oh, no, stay a while longer," you may sit down. But if they don't say anything, you've got to get up and go! Have you got that into your head?

SARAH MAUD (*Mournfully*): It seems as if this whole dinner party sets right square on top of me! Maybe I could manage my own manners, but managing nine manners is worse than staying at home.

MRS. RUGGLES (*Cheerfully*): Don't fret! I know you'll get along just fine. (*Looks at clock on wall*) It's time for you to go now. (*Children line up and file off.* MRS. RUGGLES *starts to follow them offstage, giving directions till the last child is out of sight.*) Remember—don't all talk at once! Susan, keep your hanky in your lap for Peory. Cornelius, hold your head up! Sarah Maud, don't take your eyes off Larry! Larry, you keep tight hold of Sarah Maud and whatever you do, all of you, never forget for one second—(*Shouting*) That your mother was a McGrill!*!* (*Exits after children. Curtain.*)

* * * * *

SCENE 4

BEFORE RISE: NARRATOR *enters, walks center.*

NARRATOR: There never was such a party! There were turkey and chicken with delicious gravy and stuffing, and half a dozen vegetables, with cranberry jelly, and celery and pickles; and after all that, in came plum pudding, mince pie, and ice cream; and more nuts and raisins and oranges than anyone could possibly eat. Then best of all was the tree and the presents! By nine o'clock, the Ruggles children were exhausted and could hardly stagger home with their boxes, bags, bundles, and packages. It was certainly a Christmas the children would never, never forget. (NARRATOR *steps aside, as children walk across the stage, each one laden with gifts.*)

SARAH MAUD (*Carrying large paper bag in one hand, and holding onto LARRY with other*): This bag of oranges Mrs. Bird sent home to Ma is so heavy I can hardly carry it!

LARRY: I can't wait to play with my Noah's Ark and all the animals!

CORNELIUS: Would you believe it? Everyone had his own butter, and there were pictures stuck right fast onto the dishes!

PETER (*Taking watch out of pocket*): Wait a minute, everybody! I have to see what time it is on my new watch!

CORNELIUS: You'll wear that watch out taking it in and out of your pocket. Be careful you don't break it before Ma sees it!

CORNELIUS: If he does break it, I can fix it with my new set of tools.

PEORIA (*Twirling around*): I can hardly wait to wear my beautiful new dress!

SUSAN: Me, too! And I'll bet my new coat is as warm as toast!

KITTY: I love my doll baby! She has the most beautiful clothes in the world!

EILY: I think mine are the prettiest, aren't they, Sarah Maud?

SARAH MAUD: Everything's just lovely, Eily. Now come along while we can still walk! Ma will be worried about us. And remember, not any of you is to tell her that Larry got stuck in the hall rack behind all those canes and umbrellas.

CORNELIUS: We won't! We won't!

KITTY: I wish Ma could have had some of that wonderful dinner and tasted that plum pudding!

PETER: Don't worry. She did! Mr. Bird told me they sent a whole dinner over to our house, with ice cream and everything.

PEORIA: I'm glad! I hope she got a drumstick like mine.

LARRY: And I got the wishbone! (*Chanting as they exit*) I got the wishbone! I got the wishbone!

NARRATOR (*As children exit*): And if the Ruggles children had a wonderful time, Carol Bird, their little hostess, enjoyed it even more. Carol and her mother talked it over when Mrs. Bird came in to say good night. (*Exits*)

* * * * *

SETTING: *Same as Scene 2.*

AT RISE: CAROL *is propped up on pillows.* MRS. BIRD *sits on edge of bed.*

CAROL: Wasn't it a lovely, lovely time, Mother?

MRS. BIRD: It certainly was, darling, but I'm afraid you've had enough excitement for one day.

CAROL: Everything was just exactly right! I'll never forget little Larry's face when he saw the turkey, nor Peter's when he looked at his watch! And, Mother, did you see Kitty's smile when she kissed her dolly, and Sarah Maud's eyes when she saw her new books?

MRS. BIRD: We mustn't talk any longer about it tonight, dear. You're far too tired.

CAROL (*Happily*): I'm not so tired. In fact, I've felt fine all day, not a pain anywhere. I think the party has done me good.

MRS. BIRD: I hope so. It *was* a wonderful day. Now, I'm going to close the door for a little while so you can get some rest. Then there's a little surprise for you later.

CAROL: Surprise?

MRS. BIRD: Yes, dear. The carolers did not come this way last night, so they're paying us a special visit this evening just so you may hear your favorite carol.

CAROL: Wonderful, Mother, wonderful! I will stay awake to hear them.

MRS. BIRD: They'll be here soon. We asked them to come before ten o'clock.

CAROL: I'll listen to every word. Good night, Mother. Thank you for such a happy, happy day!

MRS. BIRD: Good night, my precious Christmas Carol. Good night. (*Curtain closes, as* MRS. BIRD *leans over to kiss* CAROL.)

* * * * *

LEADER (*Before curtain,* LEADER *enters.* CAROLERS *follow, and all stand center.*): We are here, as you know, by special invitation to sing for little Carol Bird. Ten Christmases ago, the music of one of our caroling groups inspired Mrs. Bird to name her baby daughter Carol. So tonight, we'll sing the same carols that were sung on the day she was born. (*Raises hand and directs* CAROLERS *in singing "Deck the Halls" as in Scene 1.*)

1ST CAROLER: It's after ten o'clock. I do hope she heard us.

2ND CAROLER: Yes! I hope she was still awake! (*To* LEADER) Do you think Carol heard the music?

LEADER (*Looking up in the direction of* CAROL's *window*): I can't be sure. Perhaps she *has* fallen asleep! But somehow, even if she is asleep, I feel quite sure she has heard the music! (*All exit, softly humming carol.*)

THE END

Production Notes

THE BIRDS' CHRISTMAS CAROL

Characters: 9 male; 9 female; 2 male or female for Narrator and Leader of Carolers; as many male and female extras as desired for Carolers.

Playing Time: 25 minutes.

Costumes: Everyday dress of the late nineteenth century. Carolers wear outdoor winter clothing (cloaks, muffs, bonnets for girls; warm jackets, knickers, caps for boys). Carol wears bathrobe and nightgown. Nurse wears uniform. The Ruggles children are dressed as indicated in text—on the whole, they should be wearing rather elaborate, odd-looking clothing.

Properties: Letter; large paper bag of oranges, watch, dolls, various packages wrapped in Christmas paper for Ruggles children.

Setting: Scene 1, Before Rise: Street in a big city, played before the curtain. There may be cardboard cutouts of street lights, and outline of house with lighted windows pinned to curtain. At Rise: The Bird's living room, furnished in 19th century style. There is rocking chair center, a clock on mantel or wall, and small decorated Christmas tree, with Christmas presents under it, at right. Scenes 2 and 4: Carol's bedroom. A bed is center, with chair next to it. Bed has blanket and a couple of pillows. Scene 3: The Ruggles home. Seven chairs, a coal hod, and a wood box are lined up across stage. Clock is on wall.

Lighting and Sound: No special effects.